William A Kelsey

Printers' Dictionary and Guide Book

Containing Webster's spelling and division of the most used words of the English language and chapters on job work, punctuation, useful receipts

William A Kelsey

Printers' Dictionary and Guide Book

Containing Webster's spelling and division of the most used words of the English language and chapters on job work, punctuation, useful receipts

ISBN/EAN: 9783337251994

Printed in Europe, USA, Canada, Australia, Japan

Cover: Foto ©Lupo / pixelio.de

More available books at **www.hansebooks.com**

Excelsior Type Case

IMPROVED
Patent Plan.

The capitals near the small letters. More convenient and **SAVES TIME.** Thirty-two extra spaces at top for italics, accents, signs, etc.

PRICE 65 CENTS EACH.

...THE...

Combination Cabinet and Stand

PRICE $7.00

Holds 20 Excelsior Type Cases. Stand top to hold cases to set from. Well made solid and durable. Holds any two-third case. An excellent article for any printer, Price $7.00. Or filled with 20 Excelsior Cases, $20.00.

PRINTERS' DICTIONARY AND GUIDE BOOK

CONTAINING WEBSTER'S SPELLING AND DIVISION OF THE
MOST USED WORDS OF THE ENGLISH LANGUAGE
AND CHAPTERS ON JOB WORK, PUNCTUATION,
USEFUL RECEIPTS, ETC. NOT COMPLETE,
TREATISES, BUT A BRIEF, HANDY
GUIDE, FOR EVERY DAY
USE, FOR PROFESSIONAL
OR AMATEUR.

ENTERED ACCORDING TO ACT OF CONGRESS, IN THE YEAR 1892, IN THE
OFFICE OF THE LIBRARIAN OF CONGRESS, AT WASHINGTON.

PRICE 25 CENTS.

KELSEY PRESS CO., PUBLISHERS,
MERIDEN, CONN.

CARDS

FOR PRINTERS, CARD WRITERS AND ADVERTISERS.

EVERY DESCRIPTION OF

Fine Bristols, Bevel Edges, Tickets, Cheap Cards, Etc.

Our Specialty is Original Designs.

Embossed Cards and Unique Patented Styles.

PICTURE ADVERTISING CARDS.

Remit 22 cents in stamps and we will mail our full set of priced and numbered samples of cards, papers, envelopes and tags.

Address,

KELSEY PRESS CO.,
MERIDEN, CONN.

DIRECTIONS FOR AMATEUR PRINTERS.

FURNISHED WITH PRESSES MADE BY THE
KELSEY PRESS CO., Meriden, Connecticut, U. S. A.,
MANUFACTURERS AND DEALERS IN
PRINTING MATERIAL OF EVERY KIND.

☞ Send stamp for large Price-Catalogue of Type, Paper, Cards, etc. ☜

BEGIN your work without *haste*, thus you will better learn the details. Printing is easy and simple, and rapid, after first day. Print only *one line* for your first attempt, to see how all the parts work.

THE PRESS.—Should be firmly fastened down with **screws**. Oil thoroughly at working points before use, and weekly thereafter. Place near a window, if convenient, in good light.

THE TYPE.—In opening packages lay them on a table and unroll carefully; let them stand upright on the paper and place something heavy along each side to keep them from falling. Carefully remove the string around the font. If the type is quite small or seems loose, saturate a sponge with water and let a few drops fall on every part of the faces, which will run between the letters, making them adhere together and stand up. (Such wetting is often done to forms that must be moved about.) The letters of a kind generally will be found together; in separating them go through a row or line before commencing another. Arrange type in cases as shown in diagram of case elsewhere. If any letters are missing, look over the case as similar appearing letters like b, d, p, q, and n, u, v, frequently become mixed by inexperienced hands. Two or more fonts may be put in one case if *considerably* different in size so as to be readily distinguished.

TO SET TYPE.—For most type forms a composing stick is used. The movable **slide is set at a point** leaving space inside the width of the desired form. Fasten slide firmly by the screw. Hold stick in left hand, open side from you, slide to the left. Commence setting in the letters at the left with *nicks* in the side of the type *from* you. After each word place a medium sized **space** (3 m, the size of which three placed together will make a square or ' m), which gives **distance** between the words when printed. At end of line if there is some **space**, yet not enough to allow part of a word, *properly* divided, increase **space** between words by thin space and have about *uniform* space between words. Every line should be spaced out so as to be tight in the stick, and sometimes spaces have to be cut out of card. By carefully examining printed matter similar to such as you are setting, you will observe how to space. Between lines, if space is desired, put one or more *leads,* pieces of thin strips of metal, cut length of form you are setting. When several lines are set, place a lead at top and bottom, set stick down, grasp the form at the side from you with the first finger of each hand, and the side towards you with the thumbs, letting the second fingers come against the ends of the lines; pressing tightly on all sides lift carefully from the stick and place in chase. Experience enables us to thus handle a stick *full.* Repeat this till form is completed in chase. Forms may be set without a composing stick, by arranging furniture in chase to size desired, picking out words from case and placing in chase as fast as set. In this way the fingers are used as a composing stick.

LOCKING UP FORM.—Having completed a form in the chase, which should set before you with screws towards you, and top line of form towards you, or else to the left, place it as near centre of chase as possible. Outside the form, the long way of the chase, fill up with long pieces of wood furniture, and at the ends fill up with metal furniture, hollow metal blocks. Iron strips are provided for the screws to bear on in locking up Make sure the lines are all the same length and everything properly justified, that is true and square, so that pressure will hold all evenly. Now turn screws just enough to press form lightly together, then lay a *smooth surfaced* block (planer) upon the form and strike *light* blows on top with a mallet to push down any letters which may stick up above others. Now lock up firmly by the screws, holding the fingers of one hand firmly on the furniture near the screws to prevent it from springing up. Bottom of chase must be cleaned of dirt or rust occasionally. Never allow type or furniture to project below bottom level of chase as it will prevent locking in bed properly.

PRESS WORK.—Slide the chase into position on press. Cut out a sheet of medium heavy paper, width of platen, and long enough for the ends to turn over and be fastened by the bands, drawing it down smooth and tight over the platen. Under this outside sheet place from three to six more sheets of paper according to job. The additional sheets need only be just the size of the platen. For light, small forms, cards, etc., only three or four sheets are necessary. For heavy forms, electrotypes, large forms, etc., use five or six sheets. Sheets of soft bedding, such as blotting paper, rubber sheeting, woolen cloth, are sometimes used on heavy forms, under the first platen sheet, but never on small printing. All being ready, put on the impression without ink once, working carefully lest impression be too heavy and injure the type. Be careful that the grippers are set so to just catch *edges* of the sheet, but not hit and injure the type form. Care should be taken never to throw lower impression screws too far forward and thus prevent full leverage of press. Turn on impression screws to bring out a firm impression. Clean ink table of all dirt, put on ink about the size of a pea and with the roller, also well cleaned, roll it out *thin and even* on the table.

Amateurs generally use *too much ink*; use little, roll it out well and pass roller more times over the type; especially in fine work do that. Ink must be distributed on the table by hand, either with one of the press rollers or hand roller; it is best to have a hand roller for it. Now pass the roller over the type, forward and back, lay a sheet of paper on platen and take an impression. If not clear, or if uneven, regulate by the impression screws. When a clear impression is obtained, look it over for errors; this is "proof-reading." Mark all errors on the margin of sheet. Remove the chase from press, unlock the form so that wrong letters may be pulled out and changes made. Here bodkin and tweezers are needed. Lock up and put to press as before. Take a light impression of form on the platen sheet, which will show exactly where it will come every time, and guide you in fixing *feed guides*. The latter are for edges of paper to rest against when printing. Paste a quad, or very thin strip of wood on platen sheet just far enough below the printing to give a proper margin, one at the end the same, and feed the sheets against these in printing. The *Steel Gauge Pins* are a better article for this and being *adjustable* are a great convenience. Type sometimes varies in height slightly, and if certain lines or letters print too heavy or too light, remedy as follows:—First, be sure the pressure is *even*, then if a line or word is too heavy, a thickness of paper should be cut out of the second platen sheet where that part strikes it; if a line or wood is too light a thickness of paper must be pasted on the platen where that part strikes. Cuts are sometimes so low that they must have one or more thicknesses of paper on the *bottom* of them to bring them up type high. The impressions should be so well adjusted, on nearly all jobs, that the printing will be perfectly clear upon face without showing any impression on back of paper or cards. Generally jobs will dry in an hour; at other times they have to lie a day before use.

CLEANING TYPE.—Type should be always cleaned *immediately* after using. Remove chase from press and *before unlocking* form, take a rag wet with benzine or turpentine and carefully wipe the faces of the whole till no ink or smut remains. Use a brush if the type gets filled up badly; a tooth brush is good. The ink table should be washed in the same way when it becomes too dirty to work well, but will not need it so often if a paper is spread over it when not in use to keep off dust. Good work is not possible if ink table is not kept bright.

DISTRIBUTING TYPE.—After cleaning, unlock form, and taking a line at a time, by the aid of a lead or rule, hold it in left hand, and taking off a letter at a time drop it into its place in case, so proceeding till form is distributed.

ROLLERS.—Our Rollers are of patent composition. They should be washed with benzine, turpentine or kerosene oil. Clean with a soft rag wet with one of these liquids. *Keep them in a cool dry, tight box.* It is important to work with a *clean* roller. If it has become dirty, dusty, or otherwise, clean it and then let it stand an hour before use. Sometimes ink gets stiff and does not distribute well; heat it gently by fire, but be careful not to heat roller. Sometimes rollers, owing to state of atmosphere, do not take ink well; pass *slowly* over ink table and they will do fairly well, though they may not work *right* till atmosphere changes. *Secure new rollers when old ones become hard.* CAUTION: Do not attempt to print with old, dried up, hardened rollers, as good results are not possible. The *best* wash for rollers is benzine.

ROLLER MAKING.—It is cheaper for amateurs, generally, to buy rollers ready made, as they are sure of good ones, and at small expense and trouble. But parties at remote points may wish to make their own. RECIPE—One pound *best* glue; one quart *best* sugar-house syrup; one pint of glycerine. Soak glue in rain water till pliant, then drain *thoroughly*; then melt it over a slow fire in a regular glue pot. When glue is *well melted* add syrup, boil about thirty minutes, stir thoroughly and skim off any impurities that rise. Add the other ingredients about five minutes before removing from the fire. Pour the composition slowly and while hot. The moulds may be bought ready made, or prepared as follows: Sheet brass, about one-sixteenth of an inch thick, very smoothly finished for inside, is rolled into a cylinder the desired diameter, and neatly soldered. The mould sets straight up on end, the roller stock in centre. Hold both in place and pour composition in at one side. Set whole away carefully, let stand twenty-four hours, then draw out and use. Sometimes new rollers are too "green" to use for several days.

PRINTING IN COLORS.—Amateurs do well with color work, after due experience; but colored inks seldom work quite as easily as black. Yet color work is attractive, and, as before stated, it may be attempted when the amateur has become fairly versed in plain work. Use *good* colored inks, and the type used had better be plain.

GOLD OR BRONZE PRINTING.—Is done by lightly brushing over printing, when first done, before dry with bit of cotton dipped in bronze powder. The bronze sticks to the ink, and when dried the surplus bronze may be brushed off, leaving the lettering elegantly gilded, silvered or coppered. SIZE is generally used instead of ink in this work, as it is more sticky and holds the bronze better.

AN IMPORTANT POINT.—SELECTION AND CARE OF TYPE.—Plain type wears best, and should form the larger part of the printer's stock though a few styles of fancy text or shaded type are desirable. Light faced type prints clearer and most satisfactory as a general thing. But proper *use* of type is most important. *Great care* must be taken that it is not subjected to unnecessary pressure, and that every letter and point is carefully planed down, that it may not be worn by the extra pressure coming on it if above others. Never run a card with impression so heavy that it shows through distinctly on the back of card. The same rule applies to paper to a certain extent, though in printing a full form of small type so much soft bedding is used on platen that the type will usually emboss though slightly. Proper attention to the care of type *pays*, for it secures long wear. Never buy type cast from inferior metal no matter how cheap. The best is the cheapest. Our Nickel Alloy Metal is most durable.

PRICES TO GET FOR PRINTING.—It is not possible to lay down invariable rules or prices. Competition is often close and prices vary in different localities. Far West or South higher prices rule on account of being further away from source of supplies, etc. We quote average prices for leading articles, which will enable any one to estimate cost of most any job. Visiting cards, 50 on good Bristol 50c.; if with address 10c. extra. Business cards, ordinary plain card,100 for $1.25 to $3.00; 1,000 for $3.00 to $7.00 according to size of card and amount of composition. Small Hand-bills, about three by five inches, 100 about $1.25; 1,000 about $3.50. Note size circulars, half sheet, one side printed, 100 about $2.25; 1,000 about $4.50. Note heads, 100 about $1.50; 1,000 about $3.50. Envelopes, for printing simply ordinary small card in corner, 100 for about 75c; 1,000 for about $3.25. Tags, about same as envelopes. Bill Heads, about $2.50, per ream.

VARIOUS HINTS.—If amateurs will visit regular printing offices and see how *professionals* do their work, they will gain many ideas. To cut up brass rule and leads a fine saw is good, or if you have much to cut a rule and lead cutter will be a valuable addition to your plant.. In printing large lots of labels, etc. set duplicate forms to save press work. A large poster may be printed in parts, a chase full at a time. White ink is used for mixing with colors to produce tints.

ADVERTISING DODGES.—A neat spicy announcement will be noticed and read, while a dry commonplace one will not. Aim at novelty. It is a good idea to make a card that will be kept. Print the advertisement on one side and something attractive on the other. We have seen cards scattered with the words on back in large type, STOP LYING! Many would save them for the fun of turning them up to a friend who was judged to be telling a "fishy story." An advertisement headed ARE YOU AWAKE? will draw attention. Many such novelties *pay*. A card bearing on the back one of the little forms giving "Curious Bible Facts," "Language of Flowers," "Wedding Anniversaries," "Handkerchief Flirtation," and the like, will be preserved by many, and so form a good advertisement.

HOW TO START AND CONDUCT A SMALL PAPER.—Arrange a definite plan, to begin with. Give your paper some distinguishing feature, and not follow in the old ruts. If you are personally interested in some particular art, science or sport, you can, if you have energy, make your journal popular among others interested in the same subject. Or a paper can be made popular by making the leading matter village news, wit and humor, puzzles, rebuses, and the like. Church papers help the work much. Subjects are plenty. Choose one to your taste or ability, and make it your specialty. Make your paper *alive* with that subject, and fill the space not occupied therewith by pleasant miscellany. In a small sheet long, prosy articles appear out of place. It is seldom that a single article should occupy more than a page of a paper, and a column and a half article should be considered long.

Having perfected your plan for conducting a paper, you choose a name for it, which requires considerable thought. You want one appropriate to your leading subject. Let it be as *short* and striking as possible. There is much in a name. Whether you propose to circulate the paper free, as an advertisement or otherwise, or to make money out of it, it is best to fix upon it a subscription price; it gives it an apparent value even if given away. If you desire to make the project pay it can be done. Circulate specimens freely among those liable to subscribe. Fix your subscription price high enough to enable you to give agents a commission for securing clubs.

We would advise the admittance of a limited amount of advertising in every paper. Condense it as much as possible, and let it be the *very last* part of the paper. Advertisements should be set in six point type. That should be the standard. Twelve lines of six point measure one inch. If advertisers desire a displayed advertisement, that is one which is not set in uniform style, but requires increased space between lines or large type, charge by the inch, an inch costing the same as twelve lines in six point. We consider ten cents per line a low enough rate for advertisements in any paper of ten thousand circulation or less. For three insertions make ten per cent. off, for six or more make twenty-five per cent. off. In exchanging advertisements with other publishers, line for line is a fair plan unless the circulations vary quite largely.

A folio or four-page paper is the preferable form. If two columns to page, each page should be about seven and one-quarter inches long by four and three-quarter inches wide. This to include rules, head lines, etc. A good width for columns is thirteen em pica, or two and one-eighth inches. If three columns to page, each page should be eight and one-half inches long by six and a half inches wide. The reading matter should be set in eight or ten point, leaded, that is with leads between the lines, which spaces matter out and gives it a lighter appearance. Often an article has to be set without leads, rendering it "solid," to get it into a given space. A pound of type will average to occupy a space of three and one-half square inches, but by leading with six-to-pica leads, it increases about twenty-five per cent. In average composition the liability to run short on certain letters sooner than others, necessitates increasing of fonts twenty-five per cent. Hence for each three and one-half inches space, provide one and one-fourth pounds of type for solid matter, or one pound for leaded matter as leads will compensate for the allowance of twenty-five per cent. in solid matter. We consider the best appearing paper is obtained by using ten point for reading matter and six point for advertisements. Eight point is sometimes used on reading matter and it appears well.

What is needed in the way of rules, dashes, etc. will be suggested by a careful examination of any paper similar to what you propose to publish.

TECHNICAL TERMS USED BY PRINTERS.—Blanket—The covering used on the platen, and held in place by the iron bands. **Body**—Applied to the sizes of shanks of type, as six and eight point, etc. **Condensed Letter**—Type with narrow face higher than wide. **Copyright**—An author or designer may obtain exclusive right to use his work by paying one dollar to the government. For full particulars apply to *The Librarian of Congress, Washington, D.C.* **Em**—The square of the body of type. **En**—Half the width of an em. **Extended Letter**—Type with broad face; wider than its height. **Font of Type**—One complete set of letters, points, spaces, and usually figures, make a FONT, or it may contain many sets. To show the *proportion* of letters we give number which *averages* to be in a 10 A 20 a font:—A 10, B 4, C 5, D 6, E 12, F 4, G 4, H 6, I 10, J 2, K 2, L 7, M 6, N 10, O 10, P 4, Q 2, R 10, S 10, T 10, U 4, V 3, W 3, X 2, Y 3 Z 2, Æ 1, Œ 1, & 4, $ 3, £ 1. Figures 5 each- a20, b 8, c 11, d 12, e 25, f 8, g 8, h 13, i 20, j 5, k 5, l 13, m 11, n 20, o 20, p 8, q 4, r 20, s 20, t 20, u 11, v 6, w 8, x 4, y 8 z 4, æ 2, œ 2, ff 2, fl 2, ffl 2, fi 2, ffi 2, , 20, ; 4, . 10, - 6, ' 6, ! 4, ? 4, : 4, **Galley**—A light movable tray to receive forms as they are set up before ready for chase, or to hold matter not in immediate use. **Justifying**—Spacing of lines to exact measure in uniformity with their fellows. **Pressing Sheets**—Done in large offices with hydraulic presses, to remove the impressions of type on backs of sheets. Amateurs can do the same with a hot flat-iron. Place the sheet on a smooth board, printed side down; over that place a blank sheet and a pass the iron over it once or more. **Proof-reading**—Searching for errors and marking them for corrections. **Quads**—Pieces of type metal same size body of type, but cast low with no face for giving blank space between words, and at end of lines, etc.; there are four sizes: one, two and three-em and en quads. **Spaces**—Same as quads, but thinner: there are four sizes, three, four and five-em and hair spaces. **Wood Type**—Generally made of cherry; works as accurately as metal type; has several advantages for type of large size; cheaper because it lasts longer, the metal type being easily injured in falling on account of weight.

Difficulty sometimes being experienced in learning differences in letters of Text type, we append alphabets of caps and lower case in their order.

𝔄 𝔅 ℭ 𝔇 𝔈 𝔉 𝔊 ℌ 𝔍 𝔍 𝔎 𝔏 𝔐 𝔑 𝔒 𝔓 𝔔 ℜ 𝔖
𝔗 𝔘 𝔙 𝔚 𝔛 𝔜 ℨ & a b c d e f g h i j k l m n o p
q r s t u v w x y z

Hints on Job Printing.

"Cheap Printing."—We would very seriously warn every young (or old) printer against this dangerous pitfall. Presses, Type, etc., cost money and all work executed should pay so good a profit that they may be renewed as occasion requires. In estimating the price for a certain job, this is the plan of one successful office in our knowledge:—Figure 35 cents per hour for time necessary to set up jobs, $1.00 for the first thousand impressions of press-work and 50 cents for each additional thousand; for paper or card board used, 25 per cent., profit is charged over cost of same after paying all freight or express charges. Customers demanding special cuts for their jobs are required to pay cost of same, or half the cost if the printer cares to keep them for future use in the office and is willing therefore to bear half the immediate expense. The foregoing rules apply to large work. Small cards and numerous fancy jobs pay greater profits; at least half the price should be profit and in some cases two thirds or more.

To Set a Job.—It is better to pencil out the job on paper about the size which will be used, arranging the lines long and short, large and small, about as they are desired to appear printed. Then decide what type shall be used for the principal lines throughout, before commencing the composition. We jot down a few points to be remembered. The princepal display lines should be larger and longer than all others. No two large lines of same length should be close togather. Be careful to space out more in lines of broad face, extended, type, than with slim, condensed letters. A thiner space is required after a word followed by a comma or period because the space over the point makes the printing look more open. When extra spacing a line, to fill out, increase space after letters which end full, like E H M N Z etc., rather than after such as A C J L O etc.

Tricks worth knowing.—Following are a few devices, (make-shifts or tricks of the trade as it were,) which are often serviceable. If commas run short in a font semi-colons are sometimes used by cutting off the dot. Periods are made from colons. Letters I may be made by cutting off part of the L; P of B; L of E; F of E; O of Q; etc. In setting figures the 6 inverted can be used as a 9 or the 9 as a 6. The letter **n** can be inverted for an **u** and vice **versa**. The following lines show **two very** pretty dodges:—

> SPRING ∴ OPENINGS ∴ READY <

The end ornaments are simply capital V and those between are made with four periods. Likewise the capital I of gothic fonts may be used as the V is used, or for a short black dash between lines. The following very neat and odd borders are set simply of brass rule with small o and asterisks:—

○ ○ ○ ○ ○ ○ ○ ○ ○ ○ ○ ○ ○ ○ ○   ✸ ✸ ✸ ✸ ✸ ✸ ✸ ✸ ✸ ✸ ✸

German proper names often require double dots over the vowels and they are readily made by setting a colon above the letters in this manner ö ü. The french c can be made by inverting a figure ɔ.

Wedding Cards.—These appear best when printed in script type. Wooden wedding cards may be made appropriate by introducing one line of the rustic type which imitates wood work. Tin or Silver wedding cards should be printed with silver bronze. For Golden Wedding use gold bronze.

Dusty Cases.—To clean type cases without removing type use bellows, a rubber ball, or an insect powder blower.

Punctuation.

We propose simply to notice a few points specially important to printers **only**, **as** the regular rules of punctuation are quite common. The use of parenthesis is giving away largely to the comma and generally to the benefit of the appearance of printing. When the former is used, if a point follows the words enclosed it should be outside the parenthesis, thus: (the aforesaid party),

Some printers appear to mis-understand the use of the period and comma together ., It should be used after an abbreviation only and where wording follows which would only demand a comma preceding if the abbrevated word were printed in full. Example: W. A. KELSEY & Co., the sole manufacturers. It is better not to use it on cards, headings, etc., in a display line where the abbreviated word ends the line, as the period alone appears better.

Every abbreviation demands a **period** there after, whether it be an initial or part of a word. Examples: Jan. Feb. Mon. Tue. Conn. N. Y. Fred. Geo. Chas. P. M. M. D. G. Washington. But no period follows an abbreviation when an apostrophe is used before the final letter, as Fred'k.

The exclamation and interrogation points appear better if a thin space separates them from words, or from each other if several are used together.

We close this page with a **few** diagrams of **perperly pointed** visiting cards. Many readers will deem this needless but **we have seen so many** violations of these simple rules that we are led to the step.

Ben. F. Butler, Jr.	R. Black Hayes.
Will. M. Evarts.	Sam'l Slick.
Emma May Smith.	C. D. Tooth, D. D. S.

Music Type.—The printing of sheet music is hardly to be attempted by amateurs. A font of type consists of many characters and costs about one hundred dollars. The composition is quite difficult.

Advertising Novelties.

In making an advertising card or hand bill aim to have it spicy and attractive — never common-place. A circular recently attracted our notice headed, in large type,

YOU CAN DODGE AN ELEPHANT

and under in a smaller type, "but you cant the fact that Crane the Grocer is the cheapest in town". And this same witty Crane had a batch of his prices printed on the opposite side of the sheet and to compel the reader to see it he printed at bottom of first page

☞ DON'T TURN OVER UNLESS YOU WANT TO READ THE OTHER SIDE.

Cards with an advertisement one side will be longer perserved if something of interest appears on opposite side. The following forms will prove good for the purpose:—

Curiosities of life.

Half of all who live die before seventeen.

Only one person in ten thousand lives to be one hundred years old, and but one in a hundred reaches sixty.

The married live longer than the single.

There is one soldier to every eight persons, and, out of every thousand born, only ninety-five weddings take place.

If you take a thousand persons who have reached seventy years, there are of

Clergyman, orators,..........43
Farmers....................40
Workmen...................33
Soldiers...................32
Lawyers...................28
Professors.................27
Doctors...................24

Telegraph Alphabet.

A B C D E F
G H I J K
L M N O P Q
R S T U V W
X Y Z &

Figures: 1 2 3
4 5 6 7
8 9 0

Period.
Interrogation.   Exclamation.

Color Printing.—A delightful field of work for the printer of taste and judgement! A supply of white ink is necessary for tints. To ¼ oz white add blue the size of a pea and a rich blue tint results. So red produces pink. If a light shade and dark shade of a color are to appear in a job use the same color for the dark as is employed to produce the tint. For a plain block, to tint a large surface, comman pine smoothly planed, made type high, will do. Brown ink does handsome printing. To imitate the hue of certain lithographic printing mix a little blue ink with black. Better use plain faced type only in color printing. Combinations that harmonize well are. Red with Green,—Light Blue with Dark Red,—Blue with Gold,—Blue with Brown,—Black with Green. And in three colors, Red, Yellow and Blue,—Brown, Purple and Yellow,—Black, Orange Yellow and Light Blue.

A PROOF SHEET, MARKED.

Though a v/riety of opinions exist **as to**   *a*]1
the individual by whom the **art of** print-   ⚲]2
ing was first discovered; ſet all authorities   ‚
concur in admitting Peter schoeffer to be   *Caps*]
the person who invented cast metal types,
⌐]4 havin/g learned the art of cutting the letters from the Gu/tembergs / he is also sup   ⚲]5
⚸]6 posed **to** havebeen the first who **engraved**
on copper plates. The following testimony   ‚
is preserved in the family, by Jo. Fred   ⁀]7
Faustus of Ascheffenburg :—————   *no* ¶]8
⁋[[" Peter Schoeffer of Gernsheim, perceiv-   *s.c.*]
ing his masters design, and being himself   v̌]10
11 ardently desirous to improve the art, found
              2   3   1
tr.]out (by the providence of good God) the   13
method of cutting (incidendi) the charac-   *stet.*]
ters in a matrix; that the letters might be   ‚]
as] singly cast, instead of being cut. He pri- |]12
vately cut matrices for the whole alphabet,   13
and when he showed his Master the letters   *l.c.*]
cast from these matrices, Faust was **well**   *so*]
14 ⌐well pleased with the contrivance that he   15
w.f./promised Peter to give him **his** only   *Ital*]
/daughter, Christina, in marriage/   ⊙]

A PROOF SHEET, CORRECTED.

Though a variety of opinions exist as to the individual **by whom the art** of printing was first discovered; yet all authorities concur in admitting PETER SCHOEFFER to be the person who invented cast metal types, having learned the art of cutting the letters from the Gutenbergs; he is also supposed to have been the first who engraved on copper plates. The following testimony is preserved in the family, by Jo. Fred. Faustus of Ascheffenburg: "Peter Schoeffer of Gernsheim, perceiving his master's designs, and being himself ardently desirous to improve the art, found out (by the good providence of God) the method of cutting (*incidendi*) the characters in a matrix, that the letters might be singly cast, instead of being cut. He privately cut matrices for the whole alphabet, and when he showed his master the letters cast from the matrices, Faust was so well pleased with the contrivance that he promised *Peter* to give him his only daughter, Christina, in marriage.

Correcting Marks.—The opposite page shows the first impression of the above form, with errors marked for correction. Mark No 1 means insert letter a in place of the e. No. 6 means a space wanted. No. 7 take out space. No. 8 make no paragraph. No. 9 shows two lines drawn under words meaning put in SMALL CAPITALS. One line under words means, put in *italic;* three lines means put in CAPITALS.

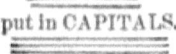

Stereotyping.—It is sometimes desirable to make a solid plate from type forms, for future use or for duplicating. Lock the form in chase and oil the type very thinly with olive oil. Now lay a wood frame around form one half inch deep, and pour into it a thick paste of plaster paris and water. In an hour raise the plaster frame and a perfect mold is found. Dry it thoroughly in an oven. Oil mold thinly, arrange a frame around it, made of iron, likewise a thin iron plate to cover it, forming a casting box of proper depth to make your stereotyping same height as type. Next pour in the melted metal, through a hole in the iron plate or frame. The metal cools at once and the stereotype is ready for press after being squared up carefully by filing. The metal is made up by melting 1 lb of lead with 2 oz of antimony. Melt lead first and add antimony in very small broken pieces. Or old type may be used, melting it and adding a ¼ 'b lead to each lb. of type. Electrotypes may be made in the same manner except that the plaster mold is dusted with plumbago, instead of being oiled, and placed in a battery and a copper "shell" made of the form. Stereotype metal is then run nto the shell to back it up.

THE
PRINTERS' DICTIONARY.

BEING A HANDY GUIDE TO THE CORRECT SPELLING AND PROPER SYLLABIC DIVISION OF ALL THE MOST USED WORDS OF THE ENGLISH LANGUAGE.

A

A-back.
Ab-a-cus.
A-baft.
Ab-al-ien-ate.
A-ban-don.
A-ban-doned.
A-ban-don-ment.
A-base.
A-base-ment.
A-bash.
A-bat-a-ble.
A-bate.
A-bate-ment.
Ab-a-tis.
Ab-ba.
Ab-ba-cy.
Abbe.
Ab-bess.
Ab-bey.
Ab-bot.
Ab-bre-vi-ate.
Ab-bre-vi-a-tion.
Ab-bre-vi-a-tor.
Ab-di-cate.
Ab-di-ca-tion.
Ab-do-men.
Ab-dom-i-nal.
Ab-duct.
Ab-duc-tion.
A-be-ce-da-ri-an.
A-bed.
Ab-er-rance.
Ab-er-rant.
Ab-er-ra-tion.
A-bet.
A-bet-tor.
A-bey-ance.
Ab-hor.
Ab-hor-rence.
Ab-hor-rent.
A-bide.

A-bil-i-ty
Ab-ject.
Ab-ject-ness.
Ab-ju-ra-tion.
Ab-jure.
Ab-la-tive.
A-ble.
A-ble-bod-ied.
Ab-lu-tion.
A-bly
Ab-ne-ga-tion.
Ab-nor-mal.
A-board.
A-bode.
A-bol-ish.
Ab-o-li-tion.
Ab-o-li-tion-ism.
Ab-o-li-tion-ist.
A-bom-i-na-ble.
A-bom-i-nate.
A-bom-i-na-tion.
Ab-o-rig-i-nal.
Ab-o-rig-i-nes.
A-bor-tion.
A-bor-tive.
A-bound.
A-bout.
A-bove.
A-brade.
A-bra-sion.
A-breast.
A-bridge.
A-bridg-ment.
A-broach.
A-broad.
Ab-ro-gate.
Ab-ro-ga-tion.
Ab-rupt.
Ab-rup-tion.
Ab-rupt-ness.
Ab-scess.
Ab-scind.
Ab-scis-sion.
Ab-scond.

Ab-scond-er.
Ab-sence.
Ab-sent.
Ab-sen-tee.
Ab-so-lute.
Ab-so-lute-ly.
Ab-so-lute-ness.
Ab-so-lu-tion.
Ab-so-lu-tism.
Ab-solve.
Ab-sorb.
Ab-sorb-ent.
Ab-sorp-tion.
Ab-sorp-tive.
Ab-stain.
Ab-ste-mi-ous.
Ab-ste-mi-ous-ly.
Ab-ste-mi-ous-ness.
Ab-sterge.
Ab-ster-gent.
Ab-ster-sion.
Ab-ster-sive.
Ab-sti-nence.
Ab-sti-nent.
Ab-stract.
Ab-strac-tion.
Ab-stract-ive.
Ab-stract-ly.
Ab-struse.
Ab-struse-ly.
Ab-surd.
Ab-surd-i-ty.
Ab-surd-ness.
A-bun-dance.
A-bun-dant.
A-buse.
A-bu-sive.
A-but.
A-but-ment.
A-but-tal.
A-byss.
Ac-a-de-mi-an.
Ac-a-dem-ic.

Ac-a-dem-ic-al.
Ac-a-de-mi-cian.
A-cad-e-mist.
A-cad-e-my.
Ac-cede.
Ac-cel-er-ate.
Ac-cel-er-a-tion.
Ac-cel-er-a-tive.
Ac-cent.
Ac-cent-u-al.
Ac-cent-u-ate.
Ac-cent-u-a-tion.
Ac-cept.
Ac-cept-a-ble.
Ac-cept-a-bil-i-ty
Ac-cept-a-ble-ness.
Ac-cept-a-bly.
Ac-cept-ance.
Ac-cep-ta-tion.
Ac-cept-er.
Ac-cess.
Ac-ces-sa-ry.
Ac-cess-i-ble.
Ac-ces-sion.
Ac-ces-so-ri-al.
Ac-ces-so-ry.
Ac-ci-dence.
Ac-ci-dent.
Ac-ci-dent-al.
Ac-ci-dent-al-ly.
Ac-claim.
Ac-cla-ma-tion.
Ac-clam-a-to-ry.
Ac-cli-mate.
Ac-cli-ma-tion.
Ac-cliv-i-ty.
Ac-com-mo-date.
Ac-com-mo-da-ting.
Ac-com-mo-da-tion.
Ac-com-pa-ni-ment.

Ac-com-pa-nist.
Ac-com-pa-ny.
Ac-com-plice.
Ac-com-plish.
Ac-com-plished.
Ac-com-plish-ment.
Ac-compt-ant.
Ac-cord.
Ac-cord-ance.
Ac-cord-ant.
Ac-cord-ing.
Ac-cord-ing-ly.
Ac-cor-di-on.
Ac-cost.
Ac-cost-a-ble.
Ac-count.
Ac-count-a-bil-i-ty.
Ac-count-a-ble.
Ac-count-a-ble-ness.
Ac-count-ant.
Ac-cou-ter.
Ac-cou-tre.
Ac-cou-ter-ments.
Ac-cou-tre-ments.
Ac-cred-it.
Ac-cre-tion.
Ac-cre-tive.
Ac-crue.
Ac-cum-ben-cy.
Ac-cum-bent.
Ac-cu-mu-late.
Ac-cu-mu-la-tion.
Ac-cu-mu-la-tive.
Ac-cu-mu-la-tor.
Ac-cu-ra-cy.
Ac-cu-rate.
Ac-cu-rate-ly.
Ac-cu-rate-ness.
Ac-curse.
Ac-curs-ed.
Ac-cus-ant.
Ac-cu-sa-tion.
Ac-cu-sa-tive.
Ac-cuse.
Ac-cus-er.
Ac-cus-tom.
Ace.
A-ceph-a-lous.
A-cerb-i-ty.
A-ces-cent.
A-cet-i-fy.
Ac-e-tim-e-try.
A-ce-tous.
Ache.
A-chiev-a-ble.

A-chieve.
A-chieve-ment.
Ach-ing.
Ach-ro-mat-ic.
Ac-id.
A-cid-i-fy.
A-cid-i-fi-a-ble.
A-cid-i-fi-ca-tion.
A-cid-i-ty.
Ac-id-ness.
A-cid-u-late.
A-cid-u-lous.
Ac-knowl-edge.
Ac-knowl-edg-ment.
Ac-me.
A-corn.
A-cou-stic.
A-cous-tics.
Ac-quaint.
Ac-quaint-ance.
Ac-qui-esce.
Ac-qui-es-cence.
Ac-qui-es-cent.
Ac-quir-a-ble.
Ac-quire.
Ac-quire-ment.
Ac-qui-si-tion.
Ac-quis-i-tive.
Ac-quis-i-tive-ness.
Ac-quit.
Ac-quit-tal.
Ac-quit-tance.
A-cre.
Ac-rid.
Ac-ri-mo-ni-ous.
Ac-ri-mo-ny.
Ac-ri-tude.
Ac-ro-bat.
A-cron-y-cal.
A-crop-o-lis.
A-cross.
A-cros-tic.
A-cros-tic-al.
Act.
Act-ing.
Ac-tion.
Ac-tion-a-ble.
Act-ive.
Act-ive-ly.
Ac-tiv-i-ty.
Act-or.
Act-ress.
Act-u-al.
Act-u-al-ly.
Act-u-a-ry.
Act-u-ate.
A-cu-le-ate.
A-cu-men.

A-cu-mi-nate.
A-cu-mi-na-tion.
A-cute.
A-cute-ness.
Ad-age.
Ad-a-gio.
Ad-a-mant.
Ad-a-mant-e-an.
Ad-a-mant-ine.
A-dapt
A-dapt-a-bil-i-ty.
A-dapt-a-ble.
Ad-ap-ta-tion.
A-dapt-ed-ness.
Add.
Ad-den-dum.
Ad-der
Ad-di-ble.
Ad-dict.
Ad-dic-tion.
Ad-di-tion.
Ad-di-tion-al.
Ad-dle.
Ad-dress.
Ad-duce.
Ad-du-cent.
Ad-du-ci-ble.
Ad-duc-tion.
A-dept.
Ad-e-qua-cy.
Ad-e-quate.
Ad-here.
Ad-her-ence.
Ad-her-en-cy.
Ad-her-ent.
Ad-her-er.
Ad-he-sion.
Ad-he-sive.
Ad-he-sive-ly.
Ad-he-sive-ness.
A-dieu.
Ad-i-po-cere.
Ad-i-pose.
Ad-it.
Ad-ja-cen-cy.
Ad-ja-cent.
Ad-jec-ti-val.
Ad-jec-tive.
Ad-jec-tive-ly.
Ad-join.
Ad-join-ing.
Ad-journ.
Ad-journ-ment.
Ad-judge.
Ad-ju-di-cate.
Ad-ju-di-ca-tion.
Ad-junct.
Ad-junc-tion.
Ad-junct-ive.
Ad-ju-ra-tion.

Ad-jure.
Ad-just.
Ad-just-ment.
Ad-ju-tan-cy.
Ad-ju-tant.
Ad-ju-vant.
Ad-meas-ure-ment.
Ad-men-su-ra-tion.
Ad-min-is-ter.
Ad-min-is-te-ri-al.
Ad-min-is-tra-tion.
Ad-min-is-tra-tive.
Ad-min-is-tra-tor.
Ad-min-is-tra-tor-ship.
Ad-min-is-tra-trix.
Ad-mi-ra-ble.
Ad-mi-ra-bly.
Ad-mi-ral.
Ad-mi-ral-ship.
Ad-mi-ral-ty.
Ad-mi-ra-tion.
Ad-mire.
Ad-mir-er.
Ad-mis-si-bil-i-ty.
Ad-mis-si-ble.
Ad-mis-sion.
Ad-mit.
Ad-mit-tance.
Ad-mix.
Ad-mix-tion.
Ad-mixt-ure.
Ad-mon-ish.
Ad-mon-ish-er.
Ad-mo-ni-tion.
Ad-mon-i-tive.
Ad-mon-i-to-ry.
Ad-mon-i-tor.
Ad-nas-cent.
A-do.
Ad-o-les-cence.
Ad-o-les-cent.
A-dopt.
A-dop-tion.
A-dopt-ive.
A-dor-a-ble.
Ad-o-ra-tion.
A-dore.
A-dor-er.
A-dorn.
A-dorn-ment.
A-drift.

A-droit.
A-droit-ly.
A-droit-ness.
Ad-sci-ti-tious.
Ad-u-la-tion.
Ad-u-la-to-ry.
A-de't.
A-du'e-'e
A-dul-ter-ate.
A-dul-ter-a-tion.
A-dul-ter-ess.
A-dul-ter-ous.
A-dul-ter-y.
A-dult-ness.
Ad-um-brate.
Ad-um-bra-tion.
Ad-un-ci-ty
A-dust.
A-dus-tion.
Ad-vance.
Ad-vance-ment.
Ad-van-tage.
Ad-van-ta-geous.
Ad-van-ta-geous-ly.
Ad-vent.
Ad-ven-ti-tious.
Ad-vent-u-al.
Ad-vent-ure.
Ad-vent-ur-er.
Ad-vent-ur-ous.
Ad-verb.
Ad-verb-i-al.
Ad-verb-i-al-ly.
Ad-ver-sa-ry.
Ad-ver-sa-tive.
Ad-verse.
Ad-verse-ly.
Ad-ver-si-ty.
Ad-vert.
Ad-vert-ence.
Ad-vert-en-cy.
Ad-vert-ent.
Ad-ver-tise.
Ad-ver-tise-ment.
Ad-ver-tis-er.
Ad-vice.
Ad-vis-a-ble.
Ad-vis-a-ble-ness.
Ad-vise.
Ad-vis-ed-ly.
Ad-vise-ment.
Ad-vis-er.
Ad-vi-so-ry.
Ad-vo-ca-cy.
Ad-vo-cate.
Ad-vo-ca-tion.
Ad-vow-ee.
Ad-vow-son.

A-dy-nam-ic.
Adz.
Adze.
Æ-o-li-an.
A-e-ri-al.
Ae-rie.
A-er-i-fi-ca-tion.
A-er-i-form.
A-er-i-dy.
A-er-og-ra-pny.
A-er-o-lite.
A-er-ol-o-gy.
A-er-o-man-cy.
A-er-om-e-try.
A-er-o-naut.
A-er-o-naut-ic.
A-er-o-naut-ics.
A-er-o-stat-ic.
A-er-o-stat-ic-al.
A-er-o-stat-ics.
A-er-os-ta-tion.
Æs-thet-ic.
Æs-thet-ics.
A-far.
A-feard.
Af-fa-bil-i-ty.
Af-fa-ble.
Af-fa-bly.
Af-fair.
Af-fect.
Af-fec-ta-tion.
Af-fect-ed.
Af-fect-ing.
Af-fec-tion.
Af-fec-tion-ate.
Af-fi-ance.
Af-fi-an-cer.
Af-fi-ant.
Af-fi-da-vit.
Af-fil-i-ate.
Af-fil-i-a-tion.
Af-fi-nage.
Af-fin-i-ty.
Af-firm.
Af-firm-a-ble.
Af-firm-ance.
Af-firm-ant.
Af-fir-ma-tion.
Af-firm-a-tive.
Af-fix.
Af-fla-tion.
Af-fla-tus.
Af-flict.
Af-flict-ed.
Af-flict-ing.
Af-flic-tion.
Af-flict-ive.
Af-flu-ence.
Af-flu-ent.
Af-flux.

Af-flux-ion.
Af-ford.
Af-fran-chise.
Af-fray.
Af-fright.
Af front.
Af-fuse.
Af-fu-sion
A-field.
A-flow.
A-foot.
A-fore.
A-fore-said.
A-fore-time.
A-fraid.
A-fresh.
Aft.
Aft-er.
Aft-er-clap.
Aft-er-crop.
Aft-er-math.
Aft-er-most.
Aft-er-noon.
Aft-er-pains.
Aft-er-piece.
Aft-er-thought.
Aft-er-ward.
Aft-er-wards.
A-gain.
A-gainst.
A-gape.
A-gate.
Age.
A-ged.
A-gen-cy.
A-gent.
Ag-glom-er-ate.
Ag-glom-er-a-tion.
Ag-glu-ti-nant.
Ag-glu-ti-nate.
Ag-glu-ti-na-tion.
Ag-glu-ti-na-tive.
Ag-grand-ize.
Ag-gran-dize-ment.
Ag-gran-diz-er
Ag-gra-vate.
Ag-gra-va-tion.
Ag-gre-gate.
Ag-gre-ga-tion.
Ag-gre-ga-tive.
Ag-gres-sion.
Ag-gress-ive.
Ag-gress-or.
Ag-griev-ance.
Ag-grieve.
Ag-group.
A-ghast.
Ag-ile.

Ag-ile-ness.
A-gil-i-ty.
Ag-i-ta-ble.
Ag-i-tate.
Ag-i-ta-tion.
Ag-i-ta-tor.
Ag-let.
Ag-nail.
Ag-nate.
Ag-na-tion.
Ag-no-men.
A-go.
A-gog.
A-go-ing.
Ag-o-nism.
Ag-o-nist-ic.
Ag-o-nist-ic-al.
Ag-o-nize.
Ag-o-ny.
A-gra-ri-an.
A-gra-ri-an-ism.
A-gree.
A-gree-a-ble.
A-gree-a-bly.
A-gree-ment.
Ag-ri-cult-ur-al.
Ag-ri-cult-ure.
Ag-ri-cult-ur-ist.
A-ground.
A-gue.
A-gu-ish.
A-gu-ish-ness.
Ah.
A-ha.
A-head.
Aid.
Aid-de-camp.
Aide-de-camp.
Aids-de-camp.
Aides-de-camp
Ail.
Ail-ment.
Aim.
Aim-less.
Air.
Air-cells
Air-gun.
Air-hole.
Air-i-ly.
Air-i-ness.
Air-ing.
Air-less.
Air-pump.
Air-y.
Aisle.
A-jar.
A-kim-bo.
A-kin.
Al-a-bas-ter.
A-lack.

A-lac-ri-ty.
Al-a-mode.
A-larm.
Al-larm-ist.
A-las.
Alb.
Al-be-it.
Al-ber-type.
Al-bes-cent.
Al-bi-no.
Al-bum.
Al-bu-men.
Al-bur-num.
Al-ca-hest.
Al-caid.
Al-chem-ic-al.
Al-che-mist.
Al-che-my.
Al-co-hol.
Al-co-hol-ic.
Al-co-ran.
Al-cove.
Al-der.
Al-der-man.
Ale.
A-lem-bic.
A-lert.
A-lert-ness.
Ale-wife.
Al-ge-bra.
Al-ge-bra-ic.
Al-ge-bra-ic-al.
Al-ge-bra-ist.
A-li-as.
Al-i-bi.
Al-ien.
Al-ien-a-ble.
Al-ien-ate.
Al-ien-a-tion.
Al-ien-a-tor.
Al-ien-ee.
A-light.
A-lign-ment.
A-like.
Al-i-ment.
Al-i-ment-al.
Al-i-ment-a-ry.
Al-i-ment-ive-ness.
Al-i-mo-ny.
Al-i-quant.
Al-i-quot.
A-live.
Al-ka-hest.
Al-ka-les-cent.
Al-ka-li.
Al-ka-lies.
Al-ka-line.
Al-ka-lize.
Al-ka-loid.

All.
Al-lay.
Al-le-ga-tion.
Al-lege.
Al-le-giance.
Al-le-gor-ic.
Al-le-gor-ic-al.
Al-le-gor-ic-al-ly.
Al-le-go-rize.
Al-le-go-ry.
Al-le-gro.
Al-le-lu-ia.
Al-le-lu-iah.
Al-le-vi-ate.
Al-le-vi-a-tion.
Al-ley.
All-fools-day.
All-hail.
Al-li-ance.
Al-li-ga-tion.
Al-li-ga-tor.
Al-lit-er-a-tion.
Al-lo-ca-tion.
Al-lo-cu-tion.
Al-lo-di-al.
Al-lo-di-um.
Al-lot.
Al-lot-ment.
Al-low.
Al-low-a-ble.
Al-low-ance.
Al-loy.
All-saints-day.
All-souls-day.
All-spice.
Al-lude.
Al-lure.
Al-lure-ment.
Al-lur-ing.
Al-lu-sion.
Al-lu-sive.
Al-lu-vi-al.
Al-lu-vi-on.
Al-lu-vi-um.
Al-ly.
Al-ma-nac.
Al-might-y.
Al-mond.
Al-mon-er.
Al-mon-ry.
Al-most.
Alms.
Alms-deed.
Alms-house.
Al-oe.
A-loft.
A-lone.
A-long.
A-long-side.
A-loof.

A-loud.
Al-pac-a.
Al-pha.
Al-pha-bet.
Al-pha-bet-ic.
Al-pha-bet-ic-al.
Al-pha-bet-i-cal-ly.
Al-pine.
Al-read-y.
Al-so.
Al-tar.
Al-tar-piece.
Al-ter.
Al-ter-ant.
Al-ter-a-tion.
Al-ter-a-tive.
Al-ter-cate.
Al-ter-ca-tion.
Al-ter-nate.
Al-ter-nate-ly.
Al-ter-na-tion.
Al-ter-na-tive.
Al-the-a.
Al-though.
Al-tim-e-try.
Al-ti-tude.
Al-to.
Al-to-geth-er.
Al-um.
A-lu-mi-na.
A-lu-mine.
Al-u-min-i-um.
A-lu-mi-num.
A-lu-mi-nous.
A-lum-nus.
Al-ve-o-late.
Al-vine.
Al-way.
Al-ways.
Am.
A-main.
A-mal-gam.
A-mal-gam-ate.
A-mal-gam-a-tion.
A-man-u-en-ses.
A-man-u-en-sis.
Am-a-ranth.
Am-a-ranth-ine.
A-mass.
Am-a-teur.
Am-a-tive-ness.
Am-a-to-ry.
A-maze.
A-maze-ment.
A-maz-ing.
Am-a-zon.
Am-a-zo-ni-an.
Am-bas-sa-dor.

Am-ber.
Am-ber-gris.
Am-bi-dex-ter.
Am-bi-dex-ter-i-ty.
Am-bi-dex-trous.
Am-bi-ent.
Am-bi-gu-i-ty.
Am-big-u-ous.
Am-big-u-ous-ly.
Am-bi-tion.
Am-bi-tious.
Am-ble.
Am-bler.
Am-bro-sia.
Am-bro-sial.
Am-bro-sian.
Am-bro-type.
Am-bu-lance.
Am-bu-la-tion.
Am-bu-la-to-ry.
Am-bus-cade.
Am-bush.
A-mel-io-rate.
A-mel-io-ra-tion.
A-men.
A-me-na-ble.
A-mend.
A-mend-a-ble.
A-mende.
A-mend-ment.
A-mends.
A-men-i-ty.
A-merce.
A-merce-a-ble.
A-merce-ment.
A-mer-cer.
A-mer-i-can-ism.
A-mer-i-can-ize.
Am-e-thyst.
Am-e-thyst-ine.
A-mi-a-bil-i-ty.
A-mi-a-ble.
A-mi-a-ble-ness.
A-mi-a-bly.
Am-i-an-thus.
Am-i-ca-ble.
A-mid.
A-midst.
A-miss.
Am-i-ty.
Am-mo-ni-a.
Am-mo-ni-ac.
Am-mo-ni-ac-al.
Am-mu-ni-tion.
Am-nes-ty.
A-mong.
A-mongst.
Am-o-rous.
A-mor-phous.

A-mount.
A-mour.
Am-phib-i-an.
Am-phib-i-ous.
Am-phi-bol-o-gy.
Am-phi-the-a-ter.
Am-phi-the-a-tre.
Am-phi-the-at-ric-al.
Am-ple
Am-pli-fi-ca-tion.
Am-pli fi-er.
Am-pli-fy.
Am-pli-tude.
Am-ply.
Am-pu-tate.
Am-pu-ta-tion.
Am-u-let.
A-muse.
A-muse-ment.
A-mus ing.
A-mu-sive.
A-myg-da-late.
A-myg-da-line.
Am-y-la-ceous.
An.
An-a-bap-tist.
A-nach-ro-nism.
An-a-con-da.
A-nac-re-on-tic.
An-a-gram.
An-a-log-ic-al.
A-nal-o-gize.
A-nal-o-gous.
A-nal-o-gy.
A-nal-y-sis.
An-a-lyst.
An-a-lyt-ic.
An-a-lyt-ic-al.
An-a-lyt-ics.
An-a-lyze.
An-a-lyz-er.
An-a-pest.
An-a-pest-ic.
A-narch-ic.
A-narch-ic-al.
An-arch-y.
A-nath-e-ma.
A-nath-e-ma-tize.
An-a-tom-ic-al.
A-nat-o-mist.
A-nat-o-my.
An-bu-ry.
An-ces-tor.
An-ces-tral.
An-ces-try.
Anch-or.
Anch-or-age.
Anch-o-ress.
Anch-o-ret.

Anch-o-rite.
An-cho-vy.
An-cient
An-cient-ly.
An-cients.
An-cil-la-ry.
And.
An-dan-te.
And-i-ron.
An-drog-y-nal.
An-drog-y-nous.
An-ec-dote.
An-ec-dot-ic-al.
A-nem-o-ne.
An-eu-rism.
A-new.
An-gel.
An-gel-ic.
An-gel-ic-al.
An-gel-ol-o-gy.
An-ger.
An-gle.
An-gler.
An-gli-can.
An-gli-cism.
An-gli-cize.
An-gling.
An-gri-ly.
An-gry.
An-guish.
An-gu-lar.
An-gu-lar-i-ty.
An-gu-la-ted.
An-ile
A-nil-i-ty.
An-i-mad-ver-sion.
An-i-mad-vert.
An-i-mal.
An-i-mal-cu-lar.
An-i-mal-cule.
An-i-mal-cu-line.
An-i-mal-cu-lum.
An-i-mal-cu-la.
An-i-mal-ism.
An-i-mal-i-ty.
An-i-mal-ize.
An-i-mate.
An-i-mat-ed
An-i-ma-tion.
An-i-ma-tor
An-i-mos-i-ty
An-ise.
An-kle.
An-nal-ist.
An-nals.
An-nats.
An-neal.
An-nex.
An-nex-a-tion.

An-ni-hi-late.
An-ni-hi-la-tion.
An-ni-ver-sa-ry.
An-no-tate.
An-no-ta-tion.
An-no-ta-tor.
An-not-to.
An-nounce.
An-nounce-ment.
An-noy.
An-noy-ance.
An-nu-al.
An-nu-al-ly.
An-nu-i-tant.
An-nu-i-ty
An-nul.
An-nu-lar.
An-nu-la-ry.
An-nu-let.
An-nul-ment.
An-nu-lose.
An-nun-ci-ate.
An-nun-ci-a-tion.
An-o-dyne.
A-noint.
A-noint-ed.
A-noint-ment.
A-nom-a-lism.
A-nom-a-lis-tic.
A-nom-a-lous.
A-nom-a-ly.
A-non.
A-non-y-mous.
An-oth-er.
An-ser-ine.
An-swer.
An-swer-a-ble.
An-swer-er.
Ant.
An-tag-o-nism.
An-tag-o-nist.
An-tag-o-nist-ic.
An-tag-o-nize.
An-tal-gic.
Ant-arc-tic.
Ant-ar-thrit-ic.
An-te.
Ant-eat-er.
An-te-ced-ence.
An-te-ced-ent.
An-te-ces-sor.
An-te-cham-ber.
An-te-date.
An-te-di-lu-vi-al.
An-te-di-lu-vi-an.
An-te-lope.
An-te-me-rid-i-an.
An-te-mun-dane.

An-ten-na.
An-te-nup-tial.
An-te pas-chal.
An-te-past.
An-te-pe-nult.
An-te-pe-nult-i-mate.
An-te-ri-or.
An-te-ri-or-i ty.
An-te-room.
An-them.
An-ther.
An-tho-log-ic-al.
An-thol-o-gy
An-tho-ny's-fire.
An-thra-cite.
An-thra-cit-ic.
An-thro-pol-o-gy.
An-thro-po-mor-phism.
An-thro-poph-a-gy.
An-ti.
An-tic.
An-ti-christ.
An-ti-chris-tian.
An-tic-i-pa.e.
An-tic-i-pa-tic n
An-tic-i-pa-tor.
An-ti-cli-max.
An-ti-do-tal.
An-ti-do-ta-ry
An-ti-dote
An-ti-feb-rile.
An-ti-ma-son.
An-ti-mo-narch ic-al.
An-ti-mo-ni-al.
An-ti-mo-ny.
An-ti-no-mi-an.
An-ti-no-mi-an-ism.
An-ti-no-my.
An-ti-pa-pal.
An-ti-par-a-lyt-ic.
An-ti-pa-thet-ic.
An-tip-a-thy.
An-tiph-o-nal.
An-ti-phon.
An-tiph-o-ny.
An-tiph-ra-sis.
An-tip-o-dal.
An-ti pode.
An-tip-o-des.
An-ti-qua-ri-an.
An-ti-qua-ry.
An-ti-quat-ed.
An-tique.

An-tiq-ui-ty.
An-ti-scor-bu-tic.
An-ti-scor-bu-tic-
  al.
An-ti-script-ur-
  al.
An-ti-sep-tic.
An-ti-slav-er-y.
An-tith-e-sis.
An-ti-thet-ic.
An-ti-thet-ic-al.
An-ti-type.
An-ti-typ-ic-al.
Ant-ler.
An-vil.
Anx-i-e-ty.
Anx-ious.
Anx-ious-ly.
A-ny
A-or-ta.
A-pace.
A-part.
A-part-ment.
Ap-a-thet-ic.
Ap-a-thy.
Ape.
A-pe-ri-ent.
Ap-er-ture.
A-pex.
A-pex-es.
A-phel-ion.
A-phe-li-a.
Aph-o-rism.
Aph-o-rist-ic.
Aph-o-rist-ic-al.
A-pi-a-ry.
A-piece.
Ap-ish.
A-poc-a-lypse.
A-poc-a-lyp-tic.
A-poc-a-lyp-tic-
  al.
A-poc-o-pe.
A-poc-ry-pha.
A-poc-ry-phal.
Ap-o-gee.
A-pol-o-get-ic.
A-pol-o-get-ic-al.
A-pol-o-gist.
A-pol-o-gize.
Ap-o-logue.
A-pol-o-gy.
Ap-oph-thegm.
Ap-o-plec-tic.
Ap-o-plex-y.
A-pos-ta-sy.
A-pos-tate.
A-pos-ta-tize.
A-pos-tle.
Ap-os-tol-ic.

Ap-os-tol-ic-al.
A-pos-tro-phe.
A-pos-tro-phize.
A-poth-e-ca-ry
Ap-o-thegm.
Ap-o-the-o-sis.
Ap-o-the-o-size.
Ap-pall.
Ap-pa-nage.
Ap-pa-ra-tus.
Ap-par-el.
Ap-par-ent.
Ap-par-ent-ly.
Ap-pa-ri-tion.
Ap-par-i-tor.
Ap-peal.
Ap-pear.
Ap-pear-ance.
Ap-pease.
Ap-pel-lant.
Ap-pel-late.
Ap-pel-la-tion.
Ap-pel-la-tive.
Ap-pel-lee.
Ap-pel-lor.
Ap-pend.
Ap-pend-age.
Ap-pend-ant.
Ap-pen-dix.
Ap-pen-dix-es.
Ap-per-tain.
Ap-pe-tence.
Ap-pe-ten-cy.
Ap-pe-tite.
Ap-pe-tize.
Ap-plaud.
Ap-plause.
Ap-ple.
Ap-pli-ance.
Ap - pli - ca- **bil-i-**
  ty.
Ap-pli-ca-ble.
Ap-pli-cant.
Ap-pli-ca-tion.
Ap-ply.
Ap-point.
Ap-point-ee.
Ap-point-ment.
Ap-por-tion.
Ap - por - tion-
  ment.
Ap-po-site.
Ap-po-si-tion.
Ap-prais-al.
Ap-praise.
Ap-praise-ment.
Ap-prais-er.
Ap-pre-cia-ble.
Ap-pre-ci-ate.
Ap-pre-ci-a-tion.

Ap-pre-hend.
**Ap - pre - hen - si -
  ble.**
Ap-pre-hen-sion.
Ap-pre-hen-sive.
Ap-pren-tice.
Ap - pren - tice -
  ship.
Ap-prise.
Ap-prize.
Ap-proach.
**Ap - proach - a -
  ble.**
Ap-pro-ba-tion.
Ap-pro-ba-tive.
Ap-pro-ba-to-ry.
Ap-pro-pri-ate.
**Ap-pro - pri - ate-
  ly.**
**Ap-pro - pri - ate-
  ness.**
Ap - pro - pri - a-
  tion.
Ap-prov-al.
Ap-prove.
Ap-prox-i-mate.
Ap - prox - i - ma-
  tion.
Ap - prox i - ma-
  tive.
Ap-pulse.
Ap-pur-te-nance.
Ap-pur-te-nant.
A-pri-cot.
A-pril.
A-pron.
Ap-ro-pos.
Apt.
Ap-ter-ous.
Apt-i-tude.
Apt-ly
Apt-ness.
A-qua-for-tis.
A-quat-ic.
Aq-ue-duct.
A-que-ous.
Aq-ui-line.
Ar-ab.
Ar-a-besque.
A-ra-bi-an.
Ar-a-bic.
Ar-a-ble.
Ar-bi-ter.
Ar-bi-tra-ble.
Ar-bit-ra-ment.
Ar-bi-tra-ry.
Ar-bi-trate.
Ar-bi-tra-tion.
Ar-bi-tra-tor.
Ar-bor.

Ar-bo-res-cent.
Ar-bo-rous.
Arc.
Ar-cade.
Ar-ca-num.
Arch.
Ar-chæ-ol-o-gy.
Ar-cha-ic.
Ar-cha-ism.
Arch-an-gel.
Arch-bish-op.
Arch-bish-op-ric.
Arch-dea-con.
Arch-duch-ess.
Arch-duke.
Arched.
Archer.
Arch-er-y.
Arch-e-typ-al.
Arch-e-type.
Arch-fiend.
Ar-chi-pel-a-go.
Ar-chi-tect.
Ar-chi-tect-ur-al.
Ar-chi-tect-ure.
Ar-chi-trave.
Ar-chives.
Arch-ness.
Arch-way.
Arc-tic.
Ar-dent.
Ar-dor.
Ard-u-ous.
A-re-a.
A-re-na.
Ar-gal.
Ar-gent.
Ar-gent-ine.
Ar-gil-la-ceous.
Ar-go-sy.
Ar-gue.
Ar-gu-ment.
Ar - gu - men - ta
  tion.
**Ar - gu ment-a-
  tive.**
A-ri-an.
A-ri-an-ism.
Ar-id.
A-rid-i-ty.
A-right.
A-rise.
Ar-is-toc-ra-cy.
A-ris-to-crat.
Ar-is-to-crat-ic.
Ar-is-to - crat - ic-
  al.
A-rith-me-tic.
Ar-ith-met-ic-al.
A-rith-me-ti-cian.

6

Ark.
Arm.
Ar-ma-da
Ar-ma-ment.
Ar-ma-ture.
Arm-ful.
Ar-mil-la-ry
Ar-min-ian.
Ar-min-ian-ism.
Ar-mip-o-tent.
Ar-mis-tice.
Arm-let.
Arm-or.
Ar-mo-rer
Ar-mo-ri-al.
Ar-mo-ry.
Arm-pit.
Arms.
Ar-my
A-ro-ma.
Ar-o-mat-ic.
Ar-o-mat-ics.
A-rose.
A-round.
A-rouse.
Ar-que-buse.
Ar-rack.
Ar-raign.
Ar-raign-ment.
Ar-range.
Ar-range-ment.
Ar-rant.
Ar-ras.
Ar-ray.
Ar-rear-age.
Ar-rears.
Ar-rest.
Ar-riv-al.
Ar-rive.
Ar-ro-gance.
Ar-ro-gant.
Ar-ro-gate.
Ar-row.
Ar-row-root.
Ar-se-nal.
Ar-se-nic.
Ar-sen-ic-al.
Ar-son.
Art.
Ar-te-ri-al.
Ar-te-ri-al-ize.
Ar-te-ry.
Art-ful.
Ar-thrit-ic.
Ar-ti-choke.
Ar-ti-cle.
Ar-tic-u-late.
Ar-tic-u-la-tion.
Ar-ti-fice.
Ar-tif-i-cer.

Ar-ti-fi-cial.
Ar-til-ler-ist.
Ar-til-ler-y.
Ar-ti-san.
Art-ist.
Ar-tist-ic.
Art-less.
Art-less-ness.
As.
As-a-fet-i-da.
As-a-fœt-i-da.
As-bes-tus.
As-cend.
As-cend-ant.
As-cend-en-cy.
As-cen-sion.
As-cent.
As-cer-tain.
As-cer-tain-a-ble
As-cet-ic.
As-cet-i-cism.
As-crib-a-ble.
As-cribe.
As-crip-tion.
Ash.
A-shamed.
Ash-en.
Ash-es.
A-shore.
Ash-y.
A-side.
As-i-nine.
Ask.
A-skance.
A-skant.
A-skew.
A-sleep.
Asp.
As-par-a-gus.
As-pect.
Asp-en.
As-per-i-ty.
As-perse.
As-per-sion.
As-phalt.
As-phalt-um.
As-phyx-i-a.
As-phyx-y.
As-pir-ant.
As-pi-rate.
As-pi-ra-tion.
As-pire.
As-pir-ing.
A-squint.
Ass.
As-sail.
As-sail-a-ble.
As-sail-ant.
As-sas-sin.
As-sas-sin-ate.

As-sas-sin-a-tion.
As-sault.
As-say
As-sem-blage.
As-sem-ble.
As-sem-bly.
As-sent.
As-sert.
As-ser-tion.
As-sert-or.
As-sess.
As-sess-ment.
As-sess-or.
As-sets.
As-sev-er-ate.
As-sev-er-a-tion.
As-si-du-i-ty.
As-sid-u-ous.
As-sign.
As-sign-a-ble.
As-sig-na-tion.
As-sign-ee.
As-sign-er.
As-sign-or.
As-sign-ment.
As-sim-i-late.
As-sim-i-la-tion.
As-sist.
As-sist-ance.
As-sist-ant.
As-size.
As-so-ci-ate.
As-so-ci-a-tion.
As-so-nant.
As-sort.
As-sort-ment.
As-suage.
As-sume.
As-sum-ing.
As-sump-tion.
As-sur-ance
As-sure.
As-ter.
As-ter-isk.
A-stern.
As-ter-oid.
Asth-ma.
Asth-mat-ic.
As-ton-ish.
As-ton-ish-ing.
As-ton-ish-ment.
As-tound.
As-tral.
A-stray.
A-stride.
As-trin-gen-cy.
As-trin-gent.
As-trol-o-ger.
As-tro-log-ic.
As-tro-log-ic-al.

As-trol-o-gy.
As-tron-o-mer.
As-tro-nom-ic-al.
As-tron-o-my.
As-tute.
A-sun-der.
A-sy-lum.
At.
Ate.
A-the-ism.
A-the-ist.
A-the-ist-ic.
A-the-ist-ic-al.
Ath-e-ne-um.
Ath-e-næ-um.
A-thirst.
Ath-lete.
Ath-let-ic.
A-thwart.
At-lan-te-an.
At-lan-tic.
At-las.
At-mos-phere.
At-mos-pher-ic.
At-mos-pher-ic-al.
At-om.
A-tom-ic.
A-tom-ic-al.
A-tone.
A-tone-ment
A-tro-cious.
A-troc-i-ty.
At-ro-phy.
At-tach.
Attaché.
At-tach-ment.
At-tack.
At-tain.
At-tain-a-ble.
At-tain-der.
At-tain-ment.
At-taint.
At-tem-per
At-tempt.
At-tend.
At-tend-ance.
At-tend-ant.
At-ten-tion.
At-tent-ive.
At-ten-u-ate.
At-ten-u-a-tion.
At-test.
At-tes-ta-tion.
At-test-or.
At-tic.
At-ti-cism.
At-tire.
At-ti-tude.
At-ti-tude-i-nize.

At-tor-ney.
At-tract.
At-trac-tion.
At-tract-ive.
At - tract - ive - ness.
At-trib-u-ta-ble.
At-trib-ute.
At-tri-bute.
At-tri-bu-tion.
At-trib-u-tive.
At-tri-tion.
At-tune.
Au-burn.
Auc-tion.
Auc-tion-eer.
Au-da-cious.
Au-dac-i-ty.
Au-di-ble.
Au-di-bly.
Au-di-ence.
Au-dit.
Au-dit-or.
Au-dit-o-ry.
Au-ger.
Aught.
Aug-ment.
Aug-men-ta-tion.
Aug-ment-a-tive.
Au-gur.
Au-gu-ri-al.
Au-gu-ry.
Au-gust.
Au-lic.
Aunt.
Au-re-o-la.
Au-re-ole.
Au-ri-cle.
Au-ric-u-lar.
Au-rif-er-ous.
Au-rist.
Au-ro-ra.
Au-ro-ral.
Aus-cul-ta-tion.
Au-spi-ces.
Au-spi-cious
Au-stere.
Au-stere-ly.
Au-ster-i-ty.
Aus-tral.
Au-then-tic.
Au-then-ti-cate.
Au - then - ti - ca - tion.
Au-then-tic-i-ty.
Au-thor.
Au-thor-ess.
Au-thor-i-ta-tive
Au-thor-i-ty.
Au-the--za-tion.

Au-thor-ize.
Au-thor-ship.
Au-to-bi - og - ra-pher.
Au-to-bi - og - ra-phy.
Au - to - bi - o-graph-ic-al.
Au-toc-ra-cy.
Au-to-crat.
Au-to-crat-ic.
Au-to-crat-ic-al.
Au-to-da-fe.
Au-to-graph.
Au-to-graph-ic.
Au-to- graph - ic-al.
Au-to-mat-ic.
Au-tom-a-ton.
Au-tumn.
Au-tum-nal.
Aux-il-ia-ry.
A-vail.
A-vail-a-ble.
Av-a-lanche.
Av-a-rice.
Av-a-ri-cious.
A-vast.
A-vaunt.
A-ve-Ma-ry.
A-ve-Ma-ri-a.
Av-e-na-ceous.
A-venge.
A-veng-er.
Av-e-nue.
A-ver.
Av-er-age.
A-ver-ment.
A-verse.
A-ver-sion.
A-vert.
A-vi-a-ry.
A-vid-i-ty
Av-o-ca-tion.
A-void.
A-void-a-ble.
A-void-ance.
A-void-er.
Av-oir-du-pois.
A-vouch.
A-vow.
A-vow-al.
A-vow-ed-ly.
A-vow-er.
A-vul-sion.
A-wait.
A-wake.
A-wak-en
A-ward.
A-ware.

A-way.
Awe.
Aw-ful.
Aw-ful-ness.
A-while.
Awk-ward.
Awk-ward-ness.
Awl.
Awn.
Awn-ing.
A-woke.
A-wry.
Ax.
Axe
Ax-i-al.
Ax-i-form.
Ax-il-la-ry.
Ax-i-om.
Ax-i-om-at-ic.
Ax-is.
Ax-es.
Ax-le.
Ax-le-tree.
Ay.
Aye.
Az-ure.

B

Baa.
Bab-ble.
Bab-bler.
Babe.
Bab-oon.
Ba-by.
Ba-by-ish
Bac - ca - lau - re-ate.
Bac-cha-nal.
Bac-cha-na-li-an.
Bach-e-lor.
Back.
Back-bite.
Back-bit-er.
Back-bone.
Back-gam-mon.
Back-ground.
Back-side.
Back-slide.
Back-ward.
Back-wards.
Back-ward-ly.
Back-ward-ness.
Back-woods-man.
Ba-con.
Bad.
Bade.
Badge.

Bad-ger.
Baf-fle.
Bag.
Bag-a-telle.
Bag-gage.
Bagn-io.
Bag-pipe.
Bail.
Bail-a-ble.
Bail-iff.
Bail-i-wick.
Bail-or.
Bail-er
Bairn.
Barn.
Bait.
Baize.
Bake.
Bak-er.
Bak-er-y.
Bak-ing.
Bal-ance.
Bal-ance-sheet.
Bal-co-ny.
Bald.
Bal-der-dash.
Bald-ness.
Bald-pate.
Bal-dric.
Bale.
Bale-fire.
Bale-ful.
Balk.
Ball.
Bal-lad.
Bal-last.
Bal-let.
Bal-loon.
Bal-lot.
Bal-lot-box.
Balm
Balm-y.
Bal-sam.
Bal-sam-ic.
Bal-us-ter.
Bal-us-trade.
Bam-boo.
Bam-boo-zle.
Ban.
Ba-na-na.
Band.
Band-age.
Ban-dan-a.
Ban-dan-na.
Band-box.
Ban-dit.
Ban-dy.
Ban-dy-leg.
Bane.
Bane-ful.

Bang.
Ban-ian.
Ban-ish.
Ban-ish-ment.
Ban-is-ter.
Bank.
Bank-a-ble.
Bank-bill.
Bank-note.
Bank-book.
Bank-er.
Bank-ing.
Bank-rupt.
Bank-rupt-cy.
Bank-stock.
Ban-ner.
Ban-quet.
Bans.
Ban-tam.
Ban-ter.
Bant-ling.
Ban-yan.
Bap-tism.
Bap-tis-mal.
Bap-tist.
Bap-tis-ter-y.
Bap-tize.
Bap-tiz-er.
Bar.
Barb.
Bar-ba-ri-an.
Bar-bar-ic.
Bar-ba-rism.
Bar-bar-i-ty.
Bar-ba-rous.
Bar-be-cue.
Bar-ber.
Bar-ber-ry
Bard.
Bare
Bare-faced.
Bare-foot.
Bare-head-ed.
Bar-gain.
Barge.
Ba-ril-la.
Bark.
Barque.
Bar-ley.
Bar-ley-corn.
Barm.
Barn.
Bar-na-cle.
Ba-rom-e-ter.
Bar-on.
Bar-on-age.
Bar-on-ess.
Bar-on-et.
Bar-on-et-cy.
Ba-ro-ni-al.

Bar-o-ny.
Ba-rouche.
Bar-rack.
Bar-ra-tor.
Bar-ra-try.
Bar-rel.
Bar-ren.
Bar-ren-ness.
Bar-ri-cade.
Bar-ri-er.
Bar-ris-ter.
Bar-row.
Bar-ter
Bar-ter-er.
Bar-y-tone.
Ba-salt.
Ba-salt-ic
Base.
Base-born.
Base-less.
Base-ment.
Base-ness.
Base-vi-ol.
Bass-vi-ol.
Bash-ful.
Bash-ful-ness.
Ba-sic.
Bas-i-lisk.
Ba-sin.
Ba-sis.
Bask.
Bas-ket.
Bass.
Bas-soon.
Bas-tard.
Bas-tard-y.
Baste.
Bas-tile.
Bas-ti-nade.
Bas-ti-na-do.
Bas-tion
Bat.
Batch.
Bate.
Ba-teau.
Bath.
Bathe.
Ba-ton.
Ba-toon.
Bat-tal-ion.
Bat-ten.
Bat-ter
Bat-ter-ing-ram.
Bat-ter-y.
Bat-ting.
Bat-tle.
Bat-tle-ax.
Bat-tle-axe.
Bat-tle-door.
Bat-tle-ment.

Baw-ble.
Bawd.
Bawd-y.
Bawl.
Bay.
Bay-ber-ry.
Bay-o-net.
Bay-ou.
Bay-rum.
Ba-zaar.
Ba-zar.
Be.
Beach
Bea-con.
Bead
Bea-dle.
Bea-gle.
Beak.
Beak-er.
Beam.
Bean.
Bear.
Bear-a-ble.
Beard.
Beard-ed.
Bear-er.
Bear-gar-den.
Bear-ing.
Bear-ish.
Beast.
Beast-ly.
Beat.
Beat-en.
Be-a-tif-ic.
Be-at-i-fi-ca-tion.
Beat-ing.
Be-at-i-tude.
Beau.
Beau I-de-al.
Beau-te-ous.
Beau-ti-ful.
Beau-ti-fy.
Beau-ty.
Bea-ver.
Be-calm.
Be-came.
Be-cause.
Be-chance.
Beck.
Beck-on.
Be-cloud.
Be-come.
Be-com-ing.
Bed.
Be-dab-ble.
Be-dash.
Be-daub.
Be-daz-zle.
Bed-bug.
Bed-cham-ber.

Bed-clothes.
Bed-ding.
Be-deck.
Be-dew.
Bed-fel-low.
Be-dim.
Be-di-zen.
Bed-lam.
Bed-lam-ite.
Bed-quilt.
Be-drag-gle.
Be-drench.
Bed-rid.
Bed-rid-den.
Bed-room.
Bed-side.
Bed-stead.
Bed-time.
Bee.
Bee-bread.
Beech.
Beech-en.
Beef.
Beef-steak.
Bee-hive.
Been.
Beer.
Bees-wax.
Beet.
Bee-tle.
Beeves.
Be-fall.
Be-fit.
Be-fit-ting.
Be-fool.
Be-fore.
Be-fore-hand.
Be-foul.
Be-friend.
Beg.
Be-get.
Beg-gar.
Beg-gar-li-ness.
Beg-gar-ly.
Beg-gar-y.
Be-gin.
Be-gin-ner.
Be-gin-ning.
Be-gird.
Be-gone.
Be-got.
Be-got-ten.
Be-grime.
Be-grudge.
Be-guile.
Be-gun.
Be-half.
Be-have.
Be-hav-ior.
Be-head.

Be-held.
Be-he-moth.
Be-hest.
Be-hind.
Be-hind-hand.
Be-hold.
Be-hold-en.
Be-hold-er.
Be-hoof.
Be-hoove.
Be-ing.
Be-la-bor.
Be-late.
Be-lat-ed.
Be-lay.
Belch.
Bel-dam.
Be-lea-guer.
Bel-fry.
Be-lie.
Be-lief.
Be-lieve.
Be-liev-er.
Bell.
Bel-la-don-na.
Belle.
Belles-let-tres.
Bel-lig-er-ent.
Bell-man.
Bell-met-al.
Bel-low.
Bel-lows.
Bell-weth-er.
Belly
Bel-ly-ache.
Bel-ly-band.
Be-long.
Be-loved.
Be-lov-ed.
Be-low.
Belt.
Be-mire.
Be-moan.
Bench.
Bench-er.
Bend.
Be-neath.
Ben-e-dict.
Ben-e-dick.
Ben-e-dic-tion
Ben-e-fac-tion.
Ben-e-fac-tor.
Ben-e-fac-tress.
Ben-e-fice.
Be-nef-i-cence.
Be-nef-i-cent.
Ben-e-fi-cial.
Ben-e-fi-ci-a-ry.
Ben-e-fit.
Be-nev-o-lence.

Be-nev-o-lent.
Be-night.
Be-nign.
Be-nig-nant.
Be-nig-ni-ty
Ben-i-son
Bent.
Be-numb.
Ben-zoin.
Be-praise.
Be-queath.
Be-quest.
Be-rate.
Be-reave.
Be-reave-ment.
Be-reft.
Ber-ga-mot.
Ber-ry.
Berth.
Ber-yl.
Be-seech.
Be-seem.
Be-set.
Be-set-ting.
Be-shrew
Be-side.
Be-sides.
Be-siege.
Be-slob-ber.
Be-smear.
Be-som.
Be-sot.
Be-sought.
Be-spat-ter.
Be-speak.
Be-sprink-le.
Best.
Bes-tial.
Be-stir.
Be-stow.
Be-stow-al.
Be-stow-ment.
Be-strew.
Be-stride.
Bet.
Be-take.
Be-tel.
Be-think.
Be-tide.
Be-time.
Be-times.
Be-to-ken.
Be-took.
Be-tray.
Be-tray-al.
Be-troth.
Be-troth-al.
Bet-ter.
Bet-ter-ment.
Bet-ters.

Bet-ty
Be-tween
Be-twixt.
Bev-el.
Bev-er-age.
Bev-y.
Be-wail.
Be-ware.
Be-wil-der.
Be-witch.
Be-witch-ing.
Bey.
Be-yond.
Bez-el.
Bi-as.
Bib.
Bib-ber
Bi-ble.
Bib-li-cal.
Bib-li-og-ra-pher.
Bib-li-o-graph-ic-al.
Bib-li-og-ra-phy.
Bib-li-o-ma-ni-ac.
Bib-u-lous.
Bi-ceph-a-lous.
Bick-er.
Bi-cy-cle.
Bi-cy-clist.
Bid.
Bid-den.
Bid-ding.
Bide.
Bi-en-ni-al.
Bier
Bi-fa-ri-ous.
Bi-fid.
Bi-form.
Bi-fur-cate.
Bi-fur-ca-ted.
Bi-fur-ca-tion.
Big.
Big-a-mist.
Big-a-my.
Big-gin.
Bight.
Big-ness.
Big-ot.
Big-ot-ed.
Big-ot-ry.
Bil-ber-ry.
Bil-bo.
Bil-boes.
Bile.
Bilge.
Bilge-wa-ter.
Bil-ia-ry.
Bi-lin-gual.

Bil-ious.
Bilk.
Bill.
Bil-let.
Bil-let-doux.
Bill-iards.
Bill-ings-gate.
Bill-ion.
Bil-low.
Bil-low-y.
Bin.
Bi-na-ry.
Bi-nate.
Bind.
Bind-er.
Bind-er-y.
Bind-ing.
Bin-na-cle.
Bi-noc-u-lar.
Bi-no-mi-al.
Bi-og-ra-pher.
Bi-o-graph-ic-al.
Bi-og-ra-phy.
Bi-ol-o-gy.
Bi-par-tite.
Bi-par-ti-tion.
Bi-ped.
Bi-quad-rate.
Bi-quad-rat-ic.
Birch.
Birch-en.
Bird.
Bird-cage.
Bird's-eye.
Bird-lime.
Birth.
Birth-day.
Birth-place.
Birth-right.
Bis-cuit.
Bi-sect.
Bi-sec-tion.
Bi-seg-ment
Bish-op.
Bish-op-ric.
Bis-muth.
Bi-son.
Bis-sex-tile.
Bis-ter.
Bis-tre.
Bit.
Bitch.
Bite.
Bit-ing.
Bit-ten.
Bit-ter.
Bit-tern.
Bit-ter-ness.
Bit-ters.
Bi-tu-men.

Bi-tu-mi-nous.
Bi-valve.
Bi-valv-u-lar.
Biv-ouac.
Blab.
Black.
Black-a-moor.
Black-art.
Black-ball.
Black-ber-ry.
Black-bird.
Black-board.
Black-cat-tle.
Black-en.
Black-guard.
Black-ish.
Black-lead.
Black-leg.
Black-let-ter.
Black-ness.
Black-smith.
Black-thorn.
Blad-der.
Blade.
Blain.
Blam-a-ble.
Blame.
Blame-less.
Blame-wor-thy.
Blanch.
Blanc-mange.
Bland.
Bland-ish.
Bland-ish-ment.
Blank.
Blank-et.
Blar-ney.
Blas-pheme.
Blas-phe-mous.
Blas-phe-my.
Blast.
Bla-tant.
Blaze.
Bla-zon.
Bla-zon-ry.
Bleach.
Bleach-er-y.
Bleak.
Blear.
Blear-eyed.
Bleat.
Bleat-ing.
Bleed.
Blem-ish.
Blench.
Blend.
Bless.
Bless-ed.
Bless-ing.
Blest.

Blew.
Blight.
Blind.
Blind-fold
Blind-man's-buff.
Blind-ness.
Blind-side.
Blink.
Bliss.
Bliss-ful.
Blis-ter.
Blithe.
Blithe-some.
Bloat.
Bloat-ed.
Block.
Block-ade.
Block-head.
Block-house.
Block-ish.
Blood.
Blood - guilt - i - ness.
Blood-heat.
Blood-hound.
Blood-less.
Blood-shed.
Blood-shot.
Blood-suck-er.
Blood-thirst-y.
Blood-ves-sel.
Blood-y.
Bloom.
Bloom-ing.
Bloom-y.
Blos-som.
Blot.
Blotch.
Blot-ter.
Blouse.
Blowse.
Blow
Blow-er.
Blow-pipe.
Blowze.
Blow-zy
Blub-ber
Blud-geon.
Blue.
Blues.
Blue-stock-ing.
Bluff.
Blu-ish.
Blun-der.
Blun-der-buss.
Blun-der-head.
Blunt.
Blunt-ly.
Blur.
Blurt.

Blush.
Blush-ing.
Blus-ter.
Blus-ter-ing.
Bo-a.
Boar
Board.
Board-er.
Board-ing-school
Boast.
Boast-ful.
Boat.
Boat-man.
Boat-swain.
Bob.
Bob-bin.
Bob-tail.
Bock-ing
Bode.
Bod-ice.
Bod-i-ly.
Bod-kin.
Bod-y.
Bod-y-guard.
Bog.
Bog-gle.
Bog-gy.
Bo-hea.
Boil.
Boil-er.
Bois-ter-ous.
Bold.
Bold-ness.
Bole
Boll.
Bol-ster.
Bolt.
Bolt-er.
Bo-lus.
Bomb.
Bom-bard.
Bom-bar-dier.
Bom-bard-ment.
Bom-ba-sine.
Bom-ba-zine.
Bom-bast.
Bom-bast-ic.
Bom-ba-zette.
Bomb-ketch.
Bond.
Bond-age.
Bond-maid.
Bond-man.
Bond-serv-ant.
Bonds-man.
Bond-wom-an.
Bone.
Bon-fire.
Bon-mot.
Bon-net.

Bon-**ny**.
Bo-nus.
Bo-ny.
Boo-**by**.
Book.
Book-bind-**er**.
Book-case.
Book-ish
Book-keep-**er**.
Book-keep-ing.
Book-sell-er.
Book-wor**m**.
Boom.
Boon.
Boor.
Boor-ish.
Boo-sy.
Boo**t**.
Boot-ee.
Booth.
Boot-jack.
Boot-less.
Boot-tree.
Boot-y.
Bo-rax.
Bor-der.
Bore.
Bo-re-as.
Born.
Borne.
Bor-ough.
Bor-row.
Boss.
Bo-som.
Bo-tan-ic.
Bo-tan-ic-al.
Bot-a-nist.
Bot-a-nize.
Bot-a-ny.
Botch.
Botch-y.
Both.
Both-er.
Bots.
Bot-tle.
Bot-tom.
Bot-tom-less.
Bot-tom-ry.
Bou-doir.
Bough.
Bought.
Bounce.
Bound.
Bound-a-ry.
Bound-en.
Bound-less.
Houn-te-ous.
Boun-ti-ful.
Boun-ty.
Bou-quet.

11

Bour-geois.
Bourn.
Bourse.
Bout.
Bo-vine.
Bow.
Bow-el.
Bow-els.
Bow-er.
Bow-er-y.
Bow-ie-knife.
Bowl.
Bow-legged.
Bowl-der.
Bow-line.
Bowl-ing-al-ley.
Bowl-ing-green.
Bow-man.
Bow-sprit.
Bow-string.
Bow-win-dow.
Box.
Box-er.
Boy.
Boy-hood.
Boy-ish.
Brace.
Brace-let.
Bra-chyg-ra-phy.
Brack-et.
Brack-ish.
Bract.
Brad.
Brag.
Brag-ga-do-ci-o.
Brag-gart.
Brah-min.
Braid.
Brain.
Brain-pan.
Brake.
Brake-man.
Bram-ble.
Bran.
Branch.
Branch-let.
Branch-y.
Brand.
Bran-dish.
Brand-new.
Bran-dy.
Brang-gle.
Bra-sier.
Brass.
Brass-y.
Brat.
Bra-va-do.
Brave.
Brav-er-y
Bra-vo.

Brawl.
Brawl-er.
Brawn.
Brawn-y.
Bray.
Braze.
Bra-zen.
Bra-zen-faced.
Bra-zier.
Breach.
Breach-y.
Bread.
Breadth
Break.
Break-age
Break-er
Break-fast.
Break-neck.
Break-wa-ter.
Bream.
Breast.
Breast-bone.
Breast-pin
Breast-plate.
Breast-work.
Breath.
Breathe.
Breath-ing.
Breath-less.
Bred.
Breech.
Breech-es.
Breech-ing.
Breed.
Breed-ing.
Breeze.
Breth-ren.
Bre-vet.
Bre-vi-a-ry.
Bre-vier.
Brev-i-ty.
Brew.
Brew-er.
Brew-er-y
Brew-house.
Brew-is.
Bribe.
Brib-er-y
Brick.
Brick-bat.
Brick-kiln.
Brick-lay-er.
Brick-mak-er
Brid-al.
Bride.
Bride-cake.
Bride-groom.
Bride-maid.
Bride-man.
Bride-well.

Bridge.
Bri-dle.
Brief.
Bri-er
Brig.
Bri-gade.
Brig-a-dier.
Brig-and.
Brig-an-tine.
Bright.
Bright-en.
Bright-ness.
Brill-ian-cy.
Brill-iant.
Brim.
Brim-ful.
Brim-ming.
Brim-stone.
Brin-ded.
Brin-dled.
Brine.
Bring.
Brin-y.
Brink.
Brisk.
Brisk-et.
Bris-tle.
Bris-tly.
Bri-tan-ni-a.
Brit-ish.
Brit-on.
Brit-tle.
Broach.
Broad.
Broad-ax.
Broad-axe.
Broad-cast.
Broad-cloth.
Broad-en.
Broad-side.
Broad-sword.
Bro-cade.
Broc-co-li.
Bro-gan.
Brogue.
Broil.
Broke.
Bro-ken.
Bro-ken-heart-ed.
Bro-ker.
Bro-ker-age.
Bron-chi-al.
Bron-chi-tis.
Bronze.
Brooch.
Brood.
Brook.
Broom.
Broom-stick.
Broth.

Broth-el.
Broth-er.
Broth-er-hood.
Broth-er-ly.
Brought.
Brow.
Brow-beat.
Brow-beat-ing.
Brown.
Brown-ish.
Brown-stud-y.
Browse.
Bru-in.
Bruise.
Bruis-er.
Bruit.
Bru-nette.
Brunt.
Brush.
Brush-wood.
Brush-y.
Bru-tal.
Bru-tal-i-ty.
Bru-tal-ize.
Brute.
Bru-ti-fy.
Bru-tish.
Bub-ble.
Bub-bly.
Buc-ca-neer.
Buck.
Buck-et.
Buck-ish.
Buck-le.
Buck-ler.
Buck-ram.
Buck-skin.
Buck-thorn.
Buck-wheat.
Bu-col-ic.
Bud.
Budge.
Budg-et.
Buff.
Buf-fa-lo.
Buf-fet.
Buf-foon.
Buf-foon-er-y.
Bug.
Bug-bear.
Bug-gy.
Bu-gle.
Bu-gle-horn.
Buhl.
Buhr-stone.
Build.
Build-ing.
Built.
Bulb.
Bulb-ous.

Bul-bul.	Burn-ing-glass.	Cab-a-la.	Cal-lous.
Bul-bule.	Bur-nish.	Cab-a-list.	Cal-low.
Bulge.	Burnt.	Cab-a-list-ic.	Calm.
Bulk.	Bur-row.	Cab-bage.	Calm-ly.
Bulk-head.	Bur-sar	Cab-in.	Calm-ness.
Bulk-i-ness.	Bur-sa-ry	Cab-i-net.	Cal-o-mel.
Bulk-y.	Burst.	Cab-i-net-mak-er.	Ca-lor-ic.
Bull.	Bur-then.		Cal-o-rif-ic.
Bull-bait-ing.	Bur-y.	Ca-ble.	Cal-u-met.
Bull-dog.	Bush.	Ca-boose.	Ca-lum-ni-ate.
Bul-let.	Bush-el.	Ca-ca-o.	Ca-lum-ni-a-tion.
Bul-le-tin.	Bush-y.	Cack-le.	Ca-lum-ni-a-tor.
Bull-fight.	Bus-i-ly.	Cac-tus.	Ca-lum-ni-ous.
Bull-finch.	Bus-i-ness.	Ca-dav-er-ous.	Cal-um-ny.
Bull-frog.	Busk.	Cad-dy.	Calve.
Bull-ion.	Busk-in.	Ca-dence.	Cal-vin-ist.
Bull-ock.	Busk-ined.	Ca-det.	Cal-vin-ist-ic.
Bull-y.	Buss.	Cæ-su-ra.	Ca-lyx.
Bull-rush.	Bust.	Cag.	Cam.
Bul-wark.	Bus-tard.	Cage.	Cam-bric.
Bum-ble-bee.	Bus-tle.	Cairn.	Came.
Bump.	Bus-y	Cai-tiff.	Cam-el.
Bum-per.	Bus-y-bod-y.	Ca-jole.	Ca-mel-o-pard.
Bump-kin.	But.	Ca-jol-er-y.	Cam-e-o.
Bun.	Butch-er.	Cake.	Cam-let.
Bunn.	Butch-er-ly.	Cal-a-bash.	Camp.
Bunch.	Butch-er-y.	Ca-lam-i-tous.	Cam-paign.
Bunch-y.	But-end.	Ca-lam-i-ty.	Cam-pan-i-form.
Bun-dle.	But-ler	Ca-lash.	Cam-pa-nol-o-gy.
Bung.	But-ment.	Cal-ca-re-ous.	Cam-pan-u-late.
Bung-hole.	Butt.	Cal-ci-na-tion.	Cam-phene.
Bun-gle.	But-ter.	Cal-cine.	Cam-phor.
Bun-gler.	But-ter-cup.	Cal-cu-late.	Cam-phor-ate.
Bun-gling.	But-ter-fly.	Cal-cu-la-tion.	Cam-phor-a-ted.
Bun-ion.	But-ter-milk.	Cal-cu-la-tive.	Can.
Bunk.	But-ter-nut.	Cal-cu-la-tor.	Ca-nal.
Bunt-ing.	But-ter-y.	Cal-cu-lous.	Ca-na-ry.
Buoy.	But-tock.	Cal-cu-lus.	Can-cel.
Buoy-an-cy.	But-ton.	Cal-dron.	Can-cel-la-tion.
Buoy-ant.	But-ton-hole.	Cal-e-fac-tive.	Can-cer.
Bur.	But-tress.	Cal-e-fac-to-ry.	Can-cer-ous.
Burr.	Bux-om.	Cal-en-dar.	Can-de-la-brum.
Bur-den.	Buy.	Cal-en-der.	Can-did.
Bur-den-some.	Buy-er.	Cal-ends.	Can-di-date.
Bur-dock.	Buzz.	Cal-en-ture.	Can-did-ly.
Bu-reau.	Buz-zard.	Calf.	Can-dle.
Bur-gess.	By.	Cal-i-ber.	Can-dle-light.
Burgh-er.	By-end	Cal-i-bre.	Can-dle-stick.
Bur-glar.	By-law.	Cal-i-co.	Can-dor.
Bur-gla-ri-ous.	By-stand-er.	Cal-i-pers.	Can-dy.
Bur-gla-ry.	By-way.	Ca-liph.	Cane.
Burg-o-mas-ter.	By-word.	Cal-iph-ate.	Cane-brake.
Bur-gun-dy.	By-zan-tine.	Cal-is-then-ics.	Ca-nine.
Bu-ri-al.		Calk.	Can-is-ter
Bu-rin.		Calk-er.	Can-ker.
Bur-lesque.	**C**	Call.	Can-kered.
Bur-ly.		Cal-lig-ra-phy.	Can-ker-worm.
Burn.		Call-ing.	Can-ni-bal.
Burn-er.	Cab.	Cal-los-i-ty.	Can-ni-bal-ism.
Burn-ing.	Ca-bal.	Cal-lus.	Can-non.

Can-non-ade.
Can-non-ball.
Can-non-eer.
Can-non-ier.
Can-non-shot.
Can-not.
Ca-noe.
Can-on.
Ca-non-ic-al.
Ca-non-ic-als.
Can-on-ist.
Can-on-i-za-tion.
Can-on-ize
Can-o-py.
Cant.
Can-ta-loupe.
Can-ta-ta.
Can-teen.
Can-ter.
Can-ti-cle.
Can-to.
Can-ton.
Can-ton-ment.
Can-vas.
Can-vass.
Can-zo-net.
Caou-tchouc.
Cap
Ca-pa-bil-i-ty.
Ca-pa-ble.
Ca-pa-bly.
Ca-pa-cious.
Ca-pac-i-ty.
Cap-a-pie.
Ca-par-i-son.
Cape.
Ca-per.
Ca-pil-la-ment.
Cap-il-la-ry.
Cap-i-tal.
Cap-i-tal-ist.
Cap-i-ta-tion.
Cap-i-tol.
Ca-pit-u-lar.
Ca-pit-u-late.
Ca-pit-u-la-tion.
Ca-pon.
Cap-pa-per.
Ca-price.
Ca-pri-cious.
Cap-size.
Cap-stan.
Cap-su-lar.
Cap-su-la-ry.
Cap-sule.
Cap-tain.
Cap-tain-cy.
Cap-tain-ship.
Cap-tion.
Cap-tious.

Cap-ti-vate.
Cap-ti-va-tion.
Cap-tive.
Cap-tiv-i-ty.
Cap-tor.
Cap-ture.
Cap-u-chin.
Car.
Car-a-bine.
Car-a-cole.
Car-at.
Car-a-van.
Car-a-van-sa-ry.
Car-a-way.
Car-bine.
Car-bon.
Car-bon-a-ceous.
Car-bon-ate.
Car-bon-ic.
Car-boy.
Car-bun-cle.
Car-cass.
Card.
Car-di-ac.
Car-di-nal.
Card-ta-ble.
Care.
Ca-reen.
Ca-reer.
Care-ful.
Care-less.
Ca-ress.
Ca-ret.
Car-go.
Car-i-ca-ture.
Car-i-ca-tur-ist.
Ca-ri-es.
Ca-ri-ole.
Ca-ri-ous.
Carl.
Car-mine.
Car-nage.
Car-nal.
Car-nal-i-ty.
Car-na-tion.
Car-nel-ian.
Car-ni-val.
Car-niv-o-rous.
Car-ol.
Ca-rot-id.
Ca-rous-al.
Ca-rouse.
Carp.
Car-pen-ter.
Car-pen-try.
Car-pet.
Car-pet-ing.
Car-riage.
Car-ri-er.
Car-ri-on.

Car-rot.
Car-ry.
Car-ry-all.
Cart.
Cart-age.
Car-tel.
Cart-er.
Car-ti-lage.
Car-ti-lag-i-nous.
Car-toon.
Car-touch.
Car-tridge.
Car-tridge-box.
Carve.
Cas-cade.
Case.
Case-hard-en.
Case-mate.
Case-ment.
Ca-se-ous.
Cash.
Cash-book.
Cash-ier.
Cash-mere.
Cas-ing.
Cask.
Cask-et.
Casque.
Cas-sa-tion.
Cas-sia.
Cas-si-mere.
Cas-sock.
Cas-so-wa-ry.
Cast.
Cas-ta-net.
Cast-a-way.
Caste.
Cas-tel-la-ted.
Cast-er.
Cas-ti-gate.
Cas-ti-ga-tion.
Cast-ing.
Cast-ing-vote.
Cas-tle.
Cas-tled.
Cas-tor.
Cas-tor-oil.
Cas-trate.
Cas-tra-tion.
Cas-u-al.
Cas-u-al-ty.
Cas-u-ist.
Cas-u-ist-ic.
Cas-u-ist-ic-al.
Cas-u-ist-ry.
Cat.
Cat-a-comb.
Cat-a-cous-tics.
Cat-a-lep-sy.
Cat-a-logue.

Cat-a-mount.
Cat-a-plasm.
Cat-a-ract.
Ca-tarrh.
Ca-tas-tro-phe.
Cat-call.
Catch.
Catch-ing.
Catch-pen-ny.
Catch-up.
Cat-sup.
Catch-word.
Cat-e-chet-ic.
Cat-e-chet-ic-al.
Cat-e-chise.
Cat-e-chism.
Cat-e-chist.
Cat-e-chu.
Cat-e-chu-men.
Cat-e-gor-ic-al.
Cat-e-go-ry.
Cat-e-na-ri-an.
Cat-e-na-ry
Cat-e-na-tion.
Ca-ter.
Ca-ter-er.
Cat-er-pil-lar.
Cat-er-waul.
Cat-fish.
Cat-gut.
Ca-thar-tic.
Ca-the-dral.
Cath-e-ter.
Cath-o-lic.
Ca-thol-i-cism.
Cath-o-lic-i-ty.
Ca-thol-i-con.
Cat-kin.
Cat-nip.
Cat-o'-nine-tails.
Cat's-paw.
Cat-tle.
Cau-cus.
Cau-dal.
Cau-dle.
Caught.
Caul.
Cau-li-flow-er.
Cau-sal-i-ty.
Cau-sa-tion.
Caus-a-tive.
Cause.
Cause-way
Caus-tic.
Caus-tic-i-ty.
Cau-ter-ize.
Cau-ter-y.
Cau-tion.
Cau-tious.
Cav-al-cade.

Cav-a-lier.
Cav-al-ry.
Cave.
Cav-ern.
Cav-ern-ous.
Ca-viare.
Cav-i-ar.
Cav-il.
Cav-i-ty.
Caw.
Cay-enne.
Ca-zique.
Cease.
Cease-less.
Ce-dar.
Cede.
Ce-dil-la.
Ceil.
Ceil-ing.
Cel-e-brate.
Cel-e-brat-ed.
Cel-e-bra-tion.
Ce-leb-ri-ty.
Ce-ler-i-ty.
Cel-er-y.
Ce-les-tial.
Cel-i-ba-cy.
Cell.
Cel-lar.
Cell-u-lar.
Cell-u-loid.
Celt.
Celt-ic.
Cem-ent.
Cem-e-ter-y.
Cen-o-taph.
Cens-er.
Cen-sor.
Cen-so-ri-ous.
Cen-sur-a-ble.
Cen-sure.
Cen-sus.
Cent.
Cen-taur.
Cen-ten-ni-al.
Cen-ter.
Cen-tre.
Cen-ter-bit.
Cen-tre-bit.
Cen-ti-grade.
Cen-ti-ped.
Cen-to.
Cen-tral.
Cen-tral-i-za-tion.
Cen-tral-ize.
Cen-tric.
Cen-tric-al.
Cen-tric-i-ty.
Cen-trif-u-gal.

Cen-trip-e-tal.
Cen-tu-ple.
Cen-tu-ri-on.
Cent-u-ry
Ce-phal-ic.
Ce-rate.
Cere.
Cer-e-bral.
Cere-cloth.
Cer-e-mo-ni-al.
Cer-e-mo-ni-ous.
Cer-e-mo-ny.
Cer-tain.
Cer-tain-ty.
Cer-tif-i-cate.
Cer-ti-fy.
Cer-ti-tude.
Ce-ru-le-an.
Ce-ruse.
Cer-vi-cal.
Ces-sa-tion.
Ces-sion.
Ce-su-ra.
Ce **su-ral.**
Ce-ta-cean.
Ce-ta-ceous.
Chafe.
Chaf-er.
Chaff.
Chaf-fer.
Chaf-finch.
Chaff-y.
Cha-fing-dish.
Cha-green.
Cha-grin.
Chain.
Chain-shot.
Chair.
Chair-man.
Chaise.
Chal-ced-o-ny.
Chal-dron.
Chal-ice.
Chalk.
Chalk-y.
Chal-lenge.
Cha-lyb-e-ate.
Cham-ber
Cham-ber-lain.
Cham-ber-maid.
Cha-me-le-on.
Cham-fer.
Cham-ois.
Cham-o-mile.
Champ
Cham-pagne.
Cham-paign.
Cham-pi-on.
Chance.
Chan-cel.

Chan-cel-lor.
Chan-cer-y.
Chan-de-lier.
Chan-dler.
Chan-dler-y.
Change.
Change-a-ble.
Change-ful.
Change-less.
Change-ling.
Chan-nel.
Chant.
Chant-i-cleer.
Chant-ry
Cha-os.
Cha-ot-ic.
Chap.
Chap-el.
Chap-el-ry
Chap-er-on.
Chap-lain.
Chap-lain-cy.
Chap-lain-ship.
Chap-let.
Chap-man.
Chaps.
Chap-ter.
Char.
Char-ac-ter.
Char - ac - ter - is-tic.
Char-ac-ter-ize.
Cha-rade.
Char-coal.
Charge.
Charge-a-ble.
Char-ger.
Char-i-ly.
Char-i-ot.
Char-i-ot-eer.
Char-i-ta-ble.
Char-i-ty.
Charl-a-tan.
Charl-a-tan-ry.
Charm.
Charm-ing.
Char-nel-house.
Chart.
Char-ter.
Chart-ist.
Char-y.
Chase.
Chasm.
Chaste.
Chas-ten.
Chas-ten-ing.
Chas-tise.
Chas-tise-ment.
Chas-ti-ty.
Chaste-ness.

Chat.
Chat-eau.
Chat-tel.
Chat-ter
Chat-ter-box.
Chat-ty.
Cheap.
Cheap-en.
Cheap-ness.
Cheat.
Check.
Check-er.
Check-er-board.
Check-ers.
Check-mate.
Cheek.
Cheer.
Cheer-ful.
Cheer-ful-ness.
Cheer-less.
Cheer-y.
Cheese.
Cheese-cake.
Chem-ic-al.
Che-mise.
Chem-ist.
Chem-is-try.
Cher-ish.
Cher-ry.
Cher-so-nese.
Cher-ub.
Che-ru-bic.
Chess.
Chess-board.
Chest.
Chest-nut.
Chev-a-lier.
Chew.
Chi-cane.
Chi-can-er-y.
Chick.
Chick-en.
Chick - en - heart-ed.
Chick-en-pox.
Chick-weed.
Chide.
Chief.
Chief-ly.
Chief-tain.
Chil-blain.
Child.
Child-bed.
Child-birth.
Child-hood.
Child-ish.
Child-less.
Chil-dren.
Chill.
Chill-i-ness.

Ch·ll-y.
Chime.
Chim-er.
Chi-me-ra.
Chi-mer-i-cal.
Chim-ney.
Chin.
Chi-na.
Chine.
Chink.
Chink-y.
Chintz.
Chip.
Chi-rog-ra-pher.
Chi-rog-ra-phy.
Chi-ro-man-cy.
Chi-rop-o-dist.
Chirp.
Chir-rup.
Chis-el.
Chit.
Chit-chat.
Chiv-al-ric.
Chiv-al-rous.
Chiv-al-ry.
Chives.
Chlo-rine.
Chock-full.
Choc-o-late.
Choice.
Choir
Choke.
Choke-damp.
Choke-full.
Choke-pear.
Chok-y.
Chol-er.
Chol-er-a.
Chol-er-a-mor-bus.
Chol-er-ic.
Choose.
Chop.
Chop-house.
Chop-ping.
Chops.
Cho-ral.
Chord.
Chore.
Chor-is-ter.
Cho-rog-ra-phy.
Cho-rus.
Chose.
Cho-sen.
Chough.
Chow-der.
Chrism.
Christ.
Chris-ten.
Chris-ten-dom.

Chris-tian.
Chris-tian-i-ty.
Chris-tian-ize.
Christ-mas.
Chro-mat-ic.
Chrome.
Chro-mi-um.
Chro-mo.
Chro-mo-lith-o-graph.
Chron-ic.
Chron-i-cle.
Chro-nol-o-ger.
Chro-nol-o-gist.
Chron-o-log-ic.
Chron-o-log-ic-al.
Chro-nol-o-gy.
Chro-nom-e-ter.
Chrys-a-lis.
Chrys-o-lite.
Chub.
Chub-bed.
Chub-by.
Chuck-le.
Chum.
Chunk.
Church.
Church-man.
Church-war-den.
Church-yard.
Churl.
Churl-ish.
Churn.
Chyle.
Chyme
Cic-a-trice.
Cic-a-trize.
Ci-der.
Ci-gar.
Cil-i-a-ry.
Cinct-ure.
Cin-der.
Cin-na-mon.
Cinque.
Cinque-foil.
Ci-on.
Ci-pher
Cir-cle.
Cir-cuit.
Cir-cu-i-tous.
Cir-cu-lar.
Cir-cu-lar-i-ty.
Cir-cu-lar-ly.
Cir-cu-late.
Cir-cu-la-tion.
Cir-cum-am-bi-ent.
Cir-cum-am-bu-late.

Cir-cum-cise.
Cir-cum-cis-ion.
Cir-cum-fer-ence.
Cir-cum-flex.
Cir-cum-flu-ence.
Cir-cum-flu-ent.
Cir-cum-fuse.
Cir-cum-fu-sion.
Cir-cum-ja-cent.
Cir-cum-lo-cu-tion.
Cir-cum-loc-u-to-ry.
Cir-cum-nav-i-gate.
Cir-cum-nav-i-ga-tion.
Cir-cum-nav-**i**-ga-tor.
Cir-cum-po-lar.
Cir-cum-scribe.
Cir-cum-scrip-tion.
Cir-cum-spect.
Cir-cum-**spec**-tion.
Cir-cum-stance.
Cir-cum-stan-tial.
Cir-cum-**stan**-tials.
Cir-cum-**val**-la-tion.
Cir-cum-vent.
Cir-cum-ven-tion.
Cir-cus.
Cis-al-pine.
Cis-at-lan-tic.
Cis-tern.
Cit.
Cit-a-del.
Ci-ta-tion.
Ci-ta-to-ry.
Cite.
Cit-i-zen.
Cit-ric.
Cit-ron.
Cit-y.
Civ-et.
Civ-ic.
Civ-il.
Ci-vil-ian.
Ci-vil-i-ty.
Civ-il-i-za-tion.
Civ-il-ize.
Civ-il-ized.
Civ-il-ly.
Clack.

Clack-er.
Clad.
Claim.
Claim-ant.
Clair-voy-ance.
Claim.
Clam-ber.
Clam-mi-ness.
Clam-my.
Clam-or.
Clam-or-ous.
Clamp.
Clan
Clan-des-tine.
Clang.
Clan-gor.
Clank.
Clap.
Clap-board.
Clap-per.
Clap-trap.
Clar-et.
Clar-i-fy.
Clar-i-net.
Clar-i-o-net.
Clar-i-on.
Clash.
Clash-ing.
Clasp.
Class.
Clas-sic.
Clas-sic-al.
Clas-si-fi-ca-tion.
Clas-si-fy.
Clat-ter.
Clat-ter-ing.
Clause.
Claw.
Clay.
Clay-ey.
Clean.
Clean-li-ness.
Clean-ly.
Cleanse.
Clear.
Clear-ance.
Clear-ing.
Clear-ly.
Cleat.
Cleav-age.
Cleave.
Cleav-er.
Clef.
Cleft.
Clem-en-cy.
Clem-ent.
Cler-gy.
Cler-gy-man.
Cler-ic-al.
Clerk.

Clerk-ship.	Cluck.	Co-di-fi-ca-tion.	Col-lapse.
Clev-er.	Clue.	Co-di-fy.	Col-lar.
Clev-is.	Clump.	Cod-dle.	Col-late.
Clev-y	Clum-sy	Co-ef-fi-cien-cy.	Col-lat-er-al.
Clew.	Clung.	Co-ef-fi-cient.	Col-la-tion.
Click.	Clus-ter.	Co-e-qual.	Col-league.
Cli-ent.	Clutch.	Co-e-qual-i-ty.	Col-lect.
Cliff.	Clut-ter.	Co-erce.	Col-lect-ed.
Cliff-y.	Clys-ter.	Co-er-cion.	Col-lec-tion.
Cli-mac-ter-ic.	Coach.	Co-er-cive.	Col-lect-ive.
Cli-mate.	Coach-man.	Co-es-sen-tial.	Col-lect-ive-ly.
Cli-max.	Co-ad-ju-tor.	Co-e-ter-nal.	Col-lect-or.
Climb.	Co-ad-ju-trix.	Co-e-ter-ni-ty.	Col-lege.
Clime.	Co-a-gent.	Co-e-val.	Col-le-gi-al.
Clinch.	Co-ag-u-late.	Co-ex-ist.	Col-le-gi-ate.
Cling.	Co-ag-u-la-tion.	Co-ex-ist-ence.	Col-le-gi-an.
Clin-ic.	Co-ag-u-la-tive.	Co-ex-ist-ent.	Col-lide.
Clin-ic-al.	Co-ag-u-lum.	Co-ex-tend.	Coll-ier.
Clink.	Coal.	Co-ex-ten-sion.	Coll-ier-y.
Clink-er.	Co-a-lesce.	Co-ex-ten-sive.	Col-lis-ion.
Clip.	Co-a-les-cence.	Cof-fee.	Col-lo-cate.
Clip-per.	Co-a-li-tion.	Cof-fee-house.	Col-lo-ca-tion.
Clip-ping.	Coal-mine.	Cof-fer.	Col-lop.
Cloak.	Coal-pit.	Cof-fin.	Col-lo-qui-al.
Clock.	Coarse.	Cog.	Col-lo-qui-al-ism.
Clock-work.	Coarse-ness.	Co-gen-cy.	Col-lo-quy.
Clod.	Coast.	Co-gent.	Col-lude.
Clod-hop-per.	Coast-er.	Cog-i-tate.	Col-lu-sion.
Cloff.	Coat.	Cog-i-ta-tion.	Col-lu-sive.
Clog.	Coat-ing.	Cog-i-ta-tive.	Co-lon.
Clois-ter.	Coax.	Cog-nate.	Colonel.
Close.	Cob.	Cogn-ac.	Colonel-cy.
Close-fisted.	Co-balt.	Cogn-iac.	Colonel-ship.
Close-ly.	Cob-ble.	Cog-ni-tion.	Co-lo-ni-al.
Close-stool.	Cob-bler.	Cog-ni-za-ble.	Col-o-nist.
Clos-et.	Cob-web.	Cog-ni-zance.	Col-o-ni-za-tion.
Clos-ing.	Coch-i-neal.	Cog-wheel.	Col-o-nize.
Clos-ure.	Coch-le-a-ry.	Co-hab-it.	Col-on-nade.
Clot.	Coch-le-a-ted.	Co-hab-it-a-tion.	Col-o-ny.
Cloth.	Cock.	Co-heir.	Col-or.
Cloths.	Cock-ade.	Co-here.	Col-or-a-ble.
Clothe.	Cock-a-trice.	Co-her-ence.	Col-or-less.
Clothes.	Cock-boat.	Co-her-en-cy.	Co-los-sal.
Cloth-ier.	Cock-er-el.	Co-her-ent.	Co-los-sus.
Cloth-ing.	Cock-fight.	Co-he-sion.	Colt.
Cloud.	Cock-horse.	Co-he-sive.	Col-ter.
Cloud-i-ness.	Cock-le.	Co-hort.	Coul-ter.
Cloud-less.	Cock-loft.	Coif.	Col-um-bine.
Cloud-y.	Cock-ney.	Coil.	Col-umn.
Clout.	Cock-pit.	Coin.	Co-lum-nar.
Clove.	Cock-roach.	Coin-age.	Co-lure.
Clo-ven.	Cock's-comb.	Co-in-cide.	Co-ma.
Clo-ven-foot-ed.	Cock-swain.	Co-in-ci-dence.	Co-ma-tose.
Clo-ver.	Co-coa.	Co-in-ci-dent.	Comb.
Clown.	Co-coa-nut.	Coke.	Com-bat.
Clown-ish.	Co-coon.	Col-an-der.	Com-bat-ant.
Cloy.	Cod.	Cold.	Com-ba-tive.
Club.	Code.	Cole-wort.	Com-bin-a-ble.
Club-foot-ed.	Cod-ger.	Col-ic.	Com-bi-na-tion.
Club-law.	Cod-i-cil.	Col-ick-y.	Com-bine.

17

Com-bus-ti-bil-i-ty.
Com-bus-ti-ble-ness.
Com-bus-ti-ble.
Com-bus-tion.
Come.
Co-me-di-an.
Com-e-dy.
Come-li-ness.
Come-ly.
Com-et.
Com-fit.
Com-fort.
Com-fort-a-ble.
Com-fort-er.
Com-fort-less.
Com-frey.
Com-ic.
Com-ic-al.
Com-ing.
Com-i-ty
Com-ma.
Com-mand.
Com-man-dant.
Com-mand-er.
Com-mand-er-y.
Com-mand-ry.
Com-mand-ing.
Com-mand-ment.
Com-mem-o-rate.
Com-mem-o-ra-tion.
Com-mem-o-ra-tive.
Com-mence.
Com-mence-ment.
Com-mend.
Com-mend-a-ble.
Com-men-da-tion.
Com-mend-a-to-ry.
Com-men-su-ra-bil-i-ty.
Com-men-su-ra-ble-ness.
Com-men-su-ra-ble.
Com-men-su-rate.
Com-men-su-ra-tion.
Com-ment.
Com-ment-a-ry.
Com-men-ta-tor.
Com-merce.
Com-mer-cial.
Com-min-gle.

Com-mi-nute.
Com-mi-nu-tion.
Com-mis-er-ate.
Com-mis-er-a-tion.
Com-mis-sa-ry.
Com-mis-sion.
Com-mis-sion-er.
Com-mis-sure.
Com-mit.
Com-mit-tal.
Com-mit-tee.
Com-mix.
Com-mixt-ure.
Com-mode.
Com-mo-di-ous.
Com-mod-i-ty.
Com-mo-dore.
Com-mon.
Com-mon-al-ty.
Com-mon-er.
Com-mon-ly.
Com-mon-place.
Com-mons.
Com-mon-weal.
Com-mon-wealth.
Com-mo-tion.
Com-mune.
Com-mu-ni-ca-ble.
Com-mu-ni-cant.
Com-mu-ni-cate.
Com-mu-ni-ca-tion.
Com-mu-ni-ca-tive.
Com-mun-ion.
Com-mu-ni-ty.
Com-mu-ta-tion.
Com-mute.
Com-pact.
Com-pan-ion.
Com-pan-ion-a-ble.
Com-pan-ion-ship.
Com-pa-ny
Com-pa-ra-ble.
Com-par-a-tive.
Com-par-a-tive-ly
Com-pare.
Com-par-i-son.
Com-part-ment.
Com-pass.
Com-pas-sion.
Com-pas-sion-ate.
Com-pat-i-bil-i-ty.

Com-pat-i-ble.
Com-pat-i-bly.
Com-pa-tri-ot.
Com-peer.
Com-pel.
Com-pel-la-tion.
Com-pend.
Com-pend-i-um.
Com-pend-i-ous.
Com-pen-sate.
Com-pen-sa-tion.
Com-pen-sa-tive.
Com-pen-sa-to-ry.
Com-pete.
Com-pe-tence.
Com-pe-ten-cy.
Com-pe-tent.
Com-pe-ti-tion.
Com-pet-i-tor.
Com-pet-i-tive.
Com-pi-la-tion.
Com-pile.
Com-pil-er.
Com-pla-cence.
Com-pla-cen-cy.
Com-pla-cent.
Com-plain.
Com-plain-ant.
Com-plaint.
Com-plai-sance.
Com-plai-sant.
Com-ple-ment.
Com-plete.
Com-plete-ly.
Com-ple-tion.
Com-plex.
Com-plex-ion.
Com-plex-i-ty.
Com-pli-ance.
Com-pli-ant.
Com-pli-ca-cy.
Com-pli-cate.
Com-pli-ca-tion.
Com-pli-ment.
Com-pli-ment-al.
Com-pli-ment-a-ry.
Com-plot.
Com-ply.
Com-po-nent.
Com-port.
Com-port-a-ble.
Com-pro-mit.
Comp-trol-ler.
Com-pul-sa-to-ry.
Com-pose.
Com-posed.
Com-pos-er.
Com-pos-ite.

Com-po-si-tion.
Com-pos-i-tor.
Com-post.
Com-pos-ure.
Com-po-ta-tion.
Com-pound.
Com-pre-hend.
Com-pre-hen-si-ble.
Com-pre-hen-sion.
Com-pre-hen-sive.
Com-press.
Com-press-i-bil-i-ty.
Com-press-i-ble.
Com-pres-sion.
Com-prise.
Com-pro-mise.
Com-pul-sion.
Com-pul-sive.
Com-pul-so-ry.
Com-punc-tion.
Com-punc-tious.
Com-put-a-ble.
Com-pu-ta-tion.
Com-pute.
Com-put-er.
Com-rade.
Con.
Con-cat-e-nate.
Con-cat-e-na-tion.
Con-cave.
Con-cav-i-ty.
Con-ca-vo-con-vex.
Con-ca-vo-con-cave.
Con-ceal.
Con-ceal-ment.
Con-cede.
Con-ceit.
Con-ceit-ed.
Con-ceiv-a-ble.
Con-ceive.
Con-cen-ter.
Con-cen-tre.
Con-cen-trate.
Con-cen-tra-tion.
Con-cen-tra-tive-ness.
Con-cen-tric.
Con-cen-tric-al.
Con-cep-tion.
Con-cern.
Con-cern-ing.
Con-cern-ment.
Con-cert.

Con-ces-sion.
Con-ces-sive.
Conch.
Conch-oid-al.
Con-chol-o-gist.
Con-chol-o-gy.
Con-cil-i-ate.
Con-cil-i-a-tion.
Con-cil-i-a-to-ry.
Con-cise.
Con-cise-ly.
Con-cis-ion.
Con-clave.
Con-clude.
Con-clu-sion.
Con-clu-sive.
Con-clu-sive-ly.
Con-coct.
Con-coc-tion.
Con-coct-ive.
Con-com-i-tance.
Con-com-i-tan-cy.
Con-com-i-tant.
Con-cord.
Con-cord-ance.
Con-cord-ant.
Con-course.
Con-crete.
Con-cre-tion.
Con-cre-tive.
Con-cu-bi-nage.
Con-cu-bine.
Con-cu-pis-cence.
Con-cur.
Con-cur-rence.
Con-cur-rent.
Con-cus-sion.
Con-cus-sive.
Con-dem.
Con - dem - na - tion.
Con - dem -na-to-ry.
Con-dem-ner.
Con-den-sa-tion.
Con-dense.
Con-dens-er.
Con-de-scend.
Con - de - scend - ing.
Con - de - scen - sion.
Con-dign.
Con-di-ment.
Con-di-tion.
Con-di-tion-al.
Con-di-tion-ed.
Con-dole.
Con-do-lence.

Con-dol-er.
Con-dor.
Con-duce.
Con-duct.
Con-duct-or.
Con-du-cive.
Con-duit.
Cone.
Con-fab-u-late.
Con - fab - u - la - tion.
Con-fect.
Con-fec-tion.
Con-fec-tion-er.
Con-fec-tion-er-y.
Con-fed-er-a-cy.
Con-fed-er-ate.
Con - fed - er - a - tion.
Con - fed - er - a - tive.
Con-fer.
Con-fer-ence.
Con-fess.
Con-fess-ed-ly.
Con-fes-sion.
Con-fes-sion-al.
Con-fess-or.
Con-fi-dant.
Con-fi-dante.
Con-fide.
Con-fi-dence.
Con-fi-dent.
Con-fi-den-tial.
Con-fi-dent-ly.
Con - fig - u - ra - tion.
Con-fine.
Con-fine-ment.
Con-firm.
Con-fir-ma-tion.
Con-firm-a-tive.
Con-firm-a-to-ry.
Con-fis-cate.
Con-fis-ca-tion.
Con-fis-ca-tor.
Con-fla-gra-tion.
Con-flict.
Con-flu-ence.
Con-flu-ent.
Con-form.
Con-form-a-ble.
Con-form-a-bly.
Con-for-ma-tion.
Con-form-i-ty.
Con-found.
Con-found-ed.
Con-front.
Con-fuse.
Con-fus-ed-ly.

Con-fu-sion.
Con-fu-ta-tion.
Con-fute.
Con-ge.
Con-geal.
Con-geal-a-ble.
Con-geal-ment.
Con-ge-la-tion.
Con-ge-ner.
Con-ge-ni-al.
Con - ge - ni - al-i-ty.
Con-gen-i-tal.
Con-ge-ri-es.
Con-ges-tion.
Con-gest-ive.
Con-glo-bate.
Con-glo-ba-tion.
Con-glom-er-ate.
Con - glom - er -a-tion.
Con-grat-u-late.
Con - grat - u - la - tion.
Con- grat -u-la-to-ry.
Con-gre-gate.
Con-gre-ga-tion.
Con-gre - ga-tion-al.
Con-gre - ga-tion-al-ism.
Con-gre -ga-tion-al-ist.
Con-gress.
Con-gres-sion-al.
Con-gru-ence.
Con-gru-ent.
Con-gru-i-ty.
Con-gru-ous.
Con-ic.
Con-ic-al.
Con-ic-al-ly.
Con-ics.
Co-nif-er-ous.
Con-ject-ur-al.
Con-ject-ure.
Con-join.
Con-joint.
Con-joint-ly.
Con-ju-gal.
Con-ju-gate.
Con-ju-ga-tion.
Con-junct.
Con-junc-tion.
Con-junc-tive.
Con-junct-ure.
Con-ju-ra-tion.
Con-jure.
Con-jur-er.

Con-nate.
Con-nat-u-ral.
Con-nect.
Con-nec-tion.
Con-nect-ive.
Con-niv-ance.
Con-nive.
Con-nois-seur.
Co-noid.
Con-nu-bi-al.
Con-quer.
Con-quer-a-ble.
Con-quer-or.
Con-quest.
Con - san -guin-e-ous.
Con - san - guin-i-ty.
Con-science.
Con-sci-en-tious.
Con-sci-en- tious-ness.
Con-scion-a-ble.
Con-scious.
Con-scious-ly.
Con-scious-ness.
Con-script.
Con-scrip-tion.
Con-se-crate.
Con-se-cra-tion.
Con-sec-u-tive.
Con - sec - u -tive-ly.
Con-sent.
Con - sen - ta - ne-ous.
Con-se-quence.
Con-se-quent.
Con-se-quen-tial.
Con-se-quen-tial-ly.
Con-se-quent-ly.
Con-ser-va-tion.
Con-serv-a-tive.
Con-serv-a-tor.
Con-serv-a-tor-y.
Con-serve.
Con-sid-er.
Con-sid-er-a-ble.
Con-sid-er-a-bly.
Con-sid-er-ate.
Con - sid - er -ate-ly.
Con - sid - er - a - tion.
Con-sid-er-ing.
Con-sign.
Con-sign-ee.
Con-sign-er.
Con-sign-or.

Con-sign-ment.
Con-sist.
Con-sist-ence.
Con-sist-en-cy.
Con-sist-ent.
Con-sist-ent-ly.
Con-sis-to-ri-al.
Cos-sist-o-ry.
Con-so-ci-a-tion.
Con-sol-a-ble.
Con-so-la-tion.
Con-sol-a-to-ry.
Con-sole.
Con-sol-i-date.
Con-sol-i-da-tion.
Con-sols.
Con-so-nance.
Con-so-nant.
Con-sort.
Con-spic-u-ous.
Con-spic-u-ous-ness.
Con-spir-a-cy.
Con-spir-a-tor.
Con-spire.
Con-sta-ble.
Con-stab-u-la-ry.
Con-stan-cy.
Con-stant.
Con-stant-ly.
Con-stel-la-tion.
Con-ster-na-tion.
Con-sti-pate.
Con-sti-pa-tion.
Con-stit-u-en-cy.
Con-stit-u-ent.
Con-sti-tute.
Con-sti-tu-tion.
Con-sti-tu-tion-al.
Con-sti-tu-tion-al-i-ty.
Con-sti-tu-tion-al-ly.
Con-sti-tu-tive.
Con-strain.
Con-strain-er.
Con-straint.
Con-strict.
Con-stric-tion.
Con-strin-gent.
Con-struct.
Con-struct-er.
Con-struc-tion.
Con-struct-ive.
Con-strue.
Con-stu-pra-tion.
Con-sub-stan-tial.
Con-sub-stan-ti-a-tion.

Con-sue-tu-di-nal.
Con-sul.
Con-su-lar.
Con-su-late.
Con-sul-ship.
Con-sult.
Con-sul-ta-tion.
Con-sult-er.
Con-sume.
Con-sum-mate.
Con-sum-ma-tion.
Con-sump-tion.
Con-sump-tive.
Con-tact.
Con-ta-gion.
Con-ta-gious.
Con-tain.
Con-tain-a-ble.
Con-tam-i-nate.
Con-tam-i-na-tion.
Con-temn.
Con-tem-ner.
Con-tem-plate.
Con-tem-pla-tion.
Con-**tem-pla**-tive.
Con-tem-pla-tor.
Con-tem-po-ra-ne-ous.
Con-tem-po-ra-ry.
Con-tempt.
Con-tempt-i-ble.
Con-tempt-i-bly.
Con-tempt-u-ous.
Con-tend.
Con-tend-er.
Con-tent.
Con-tent-ed.
Con-tent-ed-ly.
Con-**tent**-ed-ness.
Con-ten-tion.
Con-ten-tious.
Con-tent-ment.
Con-ter-mi-nous.
Con-test.
Con-text.
Con-text-ure.
Con-ti-gu-i-ty.
Con-tig-u-ous.
Con-ti-nence.
Con-ti-nent.
Con-ti-nent-al.
Con-ti-nent-ly.
Con-tin-gence.

Con-tin-gen-cy.
Con-tin-gent.
Con-tin-u-al.
Con-tin-u-al-ly.
Con-tin-u-ance.
Con-tin-u-a-tion.
Con-tin-u-a-tor.
Con-tin-ue.
Con-ti-nu-i-ty.
Con-tin-u-ous.
Con-tort.
Con-tor-tion.
Con-tour.
Con-tra-band.
Con-tract.
Con-tract-ed.
Con-tract-ile.
Con-trac-til-i-ty.
Con-trac-tion.
Con-tract-or.
Con-tra-dance.
Con-tra-dict.
Con-tra-dic-tion.
Con-tra-dic-to-ry.
Con-tra-dis-tinc-tion.
Con-tra-dis-tinct-ive.
Con-tra-**dis**-tin-guish.
Con-tral-to.
Con-tra-ri-e-ty.
Con-tra-ries.
Con-tra-ri-wise.
Con-tra-ry.
Con-trast.
Con-tra-**val**-la-tion.
Con-tra-vene.
Con-tra-ven-tion.
Con-trib-ute.
Con-tri-bu-tion.
Con-trib-u-tor.
Con-trib-u-to-ry.
Con-trite.
Con-tri-tion.
Con-triv-ance.
Con-trive.
Con-trol.
Con-trol-ler.
Con-tro-ver-sial.
Con-tro-ver-sial-ist.
Con-tro-ver-sy.
Con-tro-vert.
Con-tro-**vert**-i-ble.
Con-tu-ma-cious.

Con-tu-ma-cious-ly.
Con-tu-ma-cy.
Con-tu-mel-ious.
Con-tu-me-ly.
Con-tu-sion.
Co-nun-drum.
Con-va-les-cence.
Con-va-les-cent.
Con-vene.
Con-ven-ience.
Con-ven-ien-cy.
Con-ven-ient.
Con-vent.
Con-ven-ti-cle.
Con-ven-tion.
Con-ven-tion-al.
Con-**ven**-tion-al-ism.
Con-vent-u-al.
Con-verge.
Con-verg-ence.
Con-verg-ent.
Con-verg-ing.
Con-ver-sa-ble.
Con-ver-sant.
Con-ver-sa-tion.
Con-ver-sa-tion-al.
Con-verse.
Con-verse-ly.
Con-ver-sion.
Con-vert.
Con-**vert**-i-bil-i-ty.
Con-vert-i-ble.
Con-vex.
Con-vex-i-ty.
Con-vex-ness.
Con-vey.
Con-vey-ance.
Con-vey-an-cer.
Con-vey-an-cing.
Con-vict.
Con-vic-tion.
Con-vince.
Con-viv-i-al.
Con-viv-i-al-i-ty.
Con-vo-ca-tion.
Con-voke.
Con-vo-lu-ted.
Con-vo-lu-tion.
Con-volve.
Con-voy.
Con-vulse.
Con-vul-sion.
Con-vul-sive.
Co-ny.
Coo.

Cook.
Cook-er-y.
Cook-y.
Cool.
Cool-er.
Cool-ly.
Cool-ness.
Coo-ly.
Coo-lie.
Coomb.
Coop.
Coop-er.
Coop-er-age.
Co-op-er-ate.
Co-op-er-a-tion.
Co-op-er-a-tive.
Co-op-er-a-tor.
Co-or-di-nate.
Coot.
Co-pai-ba.
Co-pai-va.
Co-pal.
Co-par-ce-na-ry.
Co-par-ce-ny.
Co-par-ce-ner.
Co-part-ner.
Co-part-ner-ship.
Cope.
Cop-i-er.
Cop-ing.
Co-pi-ous.
Co-pi-ous-ly.
Cop-per.
Cop-per-as.
Cop-per-plate.
Cop-per-y.
Cop-pice.
Copse.
Cop-u-la-tive.
Cop-y.
Cop-y-hold.
Cop-y-ist.
Cop-y-right.
Co-quet.
Co-quet-ry.
Co-quette.
Co-quet-tish.
Cor-al.
Cor-al-line.
Cord
Cord-age.
Cord-ate.
Cor-di-al.
Cor-di-al-i-ty.
Cor-di-al-ly.
Cor-don.
Cor-du-roy.
Cord-wain-er.
Core.
Co-ri-a-ceous.

Co-ri-an-der.
Cork.
Cork-screw.
Cor-mo-rant.
Corn.
Cor-ne-a.
Cor-nel.
Cor-ner.
Cor-ner-stone.
Cor-ner-wise.
Cor-net.
Cor-net-cy.
Cor-nice.
Cor-nu-co-pi-a.
Cor-ol.
Co-rol-la.
Cor-ol-la-ry.
Cor-o-nal.
Cor-o-na-ry.
Cor-o-na-tion.
Cor-o-ner.
Cor-o-net.
Cor-po-ral.
Cor-po-ral-ly.
Cor-po-rate.
Cor-po-ra-tion.
Cor-po-ra-tor.
Cor-po-re-al.
Cor-po-re-al-ly.
Cor-po-re-i-ty.
Corps.
Corpse.
Cor-pu-lence.
Cor-pu-lent.
Cor-pus-cle.
Cor-pus-cu-lar.
Cor-rect.
Cor-rec-tion.
Cor-rect-ive.
Cor-rect-ly.
Cor-rect-ness.
Cor-rect-or.
Cor-rel-a-tive.
Cor-re-spond.
Cor - re - spond - ence
Cor - re - spond - ent.
Cor-ri-dor.
Cor-rob-o-rant.
Cor-rob-o-rate.
Cor - rob - o - ra - tion.
Cor - **rob** - o - ra - tive.
Cor-rode.
Cor-ro-sion.
Cor-ro-sive.
Cor-ru-gate
Cor-ru-ga-tion.

Cor-rupt.
Cor-rupt- i - bil-i- ty.
Cor-rupt-i-ble.
Cor-rup-tion.
Cor-sair.
Corse.
Corse-let.
Cor-set.
Cor-tege.
Cor-ti-cal.
Cor-us-cate.
Cor-us-ca-tion.
Cor-vette.
Co-sey
Cos-met-ic.
Cos-mog-o-ny.
Cos-mog-ra-pher.
Cos-mog-ra-phy.
Cos-mol-o-gist.
Cos-mol-o-gy.
Cos-mop-o-lite.
Cos-set.
Cost.
Cos-tal.
Cos-tive.
Cos-tive-ness.
Cost li-ness.
Cost-ly.
Cos-tume.
Cot.
Cote.
Cott.
Co-tem-po-ra-ne- ous.
Co-tem-po-ra-ry.
Co-te-rie.
Co-til-lon.
Co-til-lion.
Cot-tage.
Cot-ta-ger.
Cot-ter.
Cot-ton.
Cot-ton-y.
Cot-y-le-don.
Cot-y-led-o-nous.
Couch.
Cough.
Could.
Coul-ter.
Coun-cil.
Coun-cil-or.
Coun-cil-lor.
Coun-sel.
Coun-sel-or.
Coun-sel-lor.
Count.
Coun-te-nance.
Count-er.
Coun-ter-act.

Coun - ter - bal - ance.
Coun-ter-charm.
Coun - ter - cur rent.
Coun-ter-feit.
Coun-ter-feit-er
Coun-ter-mand.
Coun-ter-march
Coun-ter-mark.
Coun-ter-mine.
Coun-ter-pane.
Coun-ter-part.
Coun-ter-plot.
Coun-ter-point.
Coun-ter-poise.
Coun-ter-sign.
Coun-ter-sig-nal.
Coun-ter-ten-or.
Coun-ter-vail.
Count-ess.
Count-ing-house
Count-ing-room.
Count-less.
Coun-tri-fied.
Coun-try.
Coun-try-dance.
Coun-try-man.
Coun-try-seat.
Coun-ty.
Coup-le.
Coup-let.
Coup-ling.
Cou-pon.
Cour-age.
Cour-a-geous.
Cour-a-geous-ly.
Cou-ri-er.
Course.
Cours-er.
Court.
Court-e-ous.
Court-e-ous-ly.
Court-e-san.
Courte-sy.
Court-e-sy.
Court-ier.
Court li-ness.
Court-ly.
Court-mar-tial.
Court-ship.
Cous-in.
Cove.
Cov-e-nant.
Cov-e-nant-ee.
Cov-e-nant-er.
Cov-er.
Cov-er-ing.
Cov-er-let.
Cov-ert.

Cov-ert-ly.
Cov-ert-ure.
Cov-et.
Cov-et-ous.
Cov-et-ous-ness.
Cov-ey.
Cow.
Cow-ard.
Cow-ard-ice.
Cow-ard-li-ness.
Cow-ard-ly.
Cow-er.
Cow-hide.
Cowl.
Cow-lick.
Cow-pox.
Cow-slip.
Cow's-lip.
Cox-comb.
Cox-comb-ic-al.
Cox-comb-ry.
Coy.
Coy-ly.
Coy-ness.
Coz-en
Co-zy.
Crab.
Crab-bed.
Crab-bed-ly.
Crack.
Crack-brained.
Crack-er.
Crack le.
Crack-ling.
Cra-dle.
Craft.
Craft-i-ly
Craft-i-ness.
Crafts-man.
Craft-y.
Crag.
Crag-ged.
Crag-gy.
Cram.
Cram-bo.
Cramp.
Cram-poons.
Cran-ber-ry.
Crane.
Cra-ni-ol-o-gy.
Cra-ni-um.
Crank.
Crank-le.
Cran-ny.
Crape.
Crash.
Crate.
Cra-ter.
Craunch.
Cra-vat.

Crave.
Cra-ven.
Craw.
Craw-fish.
Crawl.
Cray-on.
Craze.
Cra-zi-ness.
Cra-zy.
Creak.
Creak-ing.
Cream.
Cream-y.
Crease.
Cre-ate.
Cre-a-tion.
Cre-a-tive.
Cre-a-tor.
Creat-ure.
Cre-dence.
Cre-den-tials.
Cred-i-bil-i-ty.
Cred-i-ble.
Cred-i-bly.
Cred-it.
Cred-it-a-ble.
Cred-it-a-bly.
Cred-it-or.
Cre-du-li-ty.
Cred-u-lous.
Creed.
Creek.
Creel.
Creep.
Cre-ole.
Cre-o-sote.
Crep-i-tate.
Crep-i-ta-tion.
Crept.
Cre-pus-cu-lar.
Cres-cent.
Cress.
Crest.
Crest-ed.
Crest-fallen.
Cre-ta-ceous.
Crev-ice.
Crew.
Crew-el.
Crib.
Crib-bage.
Crick.
Crick-et.
Cried.
Cri-er.
Crime.
Crim-i-nal.
Crim-i-nal-ly.
Crim-i-nal-i-ty.
Crim-i-nate.

Crim-i-na-tion.
Crimp.
Crim-son.
Cringe.
Crink-le.
Crip-ple.
Cri-sis.
Crisp.
Crisp-y.
Cri-te-ri-on.
Crit-ic.
Crit-ic-al.
Crit-ic-al-ly.
Crit-i-cise.
Crit-i-cism.
Cri-tique.
Croak.
Croak-er.
Crock.
Crock-er-y.
Croc-o-dile.
Cro-cus.
Croft.
Crone.
Cro-ny.
Crook.
Crook-ed.
Crook-ed-ness.
Crop.
Cro-quet.
Cro-sier.
Cross.
Cross-bow.
Cross-ex-am-ine.
Cross-eyed.
Cross-ing.
Cross-ness.
Cross-ques-tion.
Cross-road.
Cross-way.
Cross-wise.
Crotch.
Crotch-ed.
Crotch-et.
Crouch.
Croup.
Crow.
Crow-bar.
Crowd.
Crow-foot.
Crown.
Crown-glass.
Crow's-foot.
Cru-cial.
Cru-ci-ate.
Cru-ci-ble.
Cru-ci-fi-er.
Cru-ci-fix.
Cru-ci-fix-ion.
Cru-ci-form.

Cru-ci-fy.
Crude.
Crude-ly.
Crude-ness.
Cru-di-ty.
Cru-el.
Cru-el-ly.
Cru-el-ty.
Cru-et.
Cruise.
Cruis-er.
Crumb.
Crum-ble.
Crum-pet.
Crum-ple.
Crup-per.
Cru-sade.
Cru-sad-er.
Cruse.
Crush.
Crust.
Crus-ta-cean.
Crus-ta-ceous.
Crust-i-ly.
Crust-y.
Crutch.
Cry.
Crypt.
Crys-tal.
Crys-tal-line.
Crys-tal-li-za-tion.
Crys-tal-lize.
Crys-tal-log-ra-phy.
Cub.
Cu-ba-ture.
Cube.
Cu-beb.
Cu-bic.
Cu-bi-form.
Cu-bit.
Cuck-old.
Cuck-oo.
Cu-cum-ber.
Cud.
Cud-dle.
Cud-dy.
Cud-gel.
Cue.
Cuff.
Cui-rass.
Cui-ras-sier.
Cu-li-na-ry.
Cull.
Cul-len-der.
Cul-ler.
Cul-mi-nate.
Cul-mi-na-tion.
Cul-pa-ble.

Cul-pa-bil-i-ty.	Cur-tain.	Dab-bler.	**Dash.**
Cul-pa-bly.	Cur-va-tion.	Dab-ster.	**Das-tard**.
Cul-prit.	Curv-a-ture.	Dace.	Das-tard-ly.
Cul-ti-va-ble.	Curve.	Dac-tyl.	Da-ta.
Cul-ti-vate.	Cur-vet.	Dad.	Date.
Cul-ti-va-ted.	Curv-i-lin-e-al.	Dad-dy.	Da-tive.
Cul-ti-va-tion.	Curv-i-lin-e-ar.	Daf-fo-dil.	Daub.
Cul-ti-va-tor.	Curv-i-ty.	Dag-ger.	Daub-er.
Cult-ure.	Cush-ion.	Da - guerre - o -	Daub-y.
Cul-vert.	Cusp.	type.	Daugh-ter.
Cum-ber.	Cusp-i-date.	Dahl-ia.	Daunt.
Cum-ber-some.	Cusp-i-da-ted.	Dai-ly.	Daunt-less.
Cum-brous.	Cus-tard.	Dain-ti-ly.	Dau-phin.
Cum-in.	Cus-to-di-an.	Dain-ty.	Dav-it.
Cu-mu-late.	Cus-to-dy.	Dai-ry.	Daw-dle.
Cu-mu-la-tion.	Cus-tom.	Dai-sy.	Dawn.
Cu-mu-la-tive.	Cus-tom-a-ri-ly.	Dale.	Day.
Cu-ne-i-form.	Cus-tom-a-ry.	Dal-li-ance.	Day-book.
Cun-ning.	Cus-tom-er.	Dal-ly.	Day-break.
Cup.	Cus-tom-house.	Dam.	Day-light.
Cup-board.	Cut.	Dam-age.	Day-spring.
Cu-pel.	Cu-ta-ne-ous.	Dam-ask.	Daze.
Cu-pel-la-tion.	Cu-ti-cle.	Dam-ask-een.	Daz-zle.
Cu-pid-i-ty.	Cu-tic-u-lar.	Dame.	Dea-con.
Cu-po-la.	Cut-lass.	Damn.	Dea-con-ship.
Cup-ping.	Cut-ler.	Dam-na-ble.	Dead.
Cur.	Cut-ler-y.	Dam-na-bly.	Dead-en.
Cur-a-ble.	Cut-let.	Dam-na-tion.	Dead-light.
Cu-ra-coa.	Cut-purse.	Dam-na-to-ry.	Dead-ly.
Cu-ra-cy.	Cut-ter.	Damp.	Dead-ness.
Cu-rate.	Cut-throat.	Damp-er.	Deaf.
Cu-ra-tive.	Cut-ting.	Damp-ness.	Deaf-en.
Cu-ra-tor.	Cut-tle-fish.	Dam-sel.	Deaf-mute.
Curb.	Cut-wa-ter.	Dam-son.	Deaf-ness.
Curd.	Cy-cle.	Dance.	Deal.
Cur-dle.	Cyc-lic.	Dan-cer.	Dean.
Cure.	Cyc-lic-al.	Dan-dle.	Dean-er-y.
Cur-few.	Cy-clo-pe-an.	Dan-druff.	Dear.
Cu-ri-os-i-ty.	Cy-clop-ic.	Dan-dy.	Dear-ly.
Cu-ri-ous.	Cy-clo-pæ-di-a.	Dan-dy-ism.	Dear-ness.
Curl.	Cy-clo-pe-di-a.	Dan-ger.	Dearth.
Cur-lew.	Cyg-net.	Dan-ger-ous.	Death.
Curl-i-ness.	Cyl-in-der.	Dan-ger-ous-ly.	Death-bed.
Curl-y.	Cy-lin-dric-al.	Dan-gle.	Death-less.
Cur-mud-geon.	Cym-bal.	Dank.	Death-war-rant.
Cur-rant.	Cyn-ic.	Dap-per.	De-bar.
Cur-ren-cy.	Cyn-ic-al.	Dap-ple.	De-bark.
Cur-rent.	Cyn-o-sure.	Dap-pled.	De-base.
Cur-rent-ly.	Cy-press.	Dare.	De-base-ment.
Cur-ri-cle.	Cyst.	Dar-ing.	De-bat-a-ble.
Cur-ri-er.	Czar.	Dark.	De-bate.
Cur-rish.	Cza-ri-na.	Dark-en.	De-bauch.
Cur-ry.	Czar-o-witz.	Dark-ish.	Deb-au-chee.
Cur-ry-comb.		Dark ly.	De-bauch-er-y.
Curse.		Dark-ness.	De-bent-ure.
Curs-ed.	**D**	Dark-some.	De-bil-i-tate.
Cur-sive.		Dar-ling.	De-bil-i-ty.
Cur-so-ri-ly.		Darn.	Deb-it.
Cur-so-ry.	Dab.	Dar-nel.	Deb-o-nair.
Cur-tail.	Dab-ble.	Dart.	De-bouch.

De-bris.
Debt.
Debt-or.
De-but.
Dec-ade.
De-ca-dence.
De-ca-den-cy.
Dec-a-gon.
Dec-a-logue
De-camp.
De-cant.
De-can-ta-tion.
De-cant-er.
De-cap-i-tate.
De-cap-i-ta-tion.
De-cay.
De-cease.
De-ceased.
De-ceit.
De-ceit-ful.
De-ceit-ful-ly.
De-ceive.
De-cem-ber.
De-cen-cy.
De-cen-ni-al.
De-cent.
De-cent-ly.
De-cep-tion.
De-cep-tive.
De-cide.
De-cid-ed.
De-cid-ed-ly.
De-cid-u-ous.
Dec-i-mal.
Dec-i-mate.
Dec-i-ma-tion
De-ci-pher.
De-cis-ion.
De-ci-sive.
De-ci-sive-ly.
Deck.
De-claim.
De-claim-er.
Dec-la-ma-tion.
De-clam-a-to-ry.
Dec-la-ra-tion.
De-clar-a-tive.
De-clar-a-to-ry.
De-clare.
De-clen-sion.
De-clin-a-ble.
Dec-li-na-tion.
De-cline.
De-cliv-i-ty.
De-coct.
De-coc-tion.
De-col-or-a-tion.
De-com-pose.
De - com - po - si - tion.

De-com-pound.
Dec-o-rate.
Dec-o-ra-tion.
Dec-o-ra-tive.
De-co-rous.
De-co-rous-ly.
De-cor-ti-cate.
De-co-rum.
De-coy.
De-crease.
De-cree.
Dec-re-ment.
De-crep-it.
De-crep-i-tate.
De-crep-i-ta-tion.
De-crep-i-tude.
De-cre-tal.
De-cri-al.
De-cri-er.
De-cry.
De-cum-bent.
Dec-u-ple.
De-cu-ri-on.
De-cus-sate.
Ded-i-cate.
Ded-i-ca-tion.
Ded-i-ca-tor.
Ded-i-ca-to-ry.
De-duce.
De-du-ci-ble.
De-du-cive.
De-duct-ive.
De-duct.
De-duc-tion.
Deed.
Deem.
Deep.
Deep-en.
Deep-ly.
Deer.
De-face.
De-face-ment.
De-fal-ca-tion.
Def-a-ma-tion.
De-fam-a-to-ry.
De-fame.
De-fault.
De-fault-er.
De-fea-sance.
De-fea-si-ble.
De-feat.
Def-e-cate.
Def-e-ca-tion.
De-fect.
De-fec-tion.
De-fect-ive.
De-fect-ive-ly.
De-fence.
De-fend.
De-fend-ant.

De-fend-er.
De-fense.
De-fense-less.
De-fen-sive.
De-fer.
Def-er-ence.
Def-er-en-tial.
De-fi-ance.
De-fi-ant.
De-fi-cien-cy.
De-fi-cient.
Def-i-cit.
De-file.
De-file-ment.
De-fin-a-ble.
De-fine.
Def-i-nite.
Def-i-nite-ly.
Def-i-ni-tion.
De-fin-i-tive.
De-fin-i-tive-ly.
Def-la-grate.
Def-la-gra-tion.
De-flect.
De-flec-tion.
De-flour.
De-fo-li-a-tion.
De-form.
De-formed.
De-form-i-ty.
De-fraud.
De-fray.
De-funct.
De-fy.
De-gen-er-a-cy.
De-gen-er-ate.
De-gen-er-a-tion.
Deg-lu-ti-tion.
Deg ra-da-tion.
De-grade.
De-gree.
De-i-fi-ca-tion.
De-i-fy.
Deign.
De-ism.
De-ist.
De-ist-ic.
De-ist-ic-al.
De-i-ty.
De-ject.
De-ject-ed.
De-jec-tion.
De-lay.
De-lect-a-ble.
Del-e-gate.
Del-e-ga-tion.
Del-e-te-ri-ous.
Delf.
De-lib-er-ate.
De-lib-er-ate-ly.

De-lib-er-a-tion
De-lib-er-a-tive
Del-i-ca-cy.
Del-i-cate.
De-li-cious.
De-light.
De-light-ed.
De-light-ful.
De-lin-e-ate.
De-lin-e-a-tion.
De-lin-e-a-tor.
De-lin-quen-cy.
De-lin-quent.
Del-i-quesce.
Del-i-ques-cence
Del-i-ques-cent.
De-lir-i-ous.
De-lir-i-um.
De-liv-er.
De-liv-er-ance
De-liv-er-er.
De-liv-er-y.
Dell.
De-lude.
De-luge.
De-lu-sion.
De-lu-sive.
Delve.
Dem-a-gogue.
De-main.
De-mesne.
De-mand.
De-mand-ant.
De-mar-ca-tion.
De-mar-ka-tion.
De-mean.
De-mean-or.
De-ment-ed.
De-mer-it.
Dem-i-god.
Dem-i-john.
De-mise.
De-moc-ra-cy.
Dem-o-crat.
Dem-o-crat-ic.
Dem-ol-ish.
Dem-o-li-tion.
De-mon.
De-mo-ni-ac.
De-mo-ni-ac-al.
De-mon-ol-o-gy.
De-mon-stra-ble.
Dem-on-strate.
Dem - on - stra - tion.
De - mon - stra - tive.
Dem-on-stra-tor.
De-mor-al-i-za-tion.

De-mor-al-ize.
De-mul-cent.
De-mur.
De-mure.
De-mur-rage.
De-mur-rer.
De-my.
Den.
Den-drol-o-gy.
De-ni-al.
De-ni-er.
Den-i-zen.
De-nom-i-nate.
De-nom-i-na-tion.
De-nom-i-na-tive.
De-nom-i-na-tor.
De-note.
De-nounce.
De-nounce-ment.
Dense.
Den-si-ty.
Dent.
Dent-al.
Den-tic-u-la-ted.
Den-ti-frice.
Den-til.
Den-tist.
Den-tist-ry.
Den-ti-tion.
Den-u-da-tion.
De-nude.
De-nun-ci-a-tion.
De-nun-ci-a-tor.
De-nun-ci-a-to-ry.
De-ny.
De-o-dand.
De-on-tol-o-gy.
De-part.
De-part-ment.
De-part-ure.
De-pend.
De-pend-ence.
De-pend-en-cy.
De-pend-ent.
De-pict.
De-pict-ure.
De-pil-a-to-ry.
De-ple-tion.
De-plor-a-ble.
De-plore.
De-ploy.
Dep-lu-ma-tion.
De-plume.
De-po-nent.
De-pop-u-late.
De-pop-u-la-tion
De-port.

De-por-ta-tion.
De-port-ment.
De-pos-al.
De-pose.
De-pos-it.
De-pos-i-ta-ry.
Dep-o-si-tion.
De-pos-i-tor.
De-pos-i-to-ry.
De-pot.
Dep-ra-va-tion.
De-prave.
De-prav-i-ty.
Dep-re-cate.
Dep-re-ca-tion.
Dep-re-ca-to-ry.
De-pre-ci-ate.
De-pre-ci-a-tion.
Dep-re-date.
Dep-re-da-tion.
De-press.
De-pres-sion.
De-pres-sive.
Dep-ri-va-tion.
De-prive.
Depth.
Dep-u-ta-tion.
De-pute.
Dep-u-ty.
De-range.
De-ranged.
De-range-ment.
Der-e-lict.
Der-e-lic-tion.
De-ride.
De-ris-ion.
De-ri-sive.
De-ri-so-ry.
De-riv-a-ble.
Der-i-va-tion.
De-riv-a-tive.
De-rive.
Der-o-gate.
Der-o-ga-tion.
De-rog-a-to-ry.
Der-rick.
Der-vis.
Des-cant.
De-scend.
De-scend-ant.
De-scent.
De-stribe.
De-scri-er.
De-scrip-tion.
De-scrip-tive.
De-scry.
Des-e-crate.
Des-e-cra-tion.
De-sert.
Des-ert.

De-sert-er.
De-ser-tion.
De-serve.
De-served.
De-serv-ing.
Des-ha-bille.
Des-ic-cate.
Des-ic-ca-tion.
De-sid-er-ate.
De-sid-e-ra-tum.
De-sign.
Des-ig-na-tion.
De-sign-er.
De-sir-a-ble.
De-sire.
De-sir-ous.
De-sist.
Desk.
Des-o-late.
Des-o-la-tion.
De-spair.
De-spatch.
Des-per-a-do.
Des-per-ate.
Des-per-a-tion.
Des-pi-ca-ble.
De-spise.
De-spite.
De-spoil.
De-spo-li-a-tion.
De-spoil-er.
De-spond.
De-spond-en-cy.
De-spond-ent.
Des-pot.
Des-pot-ic.
Des-pot-ism.
Des-pu-ma-tion.
Des-qua-ma-tion.
Des-sert.
Des-ti-na-tion.
Des-tine.
Des-ti-ny.
Des-ti-tute.
Des-ti-tu-tion.
De-stroy.
De-struc-ti-ble.
De-struc-tion.
De-struc-tive.
Des-ue-tude.
Des-ul-to-ry.
De-tach.
De-tach-ment.
De-tail.
De-tain.
De-tect.
De-tec-tion.
De-tec-tive.
De-ten-tion.
De-ter.

De-ter-gent.
De-te-ri-o-rate.
De-te-ri-o-ra-tion.
De-ter-min-a-ble.
De-ter-min-ate.
De-ter-mi-na-tion.
De-ter-mine.
De-ter-mined.
De-ter-sive.
De-test.
De-test-a-ble.
Det-es-ta-tion.
De-throne.
De-throne-ment.
Det-i-nue.
Det-o-nate.
Det-o-nize.
Det-o-na-tion.
De-tort.
De-tor-tion.
De-tract.
De-trac-tion.
De-tract-or.
Det-ri-ment.
Det-ri-ment-al.
De-tri-tion.
De-trun-cate.
De-tru-sion.
Deuce.
Dev-as-tate.
Dev-as-ta-tion.
De-vel-op.
De-vel-op-ment.
De-vi-ate.
De-vi-a-tion.
De-vice.
Dev-il.
Dev-il-ish.
Dev-il-try.
De-vi-ous.
De-vis-a-ble.
De-vise.
Dev-is-ee.
De-vis-or.
De-void.
Devoir.
De-volve.
De-vote.
De-vot-ed.
De-vot-ed-ness.
Dev-o-tee.
De-vo-tion.
De-vo-tion-al.
De-vour.
De-vout.
De-vout ly.
Dew.
Dew-lap.

Dew-y.
Dex-ter.
Dex-tral.
Dex-ter-i-ty.
Dex-ter-ous.
Dex-ter-ous-ly.
Di-a-be-tes.
Di-a-bol-ic-al.
Di-a-crit-ic-al.
Di-a-dem.
Di-ær-e-sis.
Di-er-e-sis.
Di-ag-o-nal.
Di-ag-o-nal-ly.
Di-a-gram.
Di-al.
Di-a-lect.
Di-a-lec-tic-al.
Di-a-lec-ti-cian.
Di-a-lec-tics.
Di-al-ing.
Di-al-o-gist.
Di-a-logue.
Di-am-e-ter.
Di-a-met-ric-al.
Di-a-mond.
Di-a-pa-son.
Di-a-per.
Di-a-aph-a-nous.
Di-a-pho-ret-ic.
Di-a-phragm.
Di-ar-rhe-a.
Di-ar-rhœ-a.
Di-a-ry.
Di-a-ton-ic.
Di-a-tribe.
Dib-ble.
Dice.
Dick-y.
Dic-tate.
Dic-ta-tion.
Dic-ta-tor.
Dic-ta-to-ri-al.
Dic-ta-tor-ship.
Dic-tion.
Dic-tion-a-ry.
Dic-tum.
Did.
Di-dac-tic.
Die.
Di-er-e-sis.
Di-et.
Di-e-ta-ry.
Di-e-tet-ic.
Di-e-tet-ics.
Dif-fer.
Dif-fer-ence.
Dif-fer-ent.
Dif-fer-en-tial.
Dif-fi-cult.

Dif-fi-cul-ty.
Dif-fi-dence.
Dif-fi-dent.
Dif-fuse.
Dif-fuse-ly.
Dif-fu-sion.
Dif-fu-sive.
Dig.
Di-gest.
Di-gest-i-ble.
Di-ges-tion.
Di-gest-ive.
Dig-it.
Dig-it-al.
Dig-ni-fied.
Dig-ni-fy.
Dig-ni-ta-ry.
Dig-ni-ty.
Di-graph.
Di-gress.
Di-gres-sion.
Dike.
Di-lap-i-date.
Di-lap-i-da-tion.
Dil-a-ta-tion.
Di-late.
Di-la-tion.
Dil-a-to-ry.
Di-lem-ma.
Dil-i-gence.
Dil-i-gent.
Dil-i-gent-ly.
Di-lute.
Di-lu-tion.
Di-lu-vi-al.
Di-lu-vi-an.
Di-lu-vi-um.
Dim.
Dime.
Di-men-sion.
Di-min-ish.
Dim-i-nu-tion.
Di-min-u-tive.
Dim-is-so-ry.
Dim-i-ty.
Dim-ness.
Dim-ple.
Din.
Dine.
Din-gi-ness.
Din-gle.
Din-gy.
Din-ner.
Dint.
Di-oc-e-san.
Di-o-cese.
Di-o-ra-ma.
Dip.
Diph-the-ri-a.
Diph-thong.

Diph-thon-gal.
Di-plo-ma.
Di-plo-ma-cy.
Dip-lo-mat-ic.
Di-plo-ma-tist.
Dip-lo-mate.
Dip-per.
Dire.
Di-rect.
Di-rec-tion.
Di-rect-ly.
Di-rect-ness.
Di-rect-or.
Di-rect-o-ry.
Dire-ful.
Dirge.
Dirk.
Dirt.
Dirt-y.
Dis-a-bil-i-ty.
Dis-a-ble.
Dis-a-buse.
Dis-ad-van-tage.
Dis-ad-van-ta-geous.
Dis-af-fect.
Dis-af-fect-ed.
Dis-af-fec-tion.
Dis-a-gree.
Dis-a-gree-a-ble.
Dis-a-gree-a-bly.
Dis-a-gree-ment.
Dis-al-low.
Dis-al-low-ance.
Dis-an-nul.
Dis-ap-pear.
Dis-ap-pear-ance.
Dis-ap-point.
Dis-ap-point-ment.
Dis-ap-pro-ba-tion.
Dis-ap-prov-al.
Dis-ap-prove.
Dis-arm.
Dis-ar-range.
Dis-ar-range-ment.
Dis-ar-ray.
Dis-as-ter.
Dis-as-trous.
Dis-a-vow.
Dis-a-vow-al.
Dis-band.
Dis-be-lief.
Dis-be-lieve.
Dis-be-liev-er.
Dis-bur-den.
Dis-burse.

Dis-burse-ment.
Disc.
Dis-card.
Dis-cern.
Dis-cern-i-ble.
Dis-cern-ing.
Dis-cern-ment.
Dis-charge.
Dis-ci-ple.
Dis-ci-ple-ship.
Dis-ci-plin-a-ri-an.
Dis-ci-plin-a-ry.
Dis-ci-pline.
Dis-claim.
Dis-close.
Dis-clos-ure.
Dis-col-or.
Dis-col-or-a-tion.
Dis-com-fit.
Dis-com-fit-ure.
Dis-com-fort.
Dis-com-mode.
Dis-com-pose.
Dis-com-pos-ure.
Dis-con-cert.
Dis-con-nect.
Dis-con-nec-tion.
Dis-con-so-late.
Dis-con-tent.
Dis-con-tent-ed.
Dis-con-tent-ment.
Dis-con-tin-u-ance.
Dis-con-tin-u-a-tion.
Dis-con-tin-ue.
Dis-cord.
Dis-cord-ance.
Dis-cord-ant.
Dis-count.
Dis-coun-te-nance.
Dis-cour-age.
Dis-cour-age-ment.
Dis-course.
Dis-cour-te-ous.
Dis-cour-te-sy.
Dis-cov-er.
Dis-cov-er-a-ble.
Dis-cov-er-er.
Dis-cov-er-y.
Dis-cred-it.
Dis-cred-it-a-ble.
Dis-creet.
Dis-crep-an-cy.
Dis-crep-ance.
Dis-crep-ant.

Dis-crete.
Dis-cre-tion.
Dis-cre-tion-al.
Dis-cre-tion-a-ry.
Dis-crim-i-nate.
Dis-crim-i-na-tion.
Dis-**crim-i-na**-tive.
Dis-cur-sion.
Dis-cur-sive.
Dis-cus.
Dis-cuss.
Dis-cus-sion.
Dis-cuss-ive.
Dis-dain.
Dis-dain-ful.
Dis-ease.
Dis-em-bark.
Dis-em-bar-rass.
Dis-em-bod-ied.
Dis-em-bogue.
Dis-em-bow-el.
Dis-en-chant.
Dis-en-cum-ber.
Dis-en-gage.
Dis-en-gaged.
Dis-**en-gage**-ment.
Dis-en-tan-gle.
Dis-en-tan-gle-ment.
Dis-en-tomb.
Dis-es-teem.
Dis-fav-or.
Dis-fig-u-ra-tion.
Dis-fig-ure.
Dis-fig-ure-ment.
Dis-fran-chise.
Dis-fran-chise-ment.
Dis-gorge.
Dis-grace.
Dis-grace-ful.
Dis-guise.
Dis-gust.
Dis-gust-ful.
Dis-gust-ing.
Dish.
Dis-ha-bille.
Dis-heart-en.
Di-shev-el.
Dis-hon-est.
Dis-hon-est-y.
Dis-hon-or.
Dis-hon-or-a-ble.
Dis-in-cli-na-tion.
Dis-in-cline.
Dis-in-fect.

Dis-in-fec-tion.
Dis-in-gen-u-ous.
Dis-in-her-it.
Dis-in-te-grate.
Dis-in-te-gra-tion.
Dis-in-ter.
Dis-in-ter-est-ed.
Dis-in-ter-ment.
Dis-in-thrall.
Dis-join.
Dis-joint.
Dis-junct.
Dis-junc-tion.
Dis-junct-ive.
Disk.
Dis-like.
Dis-lo-cate.
Dis-lo-ca-tion.
Dis-lodge.
Dis-loy-al.
Dis-loy-al-ty.
Dis-mal.
Dis-man-tle.
Dis-mast.
Dis-may.
Dis-mem-ber.
Dis-**mem-ber**-ment.
Dis-miss.
Dis-miss-al.
Dis-mis-sion.
Dis-mount.
Dis-o-be-di-ence.
Dis-o-be-di-ent.
Dis-o-bey.
Dis-o-blige.
Dis-o-blig-ing.
Dis-or-der.
Dis-or-dered.
Dis-or-der-ly.
Dis-or-gan-i-za-tion.
Dis-or-gan-ize.
Dis-own.
Dis-par-age.
Dis-**par-age**-ment.
Dis-par-i-ty.
Dis-part.
Dis-pas-sion-ate.
Dis-patch.
Dis-pel.
Dis-pen-sa-ble.
Dis-pen-sa-ry.
Dis-pen-sa-tion.
Dis-pen-sa-tive.
Dis-pen-sa-to-ry.
Dis-pense.

Dis-peo-ple.
Dis-perse.
Dis-per-sion.
Dis-spir-it.
Dis-place.
Dis-play.
Dis-please.
Dis-pleas-ure.
Dis-plode.
Dis-plo-sion.
Dis-port.
Dis-pos-al.
Dis-pose.
Dis-posed.
Dis-po-si-tion.
Dis-pos-sess.
Dis-pos-ses-sion.
Dis-praise.
Dis-proof.
Dis-pro-por-tion.
Dis-pro-por-tion-al.
Dis-pro-por-tion-ate.
Dis-prove.
Dis-pu-ta-ble.
Dis-pu-tant.
Dis-pu-ta-tion.
Dis-pu-ta-tious.
Dis-pute.
Dis-qual-**i-fi-ca**-tion.
Dis-qual-i-fy.
Dis-qui-et.
Dis-qui-e-tude.
Dis-qui-si-tion.
Dis-re-gard.
Dis-rel-ish.
Dis-rep-u-ta-ble.
Dis-re-pute.
Dis-re-spect.
Dis-re-spect-ful.
Dis-robe.
Dis-rup-tion.
Dis-sat-is-**fac**-tion.
Dis-sat-is-fy.
Dis-sect.
Dis-sec-tion.
Dis-sect-or.
Dis-seize.
Dis-sem-ble.
Dis-sem-i-nate.
Dis-sem-i-na-tion.
Dis-sem-i-na-tor.
Dis-sen-sion.
Dis-sent.
Dis-sent-er.
Dis-sen-tient.

Dis-ser-ta-tion.
Dis-serv-ice.
Dis-sev-er.
Dis-sev-er-ance.
Dis-si-dence.
Dis-si-dent.
Dis-sim-i-lar.
Dis-sim-i-lar-i-ty.
Dis-si-mil-i-tude.
Dis-sim-u-la-tion.
Dis-si-pate.
Dis-si-pa-ted.
Dis-si-pa-tion.
Dis-so-ci-ate.
Dis-so-ci-a-tion.
Dis-so-lu-ble.
Dis-so-lute.
Dis-so-lute-ly.
Dis-so-lu-tion.
Dis-solve.
Dis-solv-ent.
Dis-so-nance.
Dis-so-nant.
Dis-suade.
Dis-sua-sion.
Dis-sua-sive.
Dis-syl-lab-ic.
Dis-syl-la-ble.
Dis-taff.
Dis-tain.
Dis-tance.
Dis-tant.
Dis-taste.
Dis-taste-ful.
Dis-tem-per.
Dis-tend.
Dis-ten-sion.
Dis-tich.
Dis-till.
Dis-til.
Dis-til-la-tion.
Dis-till-er.
Dis-till-er-y.
Dis-tinct.
Dis-tinc-tion.
Dis-tinct-ive.
Dis-tinct-ly.
Dis-tinct-ness.
Dis-tin-guish.
Dis-tin-guish-a-ble.
Dis-tin-guished.
Dis-tort.
Dis-tor-tion.
Dis-tract.
Dis-tract-ed.
Dis-trac-tion.
Dis-train.
Dis-traint.

Dis-tress.
Dis-tress-ing.
Dis-trib-ute.
Dis-tri-bu-tion.
Dis-trib-u-tive.
Dis-trict.
Dis-trust.
Dis-trust-ful.
Dis-turb.
Dis-turb-ance.
Dis-un-ion.
Dis-u-nite.
Dis-use.
Ditch.
Dit-to.
Dit-ty.
Di-u-ret-ic.
Di-ur-nal.
Di-van.
Di-var-i-cate.
Dive.
Di-ver.
Di-verge.
Di-ver-gence.
Di-ver-gent.
Di-vers.
Di-verse.
Di-verse-ly.
Di-ver-si-fi-ca-tion.
Di-ver-si-fy.
Di-ver-sion.
Di-ver-si-ty.
Di-vert.
Di-vert-ing.
Di-vert-ise-ment.
Di-vest.
Di-vest-ure.
Di-vid-a-ble.
Di-vide.
Div-i-dend.
Di-vid-er.
Div-i-na-tion.
Di-vine.
Di-vine-ly.
Div-ing-bell.
Di-vin-i-ty.
Di-vis-i-bil-i-ty.
Di-vis-i-ble.
Di-vis-ion.
Di-vi-sor.
Di-vorce.
Di-vulge.
Diz-en.
Diz-zi-ness.
Diz-zy.
Do.
Doc-ile.
Do-cil-i-ty.
Dock.

Dock-age.
Dock-et.
Dock-yard.
Doc-tor.
Doc-tor-ate.
Doc-tress.
Doc-tri-nal.
Doc-trine.
Doc-u-ment.
Doc-u-ment-al.
Doc-u-ment-a-ry.
Do-dec-a-gon.
Do-dec-a-he-dron.
Dodge.
Doe.
Do-er.
Does.
Doff.
Dog.
Dog-days.
Dog-ged.
Dog-ged-ly.
Dog-ger-el.
Dog-ma.
Dog-mat-ic.
Dog-mat-ic-al.
Dog-ma-tism.
Dog-ma-tist.
Dog-ma-tize.
Dog-tooth.
Dog-trot.
Doi-ly.
Do-ings.
Doit.
Dole.
Dole-ful.
Dole-some.
Doll.
Dol-lar.
Do-lor.
Dol-or-ous.
Dol-phin.
Dolt.
Dolt-ish.
Do-main.
Dome.
Do-mes-tic.
Do-mes-ti-cate.
Dom-i-cil.
Dom-i-cile.
Dom-i-cil-i-ate.
Dom-i-cil-i-a-ry.
Dom-i-nant.
Dom-i-na-tion.
Dom-i-neer.
Do-min-i-cal.
Do-min-i-can.
Do-min-ion.
Dom-i-no.

Don.
Do-nate.
Do-na-tion.
Don-a-tive.
Done.
Don-key.
Do-nor.
Doom.
Dooms-day.
Door.
Door-keep-er.
Dor-ic.
Dor-man-cy.
Dor-mant.
Dor-mer.
Dor-mer-win-dow.
Dor-mi-to-ry.
Dor-mouse.
Dor-sal.
Dose.
Dot.
Do-tage.
Do-tard.
Do-ta-tion.
Dote.
Doub-le.
Doub-le-deal-ing.
Doub-let.
Doub-loon.
Doubt.
Doubt-ful.
Doubt-ful-ly.
Doubt-less.
Dou-ceur.
Dough.
Dough-nut.
Dough-ty.
Dough-y.
Douse.
Dove.
Dove-cot.
Dove-house.
Dove-tail.
Dow-a-ger.
Dow-dy.
Dow-el.
Dow-er.
Down.
Down-cast.
Down-fall.
Down-hill.
Down-right.
Down-ward.
Down-y.
Dow-ry.
Dox-ol-o-gy.
Doze.
Doz-en.
Doz-i-ness.

Doz-y.
Drab.
Drab-ble.
Drachm.
Drach-ma.
Draff.
Draft.
Drag.
Drag-gle.
Drag-o-man.
Drag-on.
Drag-on-fly.
Dra-goon.
Drain.
Drain-age.
Drake.
Dram.
Dra-ma.
Dra-mat-ic.
Dra-mat-ic-al.
Dram-a-tist.
Dram-a-tize.
Drank.
Drape.
Dra-per.
Dra-per-y.
Dras-tic.
Draught.
Draught-horse.
Draughts-man.
Draw.
Draw-back.
Draw-bridge.
Draw-ee.
Draw-er.
Draw-ing.
Draw-ing-room.
Drawl.
Drawn.
Dray.
Dread.
Dread-ful.
Dread-ful-ly.
Dread-naught.
Dream.
Dream-y.
Dreamt.
Drear.
Drear-y.
Drear-i-ness.
Dredge.
Dredg-ing-box.
Dreg-gy.
Dregs.
Drench.
Dress.
Dress-er.
Dress-ing-room.
Dress-y.
Drib-ble.

Drib-blet.
Drib-let.
Drift.
Drill.
Drill-plow.
Drill-plough.
Drink.
Drink-er.
Drip.
Drip-pings.
Drive.
Driv-el.
Driv-el-er.
Driv-el-ler.
Driv-en.
Driv-er.
Driz-zle.
Driz-zly.
Droll.
, Droll-er-y.
Drom-e-da-ry.
Drone.
Droop.
Drop.
Drop-si-cal.
Drop-sy.
Dross.
Dross-y.
Drought.
Drouth.
Drought-y.
Drouth-y.
Drove.
Drov-er.
Drown.
Drowse.
Drow-si-ness.
Drow-sy.
Drub.
Drudge.
Drudg-er-y.
Drug.
Drug-get.
Drug-gist.
Dru-id.
Dru-id-ic-al.
Drum.
Drum-major.
Drum-mer.
Drum-stick.
Drunk.
Drunk-ard.
Drunk-en.
Drunk-en-ness.
Drupe.
Dry.
Dry-ad.
Dry-goods.
Dry-ly.
Dry-ness.

Dry-rot.
Du-al.
Du-al-i-ty
Dub.
Du-bi-ous.
Du-cal.
Duc-at.
Duch-ess.
Duch-y.
Duck.
Duck-ing.
Duct.
Duc-tile.
Duc-til-i-**ty.**
Dudg-eon.
Duds.
Due.
Du-el.
Du-el-ing.
Du-el-ling.
Du-el-ist.
Du-el-list.
Du-en-na.
Du-et.
Dug
Duke.
Duke-dom.
Dul-cet.
Dul-ci-mer.
Dull.
Dull-ard.
Dull-ness.
Dul-ness.
Du-ly.
Dumb.
Dumb-bell.
Dumb-show.
Dump-ish.
Dump-ling.
Dumps.
Dump-y.
Dun.
Dunce.
Dun-fish.
Dung.
Dun-geon.
Du-o.
Du-o-dec-i-mal.
Du-o-dec-i-mo.
Du-o-de-num.
Dupe.
Du-pli-cate.
Du-pli-ca-tion.
Du-plic-i-ty.
Du-ra-bil-i-ty.
Du-ra-ble.
Du-rance.
Du-ra-tion.
Du-ress.
Dur-ing.

Durst.
Dusk.
Dusk-y.
Dust.
Dust-y.
Du-te-ous.
Du-ti-a-ble.
Du-ti-ful.
Du-ty.
Dwarf.
Dwarf-ish.
Dwell.
Dwell-ing.
Dwin-dle.
Dye.
Dye-ing.
Dy-er.
Dy-ing.
Dy-nam-ics.
Dy-nas-ty.
Dys-en-ter-y.
Dys-pep-sy.
Dys-pep-si-a.
Dys-pep-tic.

E

Each.
Ea-ger.
Ea-gle.
Ea-glet.
Ear.
Earl.
Earl-dom.
Ear-less.
Ear-li-ness.
Ear-ly.
Earn.
Ear-nest.
Earn-ings.
Ear-ring.
Earth.
Earth-en.
Earth-ly.
Earth-quake.
Earth-y.
Ear-wax.
Ear-wig.
Ease.
Ea-sel.
Ease-ment.
Ea-si-ly.
Ea-si-ness.
East.
East-er.
East-er-ly.
East-ern.
East-ward.

Ea-sy.
Eat.
Eat-a-ble.
Eaves.
Eaves-drop-per.
Ebb.
Ebb-tide.
Eb-on.
Eb-on-y.
E-bri-e-ty
Eb-ul-li-tion.
Ec-cen-tric.
Ec-cen-tric-al.
Ec-cen-tric-i-ty.
Ec-cle-si-as-tic.
Ec-cle-si-as-tic-al.
Ech-o.
E-clat.
Ec-lec-tic.
Ec-lec-ti-cism.
E-clipse.
E-clip-tic.
Ec-logue.
E-co-nom-ic-al.
E-con-o-mist.
E-con-o-mize.
E-con-o-my.
Ec-sta-sy.
Ec-stat-ic.
Ec-u-men-ic-al.
Ed-dy.
Edge.
Edged.
Edg-ing.
Edge-tool.
Edge-wise.
Ed-i-ble.
E-dict.
Ed-i-fi-ca-tion.
Ed-i-fice.
Ed-i-fy.
E-dile.
Ed-it.
E-di-tion.
Ed-i-tor.
Ed-i-to-ri-al.
Ed-i-tor-ship.
Ed-u-cate.
Ed-u-ca-tor.
Ed-u-ca-tion.
Ed-u-ca-tion-al.
E-duce.
Eel.
Ef-face.
Ef-face-ment.
Ef-fect.
Ef-fect-ive.
Ef-fect-u-al.
Ef-fect-u-al-lv.

Ef-fect-u-ate.
Ef-fem-i-na-cy.
Ef-fem-i-nate.
Ef-fer-vesce.
Ef-fer-ves-cence.
Ef-fer-ves-cent.
Ef-fete.
Ef-fi-ca-cious.
Ef-fi-ca-cy.
Ef-fi-cien-cy.
Ef-fi-cient.
Ef-fi-gy.
Ef-flo-resce.
Ef-flo-res-cence.
Ef-flo-res-cent.
Ef-flu-ence.
Ef-flu-vi-um.
Ef-flux.
Ef-fort.
Ef-front-er-y.
Ef-ful-gence.
Ef-ful-gent.
Ef-fuse.
Ef-fu-sion.
Ef-fu-sive.
Eft.
Egg.
Eg-lan-tine.
E-go-tism.
E-go-tist.
E-go-tist-ic.
E-go-tist-ic-al.
E-gre-gious.
E-gre-gious-ly.
E-gress.
E-gres-sion.
E-gret.
E-gyp-tian.
Ei-der-down.
Eight.
Eigh-teen.
Eighth.
Eighth-ly.
Ei-ther.
E-jac-u-late.
E-jac-u-la-tion.
E-jac-u-la-to-ry.
E-ject.
E-jec-tion.
E-ject-ment.
Eke.
E-lab-o-rate.
E-lab-o-ra-tion.
E-lapse.
E-las-tic.
E-las-tic-i-ty.
E-late.
E-la-tion.
El-bow.
El-bow-chair.

Eld-er.
Eld-er-ly.
Eld-est.
El-e-cam-pane.
E-lect.
E-lec-tion.
E-lec-tion-eer.
E-lect-ive.
E-lect-or.
E-lect-or-al.
E-lec-tric.
E-lec-tric-al.
E-lec-tri-cian.
E-lec-tric-i-ty.
E-lec-tri-fy.
E - lec - tro - mag-net-ism.
E-lec-tro-type.
E-lect-u-a-ry.
El - ee - mos-y-na-ry
El-e-gance.
El-e-gant.
E-le-gi-ac.
El-e-gi-ac-al.
El-e-gist.
El-e-gy.
El-e-ment.
El-e-ment-al.
El-e-ment-a-ry.
El-e-phant.
El-e-vate
El-e-va-tion.
El-e-va-tor.
E-lev-en.
Elf.
Elf-in.
Elf-ish.
E-lic-it.
El-i-gi-bil-i-ty.
El-i-gi-ble.
E-lim-i-nate.
E-lis-ion.
E-lix-ir.
Elk.
Ell.
El-lipse.
El-lip-sis.
El-lip-tic.
El-lip-tic-al.
El-lip-tic-i-ty.
Elm
El-o-cu-tion.
El-o - cu - tion - a-ry.
El-o-cu-tion-ist.
E-lon-gate.
E-lon-ga-tion.
E-lope.
E-lope-ment.

El-o-quence.
El-o-quent.
Else.
Else-where.
E-lu-ci-date.
E-lu-ci-da-tion.
E-lu-ci-da-tor.
E-lude.
E-lu-sion.
E-lu-sive.
El-vish.
E-lys-ian.
E-lys-i-um.
E-ma-ci-ate.
E-ma-ci-a-tion.
Em-a-nate.
Em-a-na-tion.
E-man-ci-pate.
E - man - ci - pa - tion.
E-man-ci-pa-tor
Em-balm.
Em-bank.
Em-bank-ment.
Em-bar-go.
Em-bark.
Em-bar-ka-tion.
Em-bar-rass.
Em - bar - rass - ment.
Em-bas-sa-dor.
Em-bas-sy.
Em-bed.
Em-bel-lish.
Em - bel - lish - ment.
Em-bers.
Em-bez-zle.
Em-bez-zle-ment.
Em-bla-zon.
Em-bla-zon-ry.
Em-blem.
Em-blem-at-ic.
Em-blem-at-ic-al
Em-bod-y
Em-bold-en.
Em-bon-point.
Em-boss.
Em-bou-chure.
Em-bow-el.
Em-bow-er.
Em-brace.
Em-brace-ment.
Em-bra-sure.
Em-bro-cate.
Em-bro-ca-tion.
Em-broid-er.
Em-broid-er-y.
Em-broil.
Em-bry-o.

Em-en-da-tion.
Em-en-da-tor.
E-mend-a-to-ry.
Em-er-ald.
E-merge.
E-mer-gen-cy.
E-mer-gent.
E-mer-sion.
Em-er-y.
E-met-ic.
Em-i-grant.
Em-i-grate.
Em-i-gra-tion.
Em-i-nence.
Em-i-nent.
Em-i-nent-ly.
Em-is-sa-ry.
E-mis-sion.
E-mit.
Em-met.
E-mol-li-ate.
E-moll-ient.
E-mol-u-ment.
E-mo-tion.
Em-pale.
Em-pale-ment.
Em-per-il.
Em-per-or.
Em-pha-sis.
Em-pha-size.
Em-phat-ic.
Em-phat-ic-al.
Em-phat-ic-al-ly.
Em-pire.
Em-pir-ic.
Em-pir-ic-al.
Em-pir-i-cism.
Em-ploy.
Em-ploy-er.
Em-ploy-ment.
Em-po-ri-um.
Em-pow-er.
Em-press.
Em-prise.
Emp-ti-ness.
Emp-ty.
Emp-ty-ings.
Em-pyr-e-al.
Em-py-re-an.
Em-u-late.
Em-u-la-tion.
Em-u-la-tive.
Em-u-lous.
E-mul-sion.
E-mul-sive.
En-a-ble.
En-act.
En-act-ment.
En-act-or.
En-am-el.

En-am-or.
En-camp.
En-camp-ment.
En-caus-tic.
En-chain.
En-chant.
En-chant-ment.
En-chant-ress.
En-chase.
En-cir-cle.
En-clit-ic.
En-clit-ic-al.
En-close.
En-co-mi-ast.
En-co-mi-ast-ic.
En-co-mi-um.
En-com-pass.
En-core.
En-coun-ter.
En-cour-age.
En - cour - age - ment.
En-cour-a-ging.
En-croach.
En-croach-ment.
En-cum-ber.
En-cum-brance.
En-cyc-lic-al.
En-cy-clo-pe-di-a
En-cy-clo-pæ-di-a.
En-cyst-ed.
End.
En-dan-ger.
En-dear.
En-dear-ment.
En-deav-or.
En-dem-ic.
End-ing.
End-less.
En-dorse.
En-dow.
En-dow-ment.
En-due.
En-dur-a-ble.
En-dur-ance.
En-dure.
En-e-my.
En-er-get-ic.
En-er-get-ic-al.
En-er-gize.
En-er-gy.
E-ner-vate.
En-er-va-tion.
En-fee-ble.
En-fee-ble-ment.
En-feoff.
En-fi-lade.
En-force.
En-force-ment.

En-fran-chise.
En - fran - chise - ment.
En-gage.
En-gaged.
En-gage-ment.
En-gag-ing.
En-gen der.
En-gine.
En-gi-neer.
En-gin-eer-ing
En-gine-ry.
En-gird.
En-glish.
En-grain.
En-grave.
En-grav-er.
En-grav-ing.
En-gross.
En-gross-er.
En-gross-ment.
En-gulf.
En-hance.
En-hance-ment.
E-nig-ma.
E-nig-mat-ic.
E-nig-mat-ic-al.
En-join.
En-joy.
En-joy-a-ble.
En-joy-ment.
En-kin-dle.
En-large.
En-large-ment.
En-light-en.
En-list.
En-list-ment.
En-liv-en.
En-mi-ty.
En-no-ble.
En-no-ble-ment.
En-nui.
E-nor-mi-ty.
E-nor-mous.
E-nor-mous-ly.
E-nough.
En-quire.
En-rage.
En-rapt-ure.
En-rav-ish.
En-rich.
En-rich-ment.
En-roll.
En-roll-ment.
En-rol-ment.
En-sam-ple.
En-sconce.
En-shrine.
En-si-form.
En-sign.

En-sign-cy.
En-slave.
En-slave-ment.
En-sue.
En-sure.
En-tab-la-ture.
En-tail.
En-tail-ment.
En-tan-gle.
En-tan-gle-ment.
En-ter.
En-ter-prise.
En-ter-pris-ing.
En-ter-tain.
En-ter-tain-er.
En-ter-tain-ing.
En-ter-tain-ment.
En-throne.
En-throne-ment.
En-thu-si-asm.
En-thu-si-ast.
En-thu-si-ast-ic.
En-thu-si-ast -ic - al-ly.
En-tice.
En-tice-ment.
En-tire.
En-tire-ly.
En-tire-ness.
En-tire-ty.
En-ti-tle.
En-ti-ty.
En-tomb.
En-to-mol-o-gist.
En-to-mol-o-gy.
En-trails.
En-trance.
En-trap.
En-treat.
En-treat-y.
En-try.
En-twine.
En-twist.
E-nu-mer-ate.
E-nu-mer-a-tion
E-nu-mer-a-tive.
E-nun-ci-ate.
E-nun-ci-a-tion.
En-vel-op.
En-vel-ope.
En-vel-op-ment.
En-ven-om.
En-vi-a-ble.
En-vi-ous.
En-vi-ous-ly.
En-vi-ron.
En-vi-ron-ment.
En-vi-rons.
En-voy.
En-vy.

E-pact.
Ep-au-let.
Ep-au-lette.
E-phem-e-rai.
E-phem-e-ris.
Eph-od.
Ep-ic.
Ep-i-cure.
Ep-i-cu-re-an.
Ep-i-cu-rism.
Ep-i-dem-ic.
Ep-i-dem-ic-al.
Ep-i-der-mis.
Ep-i-glot-tis.
Ep-i-gram.
Ep-i-gram - mat - ic.
Ep-i - gram- mat - ic-al.
Ep - i - gram - ma-tist.
Ep-i-lep-sy.
Ep-i lep-tic.
Ep-i-logue.
E-piph-a-ny.
E-pis-co-pa-cy.
E-pis-co-pal.
E-pis-co-pa-li-an
E-pis-co-pate
Ep-i-sode.
E-pis-tle.
E-pis-to-la-ry.
Ep-i-taph.
Ep-i-thet.
E-pit-o-me.
E-pit-o-mist.
E-pit-o-miz-er.
E-pit-o-mize.
Ep-och.
Ep-ode.
E-qua-bil-i-ty.
E-qua-ble.
E-qua-bly.
E-qual.
E-qual-i-ty.
E-qual-i-za-tion.
E-qual-ize.
E-qual-ly.
E-qua-nim-i-ty.
E-qua-tion.
E-qua-tor.
E-qua-to-ri-al.
E-quer-ry.
Eq-ue-ry.
E-ques-tri-an.
E-qui-an-gu-lar
E-qui-dis-tant.
E-qui-lat-er-al.
E-qui-lib-ri-ty.
E-qui-lib-ri-um

31

E-quine.
E-qui-noc-tial.
E-qui-nox.
E-quip.
Eq-ui-page.
E-quip-ment.
E-qui-poise.
E-qui-pon-der-ance.
E-qui-pon-der-ant.
Eq-ui-ta-ble.
Eq-ui-ta-bly.
Eq-ui-ty.
E-quiv-a-lence.
E-quiv-a-lent.
E-quiv-o-cal.
E-quiv-o-cate.
E-quiv-o-ca-tion.
E-quiv-o-ca-tor.
Eq-ui-voke.
Eq-ui-voque.
E-ra.
E-ra-di-a-tion.
E-rad-i-cate.
E-rad-i-ca-tion.
E-ras-a-ble.
E-rase.
E-ras-ure.
Ere.
E-rect.
E-rec-tion.
Ere-long.
Er-got.
Er-mine.
E-ro-sion.
Err.
Er-rand.
Er-rant.
Er-rant-ry.
Er-rat-ic.
Er-ra-tum.
Err-ing.
Er-ro-ne-ous.
Er-ro-ne-ous-ly.
Er-ror.
Erst.
Er-u-bes-cent.
Er-uc-ta-tion.
Er-u-dite.
Er-u-di-tion.
E-rup-tion.
Er-up-tive.
Er-y-sip-e-las.
Er-y-si-pel-a-tous.
Es-ca-lade.
Es-cape.
Es-cape-ment.
Es-cha-rot-ic.

Es-cheat.
Es-chew.
Es-cort.
Es-cri-toir.
Es-cu-lent.
Es-cutch-eon.
Es-o-ter-ic.
Es-pal-ier.
Es-pe-cial.
Es-pe-cial-ly.
Es-pi-on-age.
Es-pla-nade.
Es-pous-al.
Es-pouse.
Es-py.
Es-quire.
Es-say.
Es-say-ist.
Es-sence.
Es-sen-tial.
Es-sen-tial-ly.
Es-tab-lish.
Es-tab-lish-ment.
Es-tate.
Es-teem.
Es-ti-ma-ble.
Es-ti-mate.
Es-ti-ma-tion.
Es-top.
Es-top-pel.
Es-trange.
Es-trange-ment.
Es-tray.
Est-u-a-ry.
Etch.
Etch-ing.
E-ter-nal.
E-ter-nal-ly.
E-ter-ni-ty.
E-ther.
E-the-re-al.
E-the-re-al-ize.
Eth-ic.
Eth-ic-al.
Eth-ic-al-ly.
Eth-ics.
E-thi-op.
E-thi-o-pi-an.
Eth-nic.
Eth-nic-al.
Eth-nog-ra-phy.
Eth-nol-o-gy.
E-ti-o-late.
Et-i-quette.
Et-y-mo-**log-ic**-al.
Et-y-mol-o-gist.
Et-y-mol-o-gy.
Et-y-mon.
Eu-cha-rist.

Eu-lo-gist
Eu-lo-gis-t.c.
Eu-lo-gize.
Eu-lo-gi-um.
Eu-lo-gy.
Eu-nuch.
Eu-phe-mism.
Eu-phon-ic.
Eu-phon-ic-al.
Eu-pho-ni-ous.
Eu-pho-ny.
Eu-ro-pe-an.
Eu-than-a-sy.
E-vac-u-ate.
E-vac-u-a-tion.
E-vade.
Ev-a-nes-cence.
Ev-a-nes-cent.
E-van-gel-ic-al.
E-van-gel-ism.
E-van-gel-ist.
E-van-gel-ize.
E-vap-o-rate.
E-vap-o-ra-tion.
E-va-sion.
E-va-sive.
Eve.
E-ven.
E-ven-ing.
E-vent.
E-vent-ful.
E-vent-u-al.
E-vent-u-ate.
Ev-er.
Ev-er-glade.
Ev-er-green.
Ev-er-last-ing.
Ev-er-more.
Ev-er-y.
Ev-er-y-where.
E-vict.
E-vic-tion.
Ev-i-dence.
Ev-i-dent.
E-vil.
E-vince.
E-vis-cer-ate.
E-voke.
Ev-o-lu-tion.
E-volve.
Ewe.
Ew-er.
Ex-ac-er-bate.
Ex-ac-er-ba-tion.
Ex-act.
Ex-ac-tion.
Ex-act-ly.
Ex-act-ness.
Ex-act-or.
Ex-ag-ger-ate.

Ex-ag-ger-a-tion.
Ex-alt.
Ex-al-ta-tion.
Ex-alt-ed.
Ex-am-i-na-tion.
Ex-am-ine.
Ex-am-in-er.
Ex-am-ple.
Ex-as-per-ate.
Ex-as-per-a-tion.
Ex-ca-vate.
Ex-ca-va-tion.
Ex-ceed.
Ex-ceed-ing.
Ex-ceed-ing-ly.
Ex-cel.
Ex-cel-lence.
Ex-cel-len-cy.
Ex-cel-lent.
Ex-cel-lent-ly.
Ex-cept.
Ex-cept-ing.
Ex-cep-tion.
Ex-cep-tion-a-ble.
Ex-cep-tion-al.
Ex-cerpt.
Ex-cess.
Ex-cess-ive.
Ex-cess-ive-ly.
Ex-change.
Ex-change-a-ble.
Ex-cheq-uer.
Ex-cise.
Ex-cise-man.
Ex-cis-ion.
Ex-ci-ta-bil-i-ty.
Ex-ci-ta-ble.
Ex-ci-ta-tion.
Ex-cite.
Ex-cit-ing.
Ex-cite-ment.
Ex-claim.
Ex-cla-ma-tion.
Ex-clam-a-to-ry.
Ex-clude.
Ex-clu-sion.
Ex-clu-sive.
Ex-clu-sive-ly.
Ex-clu-sive-ness.
Ex-cog-i-tate.
Ex-com-mu-ni-cate.
Ex-com-mu-ni-ca-tion.
Ex-co-ri-ate.
Ex-co-ri-a-tion.
Ex-cre-ment.
Ex-cres-cence.
Ex-crete.

Ex-cre-tion.
Ex-cre-tive.
Ex-cre-to-ry
Ex-cru-ci-ate.
Ex-cru-ci-a-ting.
Ex-cru-ci-a-tion.
Ex-cul-pate.
Ex-cul-pa-tion.
Ex-cul-pa-to-ry.
Ex-cur-sion.
Ex-cur-sive.
Ex-cus-a-ble.
Ex-cuse.
Ex-e-cra-ble.
Ex-e-cra-bly.
Ex-e-crate.
Ex-e-cra-tion.
Ex-e-cute.
Ex-e-cut-er.
Ex-e-cu-tion.
Ex-e-cu-tion-er.
Ex-ec-u-tive.
Ex-ec-u-tor.
Ex-ec-u-to-ry.
Ex-ec-u-trix.
Ex-e-ge-sis.
Ex-e-get-ic-al.
Ex-em-plar.
Ex-em-pla-ri-ly.
Ex-em-pla-ry.
Ex-em-pli-fi ca-tion.
Ex-em-pli-fy.
Ex-empt.
Ex-emp-tion.
Ex-e-qua-tur.
Ex-e-quies.
Ex-er-cise.
Ex-ert.
Ex-er-tion.
Ex-fo-li-ate.
Ex-fo-li-a-tion.
Ex-ha-la-tion.
Ex-hale.
Ex-haust.
Ex-haus-tion.
Ex-haust-less.
Ex-hib-it.
Ex-hib-it-er.
Ex-hi-bi-tion.
Ex-hil-a-rate.
Ex-hil-a-ra-tion.
Ex-hort.
Ex-hor ta-tion.
Ex-hor-ta-to-ry.
Ex-hort-er.
Ex-hu-ma-tion.
Ex-hume.
Ex-i-gence.
Ex-i-gen-cy.

Ex-ile.
Ex-ist.
Ex-ist-ence.
Ex-ist-ent.
Ex-it.
Ex-o-dus.
Ex-on-er-ate.
Ex-on-er-a-tion.
Ex-or-bi-tance.
Ex-or-bi-tant.
Ex-or-cise.
Ex-or-cism.
Ex-or-di-um.
Ex-ot-ic.
Ex-pand.
Ex-panse.
Ex - pan - si-bil-i-ty.
Ex-pan-si-ble.
Ex-pan-sion.
Ex-pan-sive.
Ex-pan-sive-ness.
Ex-par-te.
Ex-pa-ti-ate.
Ex-pa-tri-ate.
Ex-pa-tri-a-tion.
Ex-pect.
Ex-pect-an-cy.
Ex-pect-ant.
Ex-pec-ta-tion.
Ex-pec-to-rant.
Ex-pec-to-rate.
Ex - pec - to - ra tion.
Ex-pe-di-ence.
Ex-pe-di-en-cy.
Ex-pe-di-ent.
Ex-pe-dite.
Ex-pe-di-tion.
Ex-pe-di-tious.
Ex-pe-di-tious-ly
Ex-pel.
Ex-pend.
Ex-pen-di-ture.
Ex-pense.
Ex-pen-sive.
Ex-pe-ri-ence.
Ex-pe-ri-enced.
Ex-per-i-ment.
Ex-per-i-ment-al.
Ex - per - i -ment-al-ly
Ex-pert.
Ex-pi-a-ble.
Ex-pi-ate.
Ex-pi-a-tion.
Ex-pi-a-to-ry.
Ex-pi-ra-tion.
Ex-pire.
Ex-plain.

Ex-pla-na-tion.
Ex-plan-a-to-ry.
Ex-ple-tive.
Ex-pli-ca-ble.
Ex-pli-cate.
Ex-pli-ca-tion.
Ex-pli-ca-tive.
Ex-pli-ca-to-ry.
Ex-plic-it.
Ex-plic-it-ly.
Ex-plode.
Ex-ploit.
Ex-plo-ra-tion.
Ex-plor-a-to-ry.
Ex-plore.
Ex-plo-sion.
Ex-plo-sive.
Ex-po-nent.
Ex-port.
Ex-por-ta-tion.
Ex-port-er.
Ex-pose.
Ex-po-si-tion.
Ex-pos-i-tor.
Ex-pos-i-to-ry.
Ex-post-u-late.
Ex - post - u - la - tion.
Ex - post -u-la-to ry.
Ex-pos-ure.
Ex-pound.
Ex-pound-er.
Ex-press.
Ex-pres-sion.
Ex-press-ive.
Ex-press-ive-ly.
Ex-pugn.
Ex-pul-sion.
Ex-pul-sive.
Ex-punge.
Ex-pur-gate.
Ex-pur-ga-tion.
Ex-pur-ga-to-ry.
Ex-qui-site.
Ex-qui-site-ly.
Ex-sic-cant.
Ex-sic-cate.
Ex-sic-ca-tion.
Ex-tant
Ex-tem -po-ra-ne-ous.
Ex-tem-po-ra-ry.
Ex-tem-po-re.
Ex-tem-po-rize.
Ex-tend.
Ex-ten-si-ble.
Ex-ten-si-bil-i-ty.
Ex-ten-sion.
Ex-ten-sive.

Ex-ten-sive-ly.
Ex-tent.
Ex-ten-u-ate.
Ex-ten-u-a-tion.
Ex-te-ri-or.
Ex-ter-mi-nate.
Ex - ter - mi - na tion.
Ex-ter-mi-na-tor.
Ex-ter-nal.
Ex-ter-nals.
Ex-tinct.
Ex-tinc-tion.
Ex-tin-guish.
Ex - tin - guish ble.
Ex-tin-guish-er.
Ex - tin - guish ment.
Ex-tir-pate.
Ex-tir-pa-tion.
Ex-tol.
Ex-tort.
Ex-tor-tion.
Ex-tor-tion-ate.
Ex-tor-tion-er.
Ex-tract.
Ex-trac-tion.
Ex-tra-di-tion.
Ex-tra-ju-di-cial.
Ex-tra-ne-ous.
Ex - traor - di -na ry.
Ex-trav-a-gance.
Ex-trav-a-gant.
Ex-trav-a-sate.
Ex - trav - a - sa tion.
Ex-treme.
Ex-treme-ly.
Ex-trem-ist.
Ex-trem-i-ty.
Ex-tri-ca-ble.
Ex-tri-cate.
Ex-tri-ca-tion.
Ex-trin-sic.
Ex-trin-sic-al.
Ex-trude.
Ex-tru-sion.
Ex-u-ber-ance.
Ex-u-ber-ant.
Ex-u-ber-ant-ly.
Ex-u-da-tion.
Ex-ude.
Ex-ult.
Ex-ult-ant.
Ex-ul ta-tion.
Eye.
Eye-ball.
Eye-brow.

Eye-glass.
Eye-lash.
Eye-less.
Eye-let.
Eye-serv-ant.
Eye-sight.
Eye-sore.
Eye-tooth.
Eye-wit-ness.
Ey-rie.
Ey-ry.

F.

Fa-ble.
Fab-ric.
Fab-ri-cate.
Fab-ri-ca-tion.
Fab-ri-ca-tor.
Fab-u-list.
Fab-u-lous.
Fa-cade.
Face.
Fac-et.
Fa-ce-tious.
Fa-cial.
Fac-ile.
Fa-cil-i-tate.
Fa-cil-i-ty.
Fac-ing.
Fac-sim-i-le.
Fact.
Fac-tion.
Fac-tious.
Fac-ti-tious.
Fac-tor.
Fac-tor-age.
Fac-to-ry.
Fac-to-tum.
Fac-ul-ty.
Fade.
Fæ-ces.
Fag.
Fag-end.
Fag-ot.
Fail.
Fail-ure.
Fain.
Faint.
Faint-ly.
Faint-ness.
Fair.
Fair-ly.
Fair-ness.
Fair-y.
Faith.
Faith-ful.
Faith-ful-ly.

Faith-ful-ness.
Faith-less.
Fal-cate.
Fal-cat-ed.
Fal-chion.
Fal-con.
Fal-con-er.
Fal-con-ry.
Fall.
Fal-la-cious.
Fal-la-cy.
Fallen.
Fal-li-bil-i-ty.
Fal-li-ble.
Fall - ing - sick ness.
Fal-low.
False.
False-ly
False-hood.
Fals-i-ty.
Fal-set-to.
Fal-si-fi-ca-tion.
Fal-si-fy.
Fal-ter.
Fame.
Famed.
Fa-mil-iar.
Fa-mil-iar-i-ty.
Fa-mil-iar-ize.
Fa-mil-iar-ly.
Fam-i-ly.
Fam-ine.
Fam-ish.
Fa-mous.
Fan.
Fa-nat-ic.
Fa-nat-ic-al.
Fa-nat-i-cism.
Fan-ci-ful.
Fan-cy
Fan-dan-go.
Fane.
Fang.
Fan-tas-tic.
Fan-tas-tic-al.
Fan-ta-sy.
Far.
Farce.
Far-ci-cal.
Fare.
Fare-well.
Fa-ri-na.
Fa-ri-na-ceous.
Farm.
Farm-er.
Farm-ing.
Far-o.
Far-ra-go.
Far-ri-er.

Far-ri-er-y
Far-row.
Far-ther.
Far-thing.
Far-thin-gale.
Fas-ci-nate.
Fas-ci-na-tion.
Fash-ion.
Fash-ion-a-ble.
Fash-ion-a-bly.
Fast.
Fast-day.
Fast-en.
Fast-en-ing
Fas-tid-i-ous.
Fast-ness.
Fat.
Fa-tal.
Fa-tal-ism.
Fa-tal-ist.
Fa-tal-i-ty.
Fa-tal-ly.
Fate.
Fat-ed.
Fa-ther.
Fa-ther-land.
Fa-ther-less.
Fa-ther-ly.
Fath-om.
Fath-om-less.
Fa-tigue.
Fat-ling.
Fat-ness.
Fat-ten.
Fat-ty.
Fa-tu-i-ty.
Fat-u-ous.
Fau-cet.
Fault.
Fault-less.
Fault-y.
Faun.
Fau-na.
Fa-vor.
Fa-vor-a-ble.
Fa-vor-a-bly.
Fa-vor-er.
Fa-vor-ite.
Fa-vor-it-ism.
Fawn.
Fay.
Fe-al-ty.
Fear.
Fear-ful.
Fear-ful-ly.
Fear-less.
Fear-less-ly.
Fea-si-bil-i-ty.
Fea-si-ble-ness.
Fea-si-ble.

Feast.
Feat.
Feath-er.
Feath-er-y.
Feat-ure.
Feb-ri-fuge.
Fe-brile.
Feb-ru-a-ry.
Fe-cal.
Fe-ces.
Fec-u-lence.
Fec-u-lent.
Fec-un-date.
Fec-un-da-tion.
Fe-cun-di-ty.
Fed.
Fed-er-al.
Fed-er-a-tion.
Fed-er-a-tive.
Fee.
Fee-ble.
Fee-ble-ness.
Fee-bly.
Feed.
Feel.
Feel-er.
Feel-ing.
Feel-ing-ly.
Fee-sim-ple.
Feet.
Feign.
Feint.
Fe-lic-i-tate.
Fe-lic-i-ta-tion.
Fe-lic-i-tous.
Fe-lic-i-ty.
Fe-line.
Fell.
Fel-low.
Fel - low - creat ure.
Fel-low-feel-ing
Fel-low-ship.
Fel-ly.
Fe-lo-de-se.
Fel-on.
Fe-lo-ni-ous.
Fel-o-ny.
Felt.
Fe-male.
Fem-i-nine.
Fen.
Fence.
Fence-less.
Fen-cing.
Fend.
Fend-er.
Fen-nel.
Fen-ny.
Feoff.

Feoff-ment.
Fer-ment.
Fer-men-ta-tion.
Fer-ment-a-tive.
Fern.
Fe-ro-cious.
Fe-roc-i-ty.
Fer-re-ous.
Fer-ret.
Fer-ri-age.
Fer-ru-gi-nous.
Fer-rule.
Fer-ry.
Fer-ry-man.
Fer-tile.
Fer-til-ize.
Fer-til-i-ty.
Fer-ule.
Fer-ven-cy.
Fer-vent.
Fer-vent-ly.
Fer-vid.
Fer-vor.
Fes-tal.
Fes-ter.
Fes-ti-val.
Fes-tive.
Fes-tiv-i-ty.
Fes-toon.
Fetch.
Fete.
Fet-id.
Fet-lock.
Fet-ter.
Fe-tus.
Feud.
Feud-al.
Feud-al-ism.
Fe-ver.
Fe-ver-ish.
Few.
Few-ness.
F¹-at.
Fib.
Fi-ber.
Fi-bre.
Fi-bril.
Fi-brous.
Fick-le.
Fick le-ness.
Fic-tion.
Fic-ti-tious.
Fid-dle.
Fid-dler.
Fi-del-i-ty.
Fidg-et.
Fidg-et-y.
Fi-du-cial.
Fi-du-ci-a-ry.
Fie.

Fief.
Field.
Field-mar-shal.
Field-of-fi-cer.
Field-piece.
Fiend.
Fierce.
Fierce-ly.
Fierce-ness.
Fi-er-i-ness.
Fi-er-y.
Fife.
Fif-er.
Fif-teen.
Fifth.
Fif-ti-eth.
Fif-ty.
Fig.
Fight.
Fight-er.
Fig-ment.
Fig-u-rate.
Fig-u-ra-tion.
Fig-u-ra-tive.
Fig-ure.
Fil-a-ment.
Fil-a-ment-ous.
Fil-a-ture.
Fil-bert.
Filch.
File.
Fil-ial.
Fil-i-a-tion.
Fil-i-gree.
Fil-ings.
Fill.
Fil-let.
Fil-li-bus-ter.
Fil-lip.
Fil-ly.
Film.
Film-y.
Fil-ter.
Filth.
Filth-i-ness.
Filth-y.
Fil-trate.
Fil-tra-tion.
Fin.
Fi-nal.
Fi-nal-ly.
Fi-na-le.
Fi-nance.
Fi-nan-cial.
Fin-an-cier.
Finch.
Find.
Find-ings.
Fine.
Fine-ly.

Fine-ness.
Fin-er.
Fin-er-y.
Fi-nesse.
Fin-ger.
Fin-i-cal.
Fi-nis.
Fin-ish.
Fin-ish-ing.
Fi-nite.
Fin-ny.
Fir.
Fire.
Fire-arms.
Fire-brand.
Fire-damp.
Fire-en-gine.
Fire-fly.
Fire-man.
Fire-place.
Fire-plug.
Fire-proof.
Fire-ship.
Fire-ward.
Fire-ward-en.
Fire-wood.
Fire-works.
Fir-kin.
Firm.
Firm-a-ment.
Firm-ly.
Firm-ness.
First.
First-fruits.
First-rate.
First-ling.
Fisc-al.
Fish.
Fish-er-man.
Fish-er-y.
Fish-hook.
Fish-ing.
Fish-mon-ger.
Fish-y.
Fis-sile.
Fis-sure.
Fist.
Fist-i-cuffs.
Fist-u-la.
Fist-u-lar.
Fist-u-lous.
Fit.
Fit-ful.
Fit-ly.
Fit-ness.
Fit-ting.
Five.
Fix.
Fix-a-tion.
Fix-ed-ness.

Fix-i-ty.
Fixt-ure.
Fizz.
Fiz-zle.
Flab-bi-ness.
Flab-by.
Flac-cid.
Flac-cid-i-ty.
Flag.
Flag-el-late.
Flag-el-la-tion.
Flag-eo-let.
Fla-gi-tious.
Flag-of-fi-cer.
Flag-on.
Fla-gran-cy.
Fla-grant.
Flag-ship.
Flag-staff.
Flag-stone.
Flail.
Flake.
Flak-y.
Flam.
Flam-beau.
Flame.
Flam-ing.
Fla-min-go.
Flange.
Flank.
Flan-nel.
Flap.
Flap-jack.
Flap-per.
Flare.
Flash.
Flash-y.
Flask.
Flat.
Flat-ly.
Flat-ness.
Flat-ten.
Flat-ter.
Flat-ter-er.
Flat-ter-y.
Flat-u-lence.
Flat-u-lent.
Flaunt.
Fla-vor.
Flaw.
Flaw-y.
Flax.
Flax-en.
Flay.
Flea.
Fleam.
Fleck.
Flec-tion.
Fled.
Fledge.

Fledge-ling.
Flee.
Fleece.
Flee-cy.
Fleer
Fleet
Fleet-ing.
Fleet-ness.
Flem-ish.
Flesh.
Flesh-col-or.
Flesh-i-ness.
Flesh-ly.
Flesh-y.
Flew.
Flex.
Flex-i-bil-i-ty.
Flex-i-ble.
Flex-ion.
Flex-u-ous.
Flex-ure.
Flick-er.
Fli-er.
Flight.
Flight-i-ness.
Flight-y.
Flim-si-ness.
Flim-sy.
Flinch.
Fling.
Flint.
Flint-y.
Flip.
Flip-pan-cy.
Flip-pant.
Flip-pant-ly.
Flirt.
Flir-ta-tion.
Flit.
Flitch.
Float.
Floc-cu-lent.
Flock.
Flock-bed.
Floe.
Flog.
Flog-ging.
Flood
Flood-gate.
Floor.
Floor-ing.
Flo-ra.
Flo-ral.
Flo-ret.
Flor-id.
Flo-rid-i-ty.
Flor-in.
Flo-rist.
Flot-age.
Flo-til-la

Flot-sam.
Flot-son.
Flounce.
Floun-der.
Flour.
Flour-ish.
Flout.
Flow.
Flow-er.
Flow-er-de-luce.
Flow-er-y.
Flow-ing.
Flown.
Fluct-u-ate.
Fluct-u-a-tion.
Flue.
Flu-en-cy.
Flu-ent.
Flu-ent-ly.
Flu-id.
Flu-id-i-ty.
Fluke.
Flume.
Flum-mer-y.
Flung.
Flur-ry.
Flush.
Flus-ter.
Flute.
Flut-ist.
Flut-ter.
Flu-vi-al.
Flu-vi-at-ic.
Flux.
Flux-ion.
Fly.
Fly-blow.
Fly-leaf.
Foal.
Foam.
Foam-y.
Fob.
Fo-cal.
Fo-cus.
Fod-der.
Foe.
Fog.
Fog-gi-ness.
Fog-gy.
Fo-gy.
Foi-ble
Foil.
Foist.
Fold.
Fold-er.
Fo-li-a-ceous.
Fo-li-age.
Fo-li-ate.
Fo-li-a-tion.
Fo-li-o.

Folk.
Fol-li-cle.
Fol-low.
Fol-low-er.
Fol-ly.
Fo-ment.
Fo-men-ta-tion.
Fond
Fon-dle
Fond-ling.
Fond-ly
Fond-ness.
Font.
Food.
Fool.
Fool-er-y.
Fool-hard-y.
Fool-ish.
Fool-ish-ly.
Fool-ish-ness.
Fools-cap.
Foot.
Foot-ball.
Foot-boy.
Foot-ing.
Foot-man.
Foot-pad.
Foot-path.
Foot-step.
Foot-stool.
Fop.
Fop-per-y.
Fop-pish.
Fop-pish-ness.
For.
For-age.
For-as-much.
Fo-ray.
For-bade.
For-bear.
For-bear-ance.
For-bid.
For-bid-ding.
For-borne.
Force.
Force-meat.
For-ci-ble.
For-ci-bly.
Ford.
Ford-a-ble.
Fore.
Fore-arm.
Fore-bode.
Fore-bod-ing.
Fore-cast.
Fore-cas-tle.
Fore-close.
Fore-clos-ure.
Fore-fa-ther.
Fore-fin-ger.

Fore-go.
Fore-gone
Fore-ground.
Fore-hand-ed.
Fore head.
For-eign.
For-eign-er.
Fore-know.
Fore-knowl-edge
Fore-land.
Fore-lock.
Fore-man.
Fore-most.
Fore-noon.
Fo-ren-sic.
Fore-or-dain.
Fore-or-di-na-tion.
Fore-part.
Fore-run.
Fore-run-ner.
Fore-see.
Fore-show.
Fore-sight.
For-est.
Fore-stall.
For-est-er.
Fore-taste.
Fore-tell.
Fore-thought.
Fore-to-ken.
Fore-top.
For-ev-er.
Fore-warn.
Fore-warn-ing.
For-feit.
For-feit-a-ble.
For-feit-ure.
For-gave.
Forge.
For-ger.
For-ger-y.
For-get.
For-get-ful
For-get-ful-ness.
For-give.
For-give-ness.
For-got.
For-got-ten.
Fork.
Forked.
For-lorn.
Form.
Form-al.
Form-al-ist.
For-mal-i-ty.
For-mal-ly.
For-ma-tion.
Form-a-tive.
Form-er.

For-mer.
For-mer-ly.
For-mi-da-ble.
For-mi-da-bly.
Form-u-la.
Form-u-la-ry.
For-ni-ca-tion.
For-ni-ca-tor.
For-sake.
For-sak-en.
For-sooth.
For-swear.
Fort.
Forte.
Forth.
Forth-com-ing.
Forth-with.
For-ti-fi-ca-tion.
For-ti-fy.
For-ti-tude.
Fort-night.
For-tress.
For-tu-i-tous.
For-tu-i-ty.
Fort-u-nate.
Fort-u-nate-ly.
Fort-une.
For-ty.
Fo-rum.
For-ward.
For-ward-ness.
Fosse.
Fos-sil.
Fos-sil-if-er-ous.
Fos-ter.
Fos-ter-broth-er.
Fos-ter-child.
Foth-er.
Fought.
Foul.
Foul-ly.
Foul-ness.
Found.
Foun-da-tion.
Found-er.
Foun-der-y.
Found-ry.
Found-ling.
Fount.
Fount-ain.
Four.
Four-foot-ed.
Four-i-er-ism.
Four-score.
Four-teen.
Fourth.
Fourth-ly.
Fowl.
Fowl-er.
Fowl-ing-piece.

Fox.
Fra-cas.
Frac-tion.
Frac-tion-al.
Frac-tious.
Fract-ure.
Frag-ile.
Fra-gil-i-ty.
Frag-ment.
Frag-ment-a-ry.
Fra-grance.
Fra-grant.
Frail.
Frail-ty.
Frame.
Frame-work.
Franc.
Fran-chise.
Fran-chise-ment.
Fran-gi-ble.
Frank.
Frank-in-cense.
Frank-ly
Frank-ness.
Fran-tic.
Fra-ter-nal.
Fra-ter-ni-ty.
Fra-ter-nize.
Frat-ri-cide.
Fraud.
Fraud-u-lence.
Fraud-u-lent.
Fraught.
Fray.
Freak.
Freak-ish
Freck-le.
Freck-led.
Freck-ly.
Free.
Free-boot-er.
Free-born.
Freed-man.
Free-dom.
Free-hold.
Free-hold-er.
Free-ly.
Free-man.
Free-school.
Free-stone.
Free-think-er.
Free-will.
Freeze.
Freight.
Freight-er.
French.
French-horn.
Fren-zy.
Fre-quen-cy.
Fre-quent.

Fre-quent-a-tive.
Fres-co.
Fresh.
Fresh-en.
Fresh-et.
Fresh-ly.
Fresh-man.
Fresh-ness.
Fret.
Fret-ful.
Fret-ful-ly.
Fret-ful-ness.
Fret-work.
Fri-a-bil-i-ty.
Fri-a-ble-ness.
Fri-a-ble.
Fri-ar.
Fri-ar-y.
Fric-as-see.
Fric-tion.
Fri-day.
Friend.
Friend-less.
Friend-li-ness.
Friend-ly.
Friend-ship.
Frieze.
Frig-ate.
Fright.
Fright-en.
Fright-ful.
Fright-ful-ly.
Fright-ful-ness.
Frig-id.
Fri-gid-i-ty.
Frill.
Fringe.
Frip-per-y.
Frisk.
Frisk-i-ness.
Frisk-y.
Frith.
Frit-ter.
Fri-vol-i-ty.
Friv-o-lous.
Friz.
Friz-zle.
Fro.
Frock.
Frog.
Frol-ic.
Frol-ic-some.
From.
Frond.
Fron-des-cence.
Front.
Front-age.
Front-ier.
Front-is-piece.
Front-let.

Frost.
Frost-y.
Froth.
Froth-y.
Frounce.
Frou-sy.
Fro-ward.
Frown.
Froze.
Fro-zen.
Fruc-ti-fi-ca-tion.
Fruc-ti-fy.
Fru-gal.
Fru-gal-i-ty.
Fru-gal-ly.
Fru-gif-er-ous.
Fruit.
Fruit-age.
Fruit-er-er.
Fruit-ful.
Fruit-ful-ness.
Fru-i-tion.
Fruit-less.
Fruit-tree.
Fru-men-ty.
Frush.
Frus-trate.
Frus-tra-tion.
Frus-tum.
Fry.
Fry-ing-pan.
Fud-dle.
Fu-el.
Fu-ga-cious.
Fu-gac-i-ty.
Fu-gi-tive.
Fu-gle-man.
Fugue.
Ful-crum.
Ful-fill.
Ful-fil.
Ful-fill-ment.
Ful-fil-ment.
Full.
Full-er.
Full-ness
Ful-ness.
Ful-ly.
Ful-mi-nate.
Ful-mi-na-tion.
Ful-some.
Fum-ble.
Fume.
Fu-mi-gate.
Fu-mi-ga-tion.
Fun.
Func-tion.
Func-tion-al.
Func-tion-a-ry.
Fund.

Fun-da-ment.
Fun-da-ment-al.
Fun-da-ment-al-ly.
Fu-ner-al.
Fu-ne-re-al.
Fun-gos-i-ty
Fun-gous.
Fun-gus.
Fu-nic-u-lar.
Fun-nel.
Fun-ny.
Fur.
Fur-be-low.
Fur-bish.
Fur-cate.
Fu-ri-ous.
Fu-ri-ous-ly.
Furl.
Fur-long.
Fur-lough.
Fur-nace.
Fur-nish.
Fur-ni-ture.
Fur-ri-er.
Fur-row.
Fur-ry.
Fur-ther.
Fur-ther-ance.
Fur-ther-more.
Fur-ther-most.
Fur-thest.
Fur-tive.
Furze.
Fu-ry.
Fuse.
Fu-see.
Fu-si-bil-i-ty.
Fu-si-ble.
Fu-sil.
Fu-si-leer.
Fu-sion.
Fuss.
Fuss-y.
Fus-tian.
Fu-tile.
Fu-t'l-i-ty.
Fut-tock.
Fut ure.
Fu-tu-ri-ty.
Fuzz.
Fy.

G

Gab.
Gab-ar-dine.
Gab-ble.

Ga-bi-on.
Ga-ble.
Gad.
Gad-a-bout.
Gad-der.
Gad-fly.
Gaff.
Gag.
Gage.
Gai-ly.
Gain.
Gain-ful.
Gain-say.
Gain-say-er.
Gair-ish.
Gait.
Gait-er.
Ga-la.
Gal-ax-y.
Gale.
Gall.
Gal-lant.
Gal-lant-ly.
Gal-lant-ry.
Gal-le-on.
Gal-ler-y.
Gal-ley.
Gal-ley-slave.
Gal-lic.
Gal-li-cism.
Gal-li-gas-kins.
Gal-li-na-ceous.
Gal-li-pot.
Gall-nut.
Gal-lon.
Gal-loon.
Gal-lop.
Gal-lows.
Ga-loche.
Gal-van-ic.
Gal-van-ism.
Gal-van-ize.
Gam-ble.
Gam-bler.
Gam-boge.
Gam-bol.
Gam-brel.
Game.
Game-some.
Game-ster.
Gam-mon.
Gam-ut.
Gan-der.
Gang.
Gan-gli-on.
Gan-grene.
Gan-gre-nous.
Gangue.
Gang-way.
Gant-let.

Gaol.
Gap.
Gape.
Garb.
Garb-age.
Gar-ble.
Gar-den.
Gar-den-er.
Gar-get.
Gar-gle.
Gar-land.
Gar-lic.
Gar-ment.
Gar-ner.
Gar-net.
Gar-nish.
Gar-nish-ee.
Gar-nish-ment.
Gar-ni-ture.
Gar-ret.
Gar-ret-eer.
Gar-ri-son.
Gar-rote.
Gar-ru-li-ty.
Gar-ru-lous.
Gar-ter.
Gas.
Gas-con-ade.
Gas-e-ous.
Gash.
Gas-om-e-ter.
Gasp.
Gas-tric.
Gas-tron-o-mer.
Gas-tro-nom-ic.
Gas-tron-o-my.
Gate.
Gate-way.
Gath-er.
Gaud-i-ness.
Gaud-y.
Gauge.
Gaug-er.
Gaunt.
Gaunt-let.
Gauze.
Gave.
Gav-el.
Gawk.
Gawk-y.
Gay.
Gay-e-ty.
Gay-ly.
Gaze.
Ga-zelle.
Ga-zette.
Gaz-et-teer.
Gaz-ing-stock.
Gear.
Geese.

Gel-a-tine.
Ge-lat-i-nous.
Geld.
Gel-id.
Gem.
Gem-ma-tion.
Gen-der.
Gen-e-a-log-ic-al.
Gen-e-al-o-gist.
Gen-e-al-o-gy.
Gen-er-a.
Gen-er-al.
Gen-er-al-is-si-mo.
Gen-er-al-i-ty.
Gen-er-al-i-za-tion.
Gen-er-al-ize.
Gen-er-al-ly.
Gen-er-al-ship.
Gen-er-ate.
Gen-er-a-tion.
Gen-er-a-tive.
Gen-er-a-tor.
Ge-ner-ic.
Ge-ner-ic-al.
Gen-er-os-i-ty.
Gen-er-ous.
Gen-e-sis.
Ge-ni-al.
Ge-nie.
Gen-i-tive.
Ge-ni-us.
Ge-ni-us.
Gens-d'armes.
Gen-teel.
Gen-teel-ly.
Gen-tile.
Gen-til-i-ty.
Gen-tle.
Gen-tle-folk.
Gen-tle-folks.
Gen-tle-man.
Gen-tle-man-ly.
Gen-tle-ness.
Gen-tly.
Gen-try.
Ge-nu-flec-tion.
Gen-u-ine.
Gen-u-ine-ness.
Ge-nus.
Ge-o-cen-tric.
Ge-od-e-sy.
Ge-og-ra-pher.
Ge-o-graph-ic-al.
Ge-og-ra-phy.
Ge-o-log-ic-al.
Ge-ol-o-gist.
Ge-ol-o-gy.
Ge-om-e-try.

Ge-o-met-ri-cal.	Girl.	Gloss.	Gong.
Ge-om-e-tri-cian.	Girl-hood.	Gloss-a-ry.	Good.
Ge-om-e-try.	Girl-ish.	Gloss-i-ness.	Good-by
Geor-gic.	Girt.	Gloss-y.	Good-li-ness.
Ge-ra-ni-um.	Girth.	Glot-tis.	Good-ly.
Germ.	Gist.	Glove.	Good-ness.
Ger-man.	Give.	Glov-er.	Goods.
Ger-mane.	Giv-er.	Glow.	Good-will.
Ger-mi-nal.	Giz-zard.	Glow-ing.	Goose.
Ger-mi-nate.	Gla-cial.	Glow-worm.	Goose-ber-ry.
Ger-mi-na-tion.	Gla-cier.	Gloze.	Gore.
Ger-und.	Gla-cis.	Glue.	Gorge.
Ges-ta-tion.	Glad.	Glum.	Gor-geous
Ges-tic-u-late.	Glad-den.	Glume.	Gor-gon.
Ges-tic-u-la-tion.	Glade.	Glut.	Go-ril-la.
Gest-ure.	Glad-i-a-tor.	Glu-ten	Gor-mand-ize.
Get.	Glad-ly.	Glu-ti-nous.	Gor-mand-iz-er
Gew-gaw.	Glad-ness.	Glut-ton.	Gorse.
Ghast-li-ness.	Glad-some.	Glut-ton-ous.	Gor-y.
Ghast-ly.	Glair.	Glut-ton-y.	Gos-ling.
Gher-kin.	Glance.	Glyc-er-ine.	Gos-pel.
Ghost.	Gland.	Gly-con-ic.	Gos-sa-mer.
Ghost-ly.	Gland-ers.	Gnarl.	Gos-sip.
Gi-ant.	Gland-u-lar.	Gnarled.	Got.
Gi-ant-ess.	Gland-u-lous.	Gnash.	Goth.
Gi-ant-ly.	Glare.	Gnat.	Goth-ic.
Giaour.	Glar-ing.	Gnaw.	Gouge.
Gib-ber.	Glass.	Gneiss.	Gourd.
Gib-ber-ish.	Glass-i-ness.	Gnome.	Gour-mand.
Gib-bet.	Glass-y.	Gno-mon.	Gout.
Gib-bous.	Glaze.	Gnu.	Gout-y.
Gibe.	Gla-zier.	Go.	Gov-ern.
Gib-lets.	Glaz-ing.	Goad.	Gov-ern-ance.
Gid-di-ness.	Gleam.	Goal.	Gov-er-nante.
Gid-dy.	Glean.	Goat.	Gov-ern-ess.
Gift.	Glebe.	Goat-herd.	Gov-ern-ment.
Gift-ed.	Glee.	Gob-ble.	Gov-ern-or.
Gig.	Glen.	Gob-bler.	Gown.
Gi-gan-tic.	Glib.	Gob-let.	Grab.
Gig-gle.	Glide.	Gob-lin.	Grace.
Gild.	Glim-mer.	God.	Grace-ful.
Gild-ing.	Glim-mer-ing.	God-dess.	Grace-ful-ly.
Gill.	Glimpse.	God-fa-ther.	Grace-less.
Gil-ly-flow-er.	Glis-ten.	God-head.	Gra-cious.
Gilt.	Glit-ter.	God-less.	Gra-cious-ly.
Gim-bals.	Gloat.	God-li-ness.	Gra-da-tion.
Gim-crack.	Globe.	God-ly.	Grade.
Gim-let.	Glo-bose.	God-send.	Gra-di-ent.
Gimp.	Glo-bous.	God-son.	Grad-u-al.
Gin.	Glo-bos-i-ty.	Gog-gles.	Grad-u-al-ly.
Gin-ger.	Glob-u-lar.	Go-ing.	Grad-u-ate.
Gin-ger-bread.	Glob-ule.	Goi-ter.	Grad-u-a-tion.
Gin-ger-ly.	Gloom.	Goi-tre.	Graft.
Ging-ham.	Gloom-i-ly.	Gold.	Grain.
Gin-seng.	Gloom-y.	Gold-en.	Gra-min-e-ous.
Gip-sy.	Glo-ri-fi-ca-tion.	Gold-finch.	Gram-i-niv-o-
Gi-raffe.	Glo-ri-fy.	Gold-leaf.	rous.
Gird.	Glo-ri-ous.	Gon-do-la.	Gram-mar.
Gird-er.	Glo-ri-ous-ly.	Gon-do-lier.	Gram-ma-ri-an.
Gird-le.	Glo-ry.	Gone.	Gram-mat-i-cal.

Gram-mat-i-cal-ly.
Gram-pus.
Gran-a-ry.
Grand.
Gran-dam.
Grand-child.
Gran-dee.
Grand-eur.
Grand-fa-ther.
Gran-dil-o-quence.
Grand-ju-ry.
Grand-moth-er.
Grand-sire.
Grand-son.
Grange.
Gran-ite.
Gra-niv-o-rous.
Grant.
Grant-ee.
Grant-er.
Grant-or.
Gran-u-lar.
Gran-u-late.
Gran-u-la-tion.
Gran-ule.
Grape.
Grap-er-y.
Grape-shot.
Graph-ic.
Grap-nel.
Grap-ple.
Grasp.
Grass.
Grass-hop-per.
Grass-y.
Grate.
Grate-ful.
Grat-er.
Grat-i-fi-ca-tion.
Grat-i-fy.
Grat-ing.
Gra-tis.
Grat-i-tude.
Gra-tu-i-tous.
Gra-tu-i-ty.
Grat-u-la-tion.
Grave.
Grav-el.
Grave-ly.
Grav-er.
Grave-stone.
Grave-yard.
Grav-id.
Grav-i-tate.
Grav-i-ta-tion.
Grav-i-ty.
Gra-vy.
Gray.

Gray-beard.
Graze.
Graz-er.
Gra-zier.
Grease.
Grea-si-ness.
Grea-sy.
Great.
Great-ly.
Great-ness.
Gre-cian.
Greed-i-ly.
Greed-i-ness.
Greed-y.
Greek.
Green.
Green-gro-cer.
Green-house.
Green-sward.
Greet.
Greet-ing.
Gre-ga-ri-ous.
Gre-nade.
Gren-a-dier.
Grew.
Grey.
Grey-hound.
Grid-dle.
Grid-i-ron.
Grief.
Griev-ance.
Grieve.
Griev-ous.
Grif-fin.
Grif-fon.
Grim.
Gri-mace.
Gri-mal-kin.
Grime.
Grim-ly.
Grin.
Grind.
Grind-er.
Grind-stone.
Grip.
Gripe.
Gris-ly.
Grist.
Gris-tle.
Grist-ly.
Grit.
Grit-ti-ness.
Grit-ty.
Griz-zly.
Groan.
Groat.
Groats.
Gro-cer.
Gro-cer-y.
Grog.

Groin.
Groom.
Groove.
Grope.
Gross.
Grot.
Grot-to.
Gro-tesque.
Ground.
Ground-less.
Ground-nut.
Ground-work.
Group.
Grouse.
Grove.
Grov-el.
Grow.
Growl.
Grown.
Growth.
Grub.
Grudge.
Gru-el.
Gruff.
Gruff-ly.
Grum.
Grum-ble.
Grum-ly.
Grunt.
Gua-no.
Guar-an-tee.
Guar-an-tor.
Guar-an-ty.
Guard.
Guard-i-an.
Guard-i-an-ship.
Gu-ber-na-to-ri-al.
Gud-geon.
Guer-ril-la.
Guess.
Guest.
Guid-ance.
Guide.
Guide-post.
Guild.
Guild-er.
Guile.
Guile-ful.
Guile-less.
Guil-lo-tine.
Guilt.
Guilt-i-ness.
Guilt-less.
Guilt-y.
Guin-ea.
Guise.
Gui-tar.
Gulf.
Gulf-y

Gull.
Gul-let.
Gul-li-bil-i-ty
Gul-ly.
Gulp.
Gum.
Gum-boil.
Gum-my.
Gump.
Gump-tion.
Gun.
Gun-ner.
Gun-ner-y.
Gun-ning.
Gun-pow-der.
Gun-shot.
Gun-smith.
Gun-stock.
Gun-wale.
Gurge.
Gur-gle.
Gush.
Gus-set.
Gust.
Gus-to.
Gust-y.
Gut.
Gut-ta-per-cha.
Gut-ter.
Gut-tle.
Gut-tur-al.
Guy.
Guz-zle.
Gym-na-si-um.
Gym-nas-tic.
Gym-nas-tics.
Gyp-sum.
Gyp-sy.
Gy-ral.
Gy-ra-tion.
Gy-ra-to-ry.
Gyve.

H

Ha.
Ha-be-as Cor-pus.
Hab-er-dash-er.
Ha-bil-i-ment.
Hab-it.
Hab-it-a-ble.
Hab-it-a-tion.
Ha-bit-u-al.
Ha-bit-u-al-ly.
Ha-bit-u-ate.
Hab-i-tude.
Hack.

Hack-le.
Hack-ney.
Hack-neyed.
Hack-ney-coach.
Had.
Had-dock.
Haft.
Hag.
Hag-gard.
Hag-gish.
Hag-gle.
Hag-gler.
Ha-gi-og-ra-phy.
Hail.
Hail-stone.
Hair.
Hair-breadth.
Hair-brush.
Hair-cloth.
Hair-i-ness.
Hair-y.
Hake.
Hal-berd.
Hal-cy-on.
Hale.
Half.
Half-blood.
Half-caste.
Half-pay.
Half-pen-ny.
Hal-i-but.
Hall.
Hal-le-lu-iah.
Hal-le-lu-jah.
Hal-loo.
Hal-low.
Hal-lu-ci-na-tion.
Ha-lo.
Halt.
Halt-er.
Halve.
Halves.
Hal-yard.
Ham.
Hames.
Ham-let.
Ham-mer.
Ham-mock.
Ham-per.
Ham-strings.
Hand.
Hand-bill.
Hand-book.
Hand-cuff.
Hand-ful.
Hand-i-craft.
Hand-i-ly.
Hand-i-ness.
Hand-ker-chief.
Han-dle.

Hand-maid.
Hand-maid-en.
Hand-saw.
Hand-some.
Hand-some-ly.
Hand-spike.
Hand-y.
Hang.
Hang-er.
Hang-ings.
Hang-man.
Hank.
Hank-er.
Hank-er-ing.
Hap.
Hap-haz-ard.
Hap-less.
Hap-ly.
Hap-pen.
Hap-pi-ly.
Hap-pi-ness.
Hap-py.
Ha-rangue.
Har-ass.
Har-bin-ger.
Har-bor.
Hard.
Hard-en.
Hard-heart-ed.
Hard-i-hood.
Hard-i-ness.
Hard-ly.
Hard-ness.
Hard-ship.
Hard-ware.
Hard-y.
Hare.
Hare-bell.
Hare-brained.
Hare-lip.
Ha-rem.
Hark.
Har-le-quin.
Har-lot.
Harm.
Harm-ful.
Harm-less.
Har-mon-ic.
Har-mon-ic-al.
Har-mo-ni-ous.
Har-mo-nize.
Har-mo-ny.
Har-ness.
Harp.
Har-per.
Har-poon.
Harp-si-chord.
Har-py.
Har-ri-er.
Har-row.

Har-ry.
Harsh.
Harsh-ness.
Hart.
Harts-horn.
Har-vest.
Hash.
Has-let.
Hasp.
Has-sock.
Hast.
Haste.
Hast-en.
Has-ti-ly.
Has-ty.
Hat.
Hatch.
Hatch-el.
Hatch-et.
Hatch-way.
Hate.
Hate-ful.
Ha-tred.
Hat-ter.
Haugh-ti-ly.
Haugh-ty.
Haul.
Haunch.
Haunt.
Haut-boy.
Have.
Ha-ven.
Hav-oc.
Haw.
Hawk.
Haw-ser.
Haw-thorn.
Hay.
Hay-ing.
Hay-mow.
Hay-rick.
Hay-stack.
Haz-ard.
Haz-ard-ous.
Haze.
Ha-zel.
Ha-zi-ness.
Ha-zy.
He.
Head.
Head-ache.
Head-dress.
Head-ing.
Head-land.
Head-less.
Head-long.
Head-quar-ters.
Head-stall.
Head-strong.
Head-way.

Head-wind.
Head-y.
Heal.
Health.
Health-ful.
Health-i-ness.
Health-y.
Heap.
Hear.
Heard.
Hear-er.
Hear-ing.
Heark-en.
Hearse.
Hear-say.
Heart.
Heart-burn.
Heart-felt.
Hearth.
Heart-i-ly.
Heart-i-ness.
Heart-less.
Heart-y
Heat.
Heath.
Hea-then.
Hea-then-ish.
Hea-then-ism.
Heath-er.
Heave.
Heav-en.
Heav-en-ly.
Heaves.
Heav-i-ly.
Heav-i-ness.
Heav-y.
Heb-dom-a-dal.
He-bra-ist.
He-brew.
Hec-a-tomb.
Hec-tic.
Hec-tor.
Hedge.
Hedge-hog.
Heed.
Heed-ful.
Heed-less.
Heed-less-ness.
Heel.
He-gi-ra.
Heif-er.
Height.
Height-en.
Hei-nous.
Heir.
Heir-ess.
Heir-loom.
Held.
He-li-o-trope.
He-li-o-type.

41

Hell.
Hell-ish.
Helm.
Helm-et.
He-lot.
Help.
Help-ful.
Help-less.
Help-mate.
Help-meet.
Helve.
Hem.
Hem-i-sphere.
Hem-i-spher-ic.
Hem-i-spher-ic-al.
Hem-lock.
Hem-or-rhage.
Hemp.
Hen.
Hen-bane.
Hence.
Hence-forth.
Hence-for-ward.
He-pat-ic.
Hep-ta-gon.
Hep-tag-o-nal.
Hep-tarch-y.
Her.
Her-ald.
He-ral-dic.
Her-ald-ry.
Herb.
Her-ba-ceous.
Herb-age.
Herb-al.
Herb-al-ist.
Her-ba-ri-um.
Her-biv-or-ous.
Her-cu-le-an.
Herd.
Here.
Here-a-bouts.
Here-af-ter.
Here-at.
Here-by.
Her-e-dit-a-ment.
He-red-i-ta-ry.
Here-in.
Here-of.
Here-on.
Here-up-on.
Her-e-si-arch.
Her-e-sy.
Her-e-tic.
He-ret-ic-al.
Here-to.
Here-to-fore.
Here-with.

Her-it-a-ble.
Her-it-age.
Her-maph-ro-dite.
Her-me-neu-tics.
Her-met-ic.
Her-met-ic-al.
Her-met-ic-al-ly.
Her-mit.
Her-mit-age.
Her-ni-a.
He-ro.
He-ro-ic.
He-ro-ic-al.
Her-o-ine.
Her-o-ism.
Her-on.
Her-ring.
Hers.
Her-self.
Hes-i-tan-cy.
Hes-i-tate.
Hes-i-ta-tion.
Het-e-ro-dox.
Het-e-ro-dox-y.
Het-e-ro-ge-ne-ous.
Hew.
Hex-a-gon.
Hex-ag-o-nal.
Hex-a-he-dron.
Hex-am-e-ter.
Hex-an-gu-lar.
Hey.
Hey-day.
Hi-a-tus.
Hi-ber-nate.
Hi-ber-na-tion.
Hi-ber-ni-an.
Hic-cough.
Hick-o-ry.
Hid.
Hid-den.
Hide.
Hide-bound.
Hid-e-ous.
Hie
Hi-e-rarch.
Hi-e-rarch-al.
Hi-e-rarch-ic-al.
Hi-e-rarch-y.
Hi-e-ro-glyph.
Hi-e-ro-glyph-ic.
Hi-e-ro-glyph-ic-al.
Hi-er-o-phant.
Hig-gle.
High.
High-born.
High-flown.

High-land.
High-land-er.
High-mind-ed.
High-ness.
High-priest.
High-ly.
Hight.
Hight-en.
High-press-ure.
High-spir-it-ed.
High-way.
High-way-man.
Hi-la-ri-ous.
Hi-lar-i-ty
Hill.
Hill-ock.
Hill-y.
Hilt.
Him.
Him-self.
Hind.
Hind-er.
Hin-der.
Hin-der-ance.
Hin-drance.
Hind-most.
Hind-er-most.
Hin-doo.
Hin-du.
Hinge.
Hint.
Hip.
Hip-po-drome.
Hip-po-griff.
Hip-po-pot-a-mus.
Hip-roof.
Hire.
Hire-ling.
Hir-sute.
His.
Hiss.
Hiss-ing.
His-to-ri-an.
His-tor-ic.
His-tor-ic-al.
His-to-ri-og-ra-pher.
His-to-ri-og-ra-phy.
His-to-ry.
His-tri-on-ic.
Hit.
Hitch.
Hith-er.
Hith-er-to.
Hith-er-ward.
Hive.
Hives.
Ho.

Hoa.
Hoar.
Hoard.
Hoar-frost.
Hoar-i-ness.
Hoarse.
Hoar-y.
Hoax.
Hob-ble.
Hob-by.
Hob-gob-lin.
Hock.
Ho-cus-po-cus.
Hod.
Hodge-podge.
Hoe.
Hog.
Hog-gish.
Hogs-head.
Hoi-den.
Hoist.
Hold.
Hole.
Hol-i-day.
Ho-li-ness.
Hol-la.
Hol-lo.
Hol-loa.
Hol-land.
Hol-lands.
Hol-low.
Hol-low-ness.
Hol-ly.
Hol-ly-hock.
Holm.
Hol-o-caust.
Hol-ster.
Ho-ly.
Ho-ly-day.
Hom-age.
Home.
Home-li-ness.
Home-less.
Home-ly.
Home-made.
Ho-me-o-path-ic.
Ho-me-op-a-thy.
Home-sick.
Home-spun.
Home-stead.
Home-ward.
Hom-i-ci-dal.
Hom-i-cide.
Hom-i-ly.
Hom-i-ny.
Hom-mock.
Ho-mo-ge-ne-al.
Ho-mo-ge-ne-ous.
Hone.

Hon-est.
Hon-est-ly.
Hon-est-y
Hon-ey.
Hon-ey-comb.
Hon-ey-dew.
Hon-ey-ed.
Hon-ey-moon.
Hon-ey-suck-le.
Hon-ey-wort.
Hon-or.
Hon-or-a-ble.
Hon-or-a-bly.
Hon-or-a-ry.
Hood.
Hood-wink.
Hoof.
Hook.
Hook-ed.
Hoop.
Hoop-ing-cough.
Hoop-skirt.
Hoot
Hop.
Hope.
Hope-ful.
Hope-less.
Hop-per.
Hop-ple.
Horde.
Ho-ri-zon.
Hor-i-zon-tal.
Horn.
Horn-book.
Horn-pipe.
Horn-y.
Ho-rog-ra-phy.
Ho-rol-o-gy.
Hor-o-scope.
Hor-ri-ble.
Hor-ri-bly.
Hor-rid.
Hor-rid-ly.
Hor-rif-ic.
Hor-ror.
Horse.
Horse-back.
Horse-chest-nut.
Horse-guards.
Horse-jock-ey.
Horse-laugh.
Horse-lit-ter.
Horse-man.
Horse-man-ship.
Horse-play.
Horse-pow-er.
Horse-race.
Horse-rad-ish.
Horse-shoe.
Horse-whip.

Hor-ta-tive.
Hor-ta-to-ry.
Hor-ti-cult-ur-al.
Hor-ti-cult-ure.
Hor-ti-**cult-ur**-ist.
Ho-san-na.
Hose.
Ho-sier.
Ho-sier-y.
Hos-pi-ta-ble.
Hos-pi-ta-bly.
Hos-pi-tal.
Hos-pi-tal-i-ty.
Host.
Hos-tage.
Host-ess.
Hos-tile.
Hos-til-i-ty.
Host-ler.
Hot.
Hot-bed.
Hotch-potch.
Ho-tel.
Hot-head-ed.
Hot-house.
Hot-ly.
Hot-press.
Hough.
Hound.
Hour.
Hour-glass.
Hour-hand.
Hour-ly.
House.
House-break-er.
House-hold.
House-hold-er.
House-keep-er.
House-keep-ing.
House-maid.
House-wife.
House-wife-ry.
Hous-ing.
Hov-el.
Hov-er.
How.
How-be-it.
How-ev-**er**.
How-itz-**er**.
Howl.
Howl-**et**.
Hoy.
Hub.
Hub-**bub**.
Huck-ster.
Hud-dle.
Hue.
Huff.
Huff-y.

Hug.
Huge.
Huge-ly.
Hulk.
Hull.
Hum.
Hu-man.
Hu-mane.
Hu-man-i-ty.
Hu-man-ize.
Hu-man-kind.
Hu-man-ly.
Hum-ble.
Hum-bly.
Hum-bug.
Hum-drum.
Hu-mid.
Hu-mid-i-ty.
Hu-mid-ness.
Hu-mil-i-ate.
Hu-mil-i-a-tion.
Hu-mil-i-ty.
Hum-ming-bird.
Hu-mor.
Hu-mor-ist.
Hu-mor-ous.
Hu-mor-ous-ly.
Hu-mor-some.
Hump.
Hump-back.
Hunch.
Hun-dred.
Hun-dredth.
Hung.
Hun-ger.
Hun-gered.
Hun-gry.
Hunks.
Hunt.
Hunt-er.
Hunt-ress.
Hunts-man.
Hur-dle.
Hurl.
Hur-ra.
Hur-rah.
Hur-ri-cane.
Hur-ry.
Hurt.
Hurt-ful.
Hus-band.
Hus-band-man.
Hus-band-ry.
Hush.
Hush-mon-ey.
Husk.
Husk-i-ness.
Husk-y.
Hus-sar.
Hus-sy.

Hus-tings.
Hus-tle.
Hut.
Huz-za.
Hy-a-cinth.
Hy-brid.
Hy-dra.
Hy-drant.
Hy-draul-ic.
Hy-draul-ics.
Hy-dro-gen.
Hy-drog-ra-phy.
Hy-dro-mel.
Hy-drom-e-try.
Hy-drop-a-thy.
Hy-dro-pho-bi-a.
Hy-drop-ic-al.
Hy-dro-stat-ic.
Hy-dro-stat-ic-al.
Hy-dro-stat-ics.
Hy-e-na.
Hy-gi-ene.
Hy-men.
Hy-men-e-al.
Hy-men-e-an
Hymn.
Hy-per-bo-la.
Hy-per-bo-le.
Hy-per-bol-ic-al.
Hy-per-bo-re-an.
Hy-per-crit-ic.
Hy-per-crit-ic-al.
Hy-per-crit-i-cism.
Hy-phen.
Hyp-o-chon-dri-a.
Hyp-o-chon-dri-ac.
Hyp-o-chon-dri-ac-al.
Hy-poc-ri-sy.
Hyp-o-crite.
Hyp-o-crit-ic-al.
Hy-po-stat-ic.
Hy-pot-e-nuse.
Hy-poth-e-cate.
Hy-poth-e-ca-tion.
Hy-poth-e-sis.
Hy-po-thet-ic-al.
Hy-po-thet-ic-al-ly.
Hy-son.
Hys-sop.
Hys-ter-ic.
Hys-ter-ic-al.
Hys-ter-ics.
Hys-te-ri-a.

I

I.
I-am-bus.
I-bex.
I-bis.
Ice.
Ice-berg.
Ice-cream.
Ice-house.
Ich-neu-mon.
Ich-nog-ra-phy.
I-chor.
Ich-thy-ol-o-gy.
I-ci-cle.
I-ci-ness.
I-con-o-clast.
I-con-og-ra-phy.
I-cy.
I-de-a.
I-de-al.
I-de-al-ism.
I-de-al-i-ty.
I-den-tic-al.
I-den-tic-al-ly.
I-den-ti-fi-ca-tion.
I-den-ti-fy.
I-den-ti-ty.
Ides.
Id-i-o-cy.
Id-i-om.
Id-i-om-at-ic.
Id-i-o-syn-cra-sy.
Id-i-ot.
Id-i-ot-ic.
I-dle.
I-dle-ness.
I-dler.
I-dly.
I-dol.
I-dol-a-ter.
I-dol-a-tress.
I-dol-a-trous.
I-dol-a-try.
I-dol-ize.
I-dyl.
If.
Ig-ne-ous.
Ig-nis-Fat-u-us.
Ig-nite.
Ig-ni-tion.
Ig-no-ble.
Ig-no-min-i-ous.
Ig-no-min-y.
Ig-no-ra-mus.
Ig-no-rance.

Ig-no-rant.
Ig-no-rant-ly.
Ig-nore.
Ill.
Il-la-tion.
Il-la-tive.
Ill-bred.
Il-le-gal.
Il-le-gal-i-ty.
Il-le-gal-ly.
Il-leg-i-ble.
Il-leg-i-bly.
Il-le-git-i-ma-cy.
Il-le-git-i-mate.
Ill-fa-vored.
Il-lib-er-al.
Il-lib-er-al-i-ty.
Il-lic-it.
Il-lim-it-a-ble.
Il-lit-er-ate.
Il-lit-er-a-cy.
Ill-nat-ure.
Ill-nat-ured.
Ill-ness.
Il-log-ic-al.
Ill-starred.
Il-lude.
Il-lume.
Il-lu-mine.
Il-lu-mi-nate.
Il-lu-mi-na-tion.
Il-lu-sion.
Il-lu-sive.
Il-lu-so-ry.
Il-lus-trate.
Il-lus-tra-tion.
Il-lus-tra-tive.
Il-lus-tri-ous.
Ill-will.
Im-age.
Im-age-ry.
Im-ag-i-na-ble.
Im-ag-i-na-ry.
Im-ag-i-na-tion.
Im-ag-i-na-tive.
Im-ag-ine.
Im-bank.
Im-bank-ment.
Im-be-cile.
Im-be-cil-i-ty.
Im-bed.
Im-bibe.
Im-bit-ter.
Im-bos-om.
Im-bri-cate.
Im-bri-ca-ted.
Im-bri-ca-tion.
Im-brue.
Im-brute.
Im-bue.

Im-i-tate.
Im-i-ta-tion.
Im-i-ta-tive.
Im-i-ta-tor.
Im-mac-u-late.
Im-ma-nent.
Im-ma-te-ri-al.
Im-ma-te-ri-al-ism.
Im-ma-te-ri-al-ist.
Im-ma-te-ri-al-i-ty.
Im-ma-ture.
Im-ma-tu-ri-ty.
Im-meas-ur-a-ble.
Im-meas-ur-a-bly.
Im-me-di-ate.
Im-me-di-ate-ly.
Im-med-i-ca-ble.
Im-me-mo-ri-al.
Im-mense.
Im-mense-ly.
Im-men-si-ty.
Im-merge.
Im-merse.
Im-mer-sion.
Im-me-thod-ic-al.
Im-mi-grant.
Im-mi-grate.
Im-mi-gra-tion.
Im-mi-nent.
Im-mi-sion.
Im-mo-bil-i-ty.
Im-mod-er-ate.
Im-mod-er-ate-ly.
Im-mod-est.
Im-mod-est-ly.
Im-mod-est-y.
Im-mo-late.
Im-mo-la-tion.
Im-mor-al.
Im-mo-ral-i-ty.
Im-mor-al-ly.
Im-mor-tal.
Im-mor-tal-i-ty.
Im-mor-tal-ize.
Im-mov-a-ble.
Im-mov-a-bly.
Im-mu-ni-ty.
Im-mure.
Im-mu-ta-bil-i-ty.
Im-mu-ta-ble.
Im-mu-ta-bly.
Imp.
Im-pact.

Im-pair.
Im-pale.
Im-pal-pa-ble.
Im-pan-el.
Im-part.
Im-par-tial.
Im-par-ti-al-i-ty.
Im-par-tial-ly.
Im-pass-a-ble.
Im-pas-si-bil-i-ty.
Im-pas-si-ble.
Im-pas-sion.
Im-pas-sive.
Im-pa-tience.
Im-pa-tient.
Im-pa-tient-ly.
Im-peach.
Im-peach-a-ble.
Im-peach-ment.
Im-pec-ca-bil-i-ty.
Im-pec-ca-ble.
Im-pede.
Im-ped-i-ment.
Im-pel.
Im-pel-lent.
Im-pend.
Im-pend-ence.
Im-pend-en-cy.
Im-pend-ing.
Im-pen-e-tra-bil-i-ty.
Im-pen-e-tra-ble.
Im-pen-i-tence.
Im-pen-i-tent.
Im-per-a-tive.
Im-per-a-tive-ly.
Im-per-cept-i-ble.
Im-per-fect.
Im-per-fec-tion.
Im-per-fect-ly.
Im-pe-ri-al.
Im-per-il.
Im-pe-ri-ous.
Im-per-ish-a-ble.
Im-per-me-a-bil-i-ty.
Im-per-me-a-ble.
Im-per-son-al.
Im-per-son-ate.
Im-per-ti-nence.
Im-per-ti-nent-ly.
Im-per-tur-ba-ble.
Im-per-vi-ous.
Im-pet-u-os-i-ty.

Im-pet-u-ous.
Im-pe-tus.
Im-pi-e-ty.
Im-pinge.
Im-pi-ous.
Im-pla-ca-bil-**i**-ty.
Im-pla-ca-ble.
Im-pla-ca-bly.
Im-plant.
Im-plead.
Im-ple-ment.
Im-pli-cate.
Im-pli-ca-tion.
Im-pli-ca-tive.
Im-plic-it.
Im-plic-it-ly.
Im-plore.
Im-ply.
Im-pol-i-cy.
Im-po-lite.
Im-po-lite-ness.
Im-pol-i-tic.
Im-pon-der-a-ble.
Im-pon-der-ous.
Im-port.
Im-port-a-ble.
Im-por-tance.
Im-por-tant.
Im-por-ta-tion.
Im-port-u-nate.
Im-por-tune.
Im-por-tu-ni-ty.
Im-pose.
Im-pos-ing.
Im-po-si-tion.
Im-pos-si-bil-**i**-ty.
Im-pos-si-ble.
Im-post.
Im-post-hume.
Im-pos-tor.
Im-post-ure.
Im-po-tence.
Im-po-ten-cy.
Im-po-tent.
Im-po-tent-ly.
Im-pound.
Im-pov-er-ish.
Im-pov-er-ish-ment.
Im-prac-ti-ca-bil-i-ty.
Im-prac-**ti**-**ca**-ble.
Im-pre-cate.
Im-pre-ca-tion.
Im-preg-na-ble.
Im-preg-nate.
Im-preg-na-tion.

Im-pre-script-i-ble.
Im-press.
Im-press-i-ble.
Im-pres-sion.
Im-press-ive.
Im-press-ment.
Im-pri-mis.
Im-print.
Im-pris-*on*.
Im-pris-*on*-ment.
Im-prob-a-bil-**i**-ty.
Im-prob-a-ble.
Im-prob-a-bly.
Im-prob-i-ty.
Im-promp-tu.
Im-prop-er.
Im-prop-er-ly.
Im-pro-pri-e-ty.
Im-prov-a-ble.
Im-prove.
Im-prove-ment.
Im-prov-i-dence.
Im-prov-i-dent.
Im-prov-i-sa-tion.
Im-pro-vise.
Im-pru-dence.
Im-pru-dent.
Im-pru-dent-ly.
Im-pu-dence.
Im-pu-dent.
Im-pu-dent-ly.
Im-pugn.
Im-pulse.
Im-pul-sion.
Im-pul-sive.
Im-pu-ni-ty.
Im-pure.
Im-pu-ri-ty.
Im-pu-ta-tion.
Im-pute.
In.
In-a-bil-i-ty.
In-ac-ces-si-bil-i-ty.
In-ac-cess-i-ble.
In-ac-cu-ra-cy.
In-ac-cu-rate.
In-ac-cu-rate-ly.
In-ac-tion.
In-act-ive.
In-ac-tiv-i-ty.
In-ad-e-qua*te*.
In-ad-e-qu*acy.*
*In-ad-mis-si-*ble
*In-ad-*vert-ence.
In-ad-vert-ent.
In-ad-vert-ent-ly.

In-al-ien-a-ble.
In-ane.
In-an-i-mate.
In-a-ni-ti*on*.
In-an-i-ty.
In-ap-pli-ca-bil-i-ty.
In-ap-pli-ca-**ble**-ness.
In-ap-pli-ca-ble.
In-ap-po-site.
In-ap-pre-ci-a-ble.
In-ap-pro-pri-ate.
In-apt.
In-apt-i-tude.
In-arch.
In-ar-tic-u-late.
In-ar-ti-fi-cial.
In-as-much.
In-at-ten-tion.
In-at-ten-tive.
In-aud-i-ble.
In-au-gu-ral.
In-au-gu-rate.
In-au-gu-ra-tion.
In-au-spi-cious.
In-born.
In-bred.
In-cage.
In-cal-cu-la-ble.
In-can-des-cence.
In-can-des-cent.
In-can-ta-tion.
In-ca-pa-bil-i-ty.
In-ca-pa-ble.
In-ca-pac-i-tate.
In-ca-pac-i-ty.
In-car-cer-ate.
In-car-cer-a-tion.
In-car-nate.
In-car-na-tion.
In-case.
In-cau-tious.
In-cau-tious-ly.
In-cen-di-a-rism.
In-cen-di-a-ry.
In-cense.
In-cen-tive.
In-cep-tion.
In-cep-tive.
In-cer-ti-tude.
In-ces-sant.
In-ces-sant-ly.
In-cest.
In-cest-u-ous.
Inch.
In-cho-ate.
In-ci-dence.
In-ci-dent.

In-ci-dent-al.
In-ci-dent-al-ly.
In-cin-er-ate.
In-cip-i-en-cy.
In-cip-i-ent.
In-cis-ion.
In-ci-sive.
In-ci-sor.
In-cis-ure.
In-ci-ta-tion.
In-cite.
In-cite-ment.
In-ci-vil-i-ty.
In-clem-en-cy.
In-clem-ent.
In-cli-na-tion.
In-cline.
In-close.
In-clos-ure.
In-clude.
In-clu-sion.
In-clu-sive.
In-clu-sive-ly.
In-cog.
In-cog-ni-to.
In-co-her-ence.
In-co-her-en-cy.
In-co-her-ent.
In-com-bus-ti-bil-i-ty.
In-**com**-**bus**-**ti**-ble.
In-come.
In-com-**men**-**su**-rate.
In-com-**men**-**su**-ra-ble.
In-com-mode.
In-com-mo-di-ous.
In-com-mu-ni-ca-ble.
In-com-pa-ra-ble.
In-com-pa-ra-bly.
In-com-pas-**sion**-ate.
In-com-pat-i-bil-i-ty.
In-com-pat-i-ble.
In-com-pe-tence.
In-com-pe-ten-cy
In-com-pe-tent.
In-com-plete.
In-com-pre-hen-si-ble.
In-com-pre-hen-si-bly.
In-com-press-i-ble.

In-con-ceiv-a-ble.
In - con - ceiv - a - bly.
In-con-clu-sive.
In-con-gru-ent.
In-con-gru-i-ty.
In-con-gru-ous.
In-con-se-quent.
In-con- sid - er -a- ble.
In-con-sid-er-ate.
In - con - sid - er - ate-ly.
In-con - sid-er-a - tion.
In-con-sist-en-cy.
In-con-sist-ent.
In-con - sist - ent-ly.
In-con-sol-a-ble.
In-con-stan-cy.
In-con-stant.
In-con-test-a- ble.
In-con-test-a-bly.
In-con-ti-nence.
In-con-ti-nent.
In-con-ti-nent-ly.
In-con-tro-vert-i-ble.
In-con-tro-vert-i-bly.
In-con-ven-ience.
In-con-ven-ient.
In-cor-po-ral.
In-cor-po-re-al.
In-cor-po-rate.
In - cor - po - ra - tion.
In-cor-rect.
In-cor-ri-gi-ble.
In-cor - ri -gi-ble-ness.
In-cor-ri-gi-bly.
In-cor-rupt.
In-cor- rupt-i-bil-i-ty.
In-cor- rupt-i-ble.
In-cor-rup-tion.
In-cras-sate.
In-crease.
In- cred-i-bil-i-ty.
In-cred-i-ble.
In-cred-i-bly.
In-cre-du-li-ty.
In-cred-u-lous.
In-cre-ment.
In-crust.
In-crus-ta-tion.
in-cu-bate.
In-cu-ba-tion.

In-cu-bus.
In-cul-cate.
In-cul-ca-tion.
In-cul-pa-ble.
In-cul-pate.
In-cum-bent.
In-cum-brance.
In-cur.
In-cur-a-bil-i-ty.
In-cur-a-ble.
In-cur-a-bly.
In-cu-ri-ous.
In-cur-sion.
In-curv-ate.
In-cur-va-tion.
In-curve.
In-curv-i-ty.
In-debt-ed.
In-debt-ed-ness.
In-de-cen-cy.
In-de-cent.
In-de-cent-ly.
In-de-ci-pher - a- ble.
In-de-cis-ion.
In-de-ci-sive.
In-de-clin-a-ble.
In-de-co-rous.
In-de-co-rum.
In-deed.
In-de-fat - i - ga - ble.
In-de-fat - i - ga - bly.
In-de-fea-si-ble.
In-de-fect-i-ble.
In-de-fen-si-ble.
In-def-i-nite.
In-def-i-nite-ly.
In-del-i-ble.
In-del-i-bly.
In-del-i-ca-cy.
In-del-i-cate.
In-dem-ni-fi- ca - tion.
In-dem-ni-fy.
In-dem-ni-ty.
In-dent.
In-den-ta-tion.
In-dent-ure.
In-de-pend-ence.
In-de-pend-ent.
In-de-pend - ent - ly.
In-de-scrib-a-ble.
In-de-struc-ti-ble.
In-de-ter-mi-na- ble.
In - de - ter - mi - nate.

In-de-vout.
In-dex.
In-dex-es.
In-di-ces.
In-dia-man.
In-dian.
In-dia-rub-ber.
In-di-cate.
In-di-ca-tion.
In-dic-a-tive.
In-di-ca-tor.
In-dict.
In-dict-a-ble.
In-dict-ment.
In-dic-tion.
In-dif-fer-ence.
In-dif-fer-ent.
In-dif-fer-ent-ly.
In-di-gence.
In-dig-e-nous.
In-di-gent.
In-di-gest-i-ble.
In-di-ges-tion.
In-dig nant.
In-dig-na-tion.
In-dig-ni-ty.
In-di-go.
In-di-rect.
In-di-rec-tion.
In-di-rect-ly.
In-dis-cern-i-ble.
In-dis-creet.
In-dis-cre-tion.
In-dis - crim - i - nate.
In - dis - crim - i - nate-ly.
In-dis-crim-i- na - tion.
In-dis-pen-sa-ble.
In-dis-pen-sa-bly.
In-dis-pose.
In-dis-po-si-tion.
In-dis-pu-ta-ble.
In-dis-pu-ta-bly.
In-dis-so-lu-ble.
In-dis-so-lu-bly
In-dis-solv-a-ble.
In-dis-posed.
In-dis-tinct.
In-dis-tinct-ly.
In-dis-tinct-ness.
In-dis-tin-guish - a-ble.
In-dite.
In-di-vid-u-al.
In-di-vid-u-al-i - ty.
In-di-vid-u-al-ly.
In-di-vis-i-ble.

In-doc-ile.
In-do-cil-i-ty.
In-doc-tri-nate.
In-do-lence.
In-do-lent.
In-dom-i-ta-ble.
In-dorse.
In-dor-see.
In-dors-er.
In-dorse-ment.
In-du-bi-ta-ble.
In-du-bi-ta-bly.
In-duce.
In-duce-ment.
In-duct.
In-duc-tion.
In-duct-ive.
In-duct-ive-ly.
In-due.
In-dulge.
In-dul-gence.
In-dul-gent.
In-du-rate.
In-du-ra-tion.
In-dus-tri-al.
In-dus-tri-ous.
In-dus-tri-ous-ly.
In-dus-try.
In-dwell-ing.
In-e-bri-ate.
In-e-bri-a-tion.
In-e-bri-e-ty.
In-ed-it-ed.
In-ef-fa-ble.
In-ef-fa-bly.
In-ef-face-a-ble.
In-ef-fect-ive.
In-ef-fect-u-al.
In-ef-fi-ca-cious.
In-ef-fi-ca-cy.
In-ef-fi-cien-cy.
In-ef-fi-cient.
In-el-e-gance.
In-el-e-gant.
In-el-i-gi-bil-i-ty.
In-el-i-gi-ble.
In-e-qual-i-ty.
In-eq-ui-ta-ble.
In-ert.
In-er-ti-a.
In-ert-ness.
In-es-ti-ma-ble.
In-ev-i-ta-ble.
In-ev-i-ta-bly.
In-ex-act.
In-ex-cus-a-ble.
In-ex-cus-a-bly.
In-ex-haust-i-ble.
In-ex-o-ra-ble.
In-ex-pe-di-ence.

In-ex-pe-di-ent.
In-ex-pe-ri-ence.
In-ex-pert.
In-ex-pi-a-ble.
In-ex-pli-ca-ble.
In-ex-pli-ca-bly.
In-ex-press-i-ble.
In-ex-tin-guish-a-ble.
In-ex-tri-ca-ble.
In-fal-li-bil-i-ty.
In-fal-li-ble.
In-fal-li-bly.
In-fa-mous.
In-fa-mous-ly.
In-fa-my.
In-fan-cy.
In-fant.
In-fant-i-cide.
In-fant-ile.
In-fant-ine.
In-fant-ry.
In-fat-u-ate.
In-fat-u-a-tion.
In-fea-si-ble.
In-fect.
In-fec-tion.
In-fec-tious.
In-fect-ive.
In-fe-cund-i-ty.
In-fe-lic-i-tous.
In-fe-lic-i-ty.
In-fer.
In-fer-a-ble.
In-fer-ri-ble.
In-fer-ence.
In-fer-en-tial.
In-fe-ri-or.
In-fe-ri-or-i-ty.
In-fer-nal.
In-fer-tile.
In-fer-til-i-ty.
In-fest.
In-fi-del.
In-fi-del-i-ty.
In-fil-trate.
In-fil-tra-tion.
In-fi-nite.
In-fi-nite-ly.
In-fin-i-tes-i-mal.
In-fin-i-tive.
In-fin-i-tude.
In-fin-i-ty.
In-firm.
In-firm-a-ry.
In-firm-i-ty.
In-fix.
In-flame.
In-flam-**ma-bil-i-ty.**

In-flam-ma-ble.
In-flam-ma-tion.
In-flam-ma-to-ry.
In-flate.
In-fla-tion.
In-flect.
In-flec-tion.
In-flex-i-bil-i-ty.
In-flex-i-ble.
In-flex-i-bly.
In-flict.
In-flic-tion.
In-flo-res-cence.
In-flu-ence.
In-flu-en-tial.
In-flu-en-za.
In-flux.
In-fold.
In-form.
In-form-al.
In-for-mal-i-ty.
In-form-al-ly.
In-form-ant.
In-for-ma-tion.
In-form-er.
In-frac-tion.
In-fran-gi-ble.
In-fre-quen-cy.
In-fre-quent.
In-fringe.
In-fringe-ment.
In-fu-ri-ate.
In-fuse.
In-fu-si-bil-i-ty.
In-fu-si-ble.
In-fu-sion.
In-gen-ious.
In-gen-ious-ly.
In-ge-nu-i-ty.
In-gen-u-ous.
In-gen-u-ous-ly.
In-gen-u-ous-ness.
In-glo-ri-ous.
In-got.
In-graft.
In-graft-ment.
In-grain.
In-grate.
In-gra-ti-ate.
In-grat-i-tude.
In-gre-di-ent.
In-gress.
In-gulf.
In-hab-it.
In-hab-it-a-ble.
In-hab-it-ant.
In-hab-it-a-tion.
In-ha-la-tion.
In-hale.

In - har - mo - ni - ous.
In-here.
In-her-ence.
In-her-ent.
In-her-it.
In-her-it-a-ble.
In-her-it-ance.
In-her-it-or.
In-hib-it.
In-hi-bi-tion.
In-hos-pi-ta-ble.
In-hos-pi-tal-i-ty.
In-hu-man.
In-hu-man-i-ty.
In-hu-man-ly.
In-hu-ma-tion.
In-hume.
In-im-i-cal.
In-im-i-ta-ble.
In-im-i-ta-bly.
In-iq-ui-tous.
In-iq-ui-ty.
In-i-tial.
In-i-ti-ate.
In-i-ti-a-tion.
In-i-ti-a-tive.
In-i-ti-a-to-ry.
In-ject.
In-jec-tion.
In-ject-or.
In-ju-di-cious.
In-junc-tion.
In-jure.
In-ju-ri-ous.
In-ju-ri-ous-ly.
In-ju-ry.
In-jus-tice.
Ink.
Ink-ling.
Ink-stand.
Ink-y.
In-lace.
In-land.
In-lay.
In-let.
In-ly.
In-mate.
In-most.
Inn.
In-nate.
In-nav-i-ga-ble.
In-ner.
In-ner-most.
In-ning.
Inn-keep-er.
In-no-cence.
In-no-cent.
In-no-cent-ly.
In-noc-u-ous.

In-no-vate.
In-no-va-tion.
In-no-va-tor.
In-nox-ious.
In-nu-en-do.
In-nu-mer-a-ble.
In-nu-mer-a-bly.
In-oc-u-late.
In-oc-u-la-tion.
In-o-dor-ous.
In-of-fen-sive.
In-of-fen-sive-ly.
In-op-er-a-tive.
In-op-por-tune.
In-op-por-tune-ly.
In-or-di-nate.
In-or-di-nate-ly.
In-or-gan-ic.
In-os-cu-late.
In-os-cu-la-tion.
In-quest.
In-qui-e-tude.
In-quire.
In-quir-er.
In-quir-y.
In-qui-si-tion.
In-quis-i-tive.
In-quis - i - tive - ness.
In-quis-i-tor.
In-quis-i-to-ri-al.
In-road.
In-sa-lu-bri-ous.
In-sa-lu-bri-ty.
In-sane.
In-san-i-ty.
In-sa-ti-a-ble.
In-sa-ti-a-bly.
In-sa-ti-ate.
In-scribe.
In-scrip-tion.
In-scru-ta-bil-i-ty.
In-scru-ta-ble.
In-scru-ta-ble-ness.
In-sect.
In-sec-tiv-o-rous.
In-se-cure.
In-se-cu-ri-ty.
In-sen-sate.
In-sen-si-bil-i-ty.
In-sen-si-ble.
In-sen-si-bly.
In-sen-tient.
In-sep-a-ra-ble.
In-sert.
In-ser-tion.
In-side.

In-sid-i-ous.
In-sight.
In-sig-ni-a.
In-sig-nif-i-cance.
In-sig-nif-i-cant.
In-sin-cere.
In-sin-cere-ly.
In-sin-cer-i-ty.
In-sin-u-ate.
In-sin-u-a-tion.
In-sip-id.
In-si-pid-i-ty.
In-sist.
In-snare.
In-so-bri-e-ty.
In-so-lence.
In-so-lent.
In-so-lent-ly.
In-sol-u-bil-i-ty.
In-sol-u-ble.
In-solv-a-ble.
In-solv-en-cy.
In-solv-ent.
In-so-much.
In-spect.
In-spec-tion.
In-spect-or.
In-sphere.
In-spi-ra-tion.
In-spire.
In-spir-it.
In-spis-sate.
In-spis-sa-tion.
In-sta-bil-i-ty.
In-sta-ble.
In-stall.
In-stal-la-tion.
In-stall-ment.
In-stal-ment.
In-stance.
In-stant.
In-stan-ta-ne-ous.
In-stan-ter.
In-stant-ly.
In-state.
In-stead.
In-step.
In-sti-gate.
In-sti-ga-tion.
In-sti-ga-tor.
In-still.
In-stil.
In-stinct.
In-stinct-ive.
In-stinct-ive-ly.
In-sti-tute.
In-sti-tu-tion.
In-struct.

In-struc-tion.
In-struct-ive.
In-struct-or.
In-struct-ress.
In-stru-ment.
In-stru-ment-al.
In-stru-ment-al-i-ty.
In-sub-or-di-na-tion.
In-suf-fer-a-ble.
In-suf-fer-a-bly.
In-suf-fi-cien-cy.
In-suf-fi-cient.
In-su-lar.
In-su-lar-i-ty.
In-su-late.
In-su-la-tion.
In-sult.
In-sult-ing.
In-su-per-a-ble.
In-sup-port-a-ble.
In-sur-ance.
In-sure.
In-sur-gent.
In-sur-mount-a-ble.
In-sur-rec-tion.
In-sur-rec-tion-a-ry.
In-sus-cep-ti-ble.
In-tagl-io.
In-tan-gi-ble.
In-te-ger.
In-te-gral.
In-te-grant.
In-te-grate.
In-teg-ri-ty.
In-teg-u-ment.
In-tel-lect.
In-tel-lec-tion.
In-tel-lect-ive.
In-tel-lect-u-al.
In-tel-lect-u-al-ly.
In-tel-li-gence.
In-tel-li-gent.
In-tel-li-gent-ly.
In-tel-li-gi-ble.
In-tel-li-gi-bly.
In-tem-per-ance.
In-tem-per-ate.
In-tend.
In-tend-ant.
In-tense.
In-tense-ly.
In-ten-sion.
In-ten-si-ty.
In-ten-sive.

In-tent.
In-ten-tion.
In-ten-tion-al.
In-ten-tion-al-ly.
In-tent-ly.
In-ter.
In-ter-ca-la-ry.
In-ter-ca-late.
In-ter-ca-la-tion.
In-ter-cede.
In-ter-cept.
In-ter-cep-tion.
In-ter-ces-sion.
In-ter-ces-sor.
In-ter-ces-so-ry.
In-ter-change.
In-ter-change-a-ble.
In-ter-course.
In-ter-dict.
In-ter-dic-tion.
In-ter-est.
In-ter-est-ed.
In-ter-est-ing.
In-ter-fere.
In-ter-fer-ence.
In-ter-im.
In-te-ri-or.
In-te-ri-or-ly.
In-ter-ja-cent.
In-ter-jec-tion.
In-ter-lace.
In-ter-lard.
In-ter-leave.
In-ter-line.
In-ter-lin-e-ar.
In-ter-lin-e-al.
In-ter-lin-e-a-tion.
In-ter-link.
In-ter-loc-u-tor.
In-ter-loc-u-to-ry.
In-ter-lop-er.
In-ter-lude.
In-ter-mar-riage.
In-ter-mar-ry.
In-ter-med-dle.
In-ter-me-di-al.
In-ter-me-di-ate.
In-ter-ment.
In-ter-mi-na-ble.
In-ter-min-gle.
In-ter-mis-sion.
In-ter-mit.
In-ter-mit-tent.
In-ter-mix.
In-ter-mixt-ure.
In-ter-nal.
In-ter-nal-ly.

In-ter-na-tion-al.
In-ter-nun-ci-o.
In-ter-po-late.
In-ter-po-la-tion.
In-ter-po-lat-or.
In-ter-pose.
In-ter-po-si-tion.
In-ter-pret.
In-ter-pret-a-tion.
In-ter-pret-er.
In-ter-reg-num.
In-ter-ro-gate.
In-ter-ro-ga-tion.
In-ter-rog-a-tive.
In-ter-ro-ga-tor.
In-ter-rog-a-to-ry.
In-ter-rupt.
In-ter-rup-tion.
In-ter-sect.
In-ter-sec-tion.
In-ter-sperse.
In-ter-sper-sion.
In-ter-stice.
In-ter-sti-tial.
In-ter-text-ure.
In-ter-twine.
In-ter-twist.
In-ter-val.
In-ter-vene.
In-ter-ven-tion.
In-ter-view.
In-ter-weave.
In-tes-tate.
In-tes-ti-nai.
In-tes-tine.
In-tes-tines.
In-thrall.
In-thrall-ment.
In-thral-ment.
In-ti-ma-cy.
In-ti-mate.
In-ti-mate-ly.
In-ti-ma-tion.
In-tim-i-date.
In-tim-i-da-tion.
In-to.
In-tol-er-a-ble.
In-tol-er-a-biy.
In-tol-er-ance.
In-tol-er-ant.
In-to-na-tion.
In-tox-i-cate.
In-tox-i-ca-tion.
In-tract-a-bil-i-ty
In-tract-a-ble.
In-tran-si-tive.
In-trench.
In-trench-ment.

In-trep-id.
In-tre-pid-i-ty.
In-tri-ca-cy.
In-tri-cate.
In-trigue.
In-trigu-er.
In-trin-sic.
In-trin-sic-al.
In-trin-sic-al-ly.
In-tro-duce.
In-tro-duc-tion.
In-tro-duc-to-ry.
In-tro-spec-tion.
In-tro-vert.
In-trude.
In-trud-er.
In-tru-sion.
In-tru-sive.
In-trust.
In-tu-i-tion.
In-tu-i-tive.
In-tu-i-tive-ly.
In-tu-mes-cence.
In-twine.
In-twist.
In-un-date.
In-un-da-tion.
In-ure.
In-urn.
In-u-til-i-ty.
In-vade.
In-vad-er.
In-val-id.
In-va-lid.
In-val-i-date.
In-va-lid-i-ty.
In-val-u-a-ble.
In-va-ri-a-ble.
In-va-ri-a-bly.
In-va-sion.
In-vec-tive.
In-veigh.
In-vei-gle.
In-vent.
In-ven-tion.
In-vent-ive.
In-vent-or.
In-ven-to-ry.
In-verse.
In-verse-ly.
In-ver-sion.
In-vert.
In-vert-ed.
In-vest.
In-ves-ti-gate.
In-ves-ti-ga-tion.
In-ves-ti-ga-tor.
In-vest-i-ture.
In-vest-ment.
In-vet-er-a-cy.

In-vet-er-ate.
In-vid-i-ous.
In-vig-or-ate.
In-vig-or-a-tion.
In-vin-ci-ble.
In-vi-o-la-ble.
In-vi-o-late.
In-vis-i-bil-i-ty.
In-vis-i-ble.
In-vis-i-bly.
In-vi-ta-tion.
In-vite.
In-vit-ing.
In-vo-cate.
In-vo-ca-tion.
In-voice.
In-voke.
In-vol-un-ta-ri-ly.
In-vol-un-ta-ry.
In-vo-lu-tion.
In-volve.
In-vul-ner-a-ble.
In-ward.
In-ward-ly.
In-wards.
In-weave.
In-wrap.
In-wrought.
I-o-ta.
I-ras-ci-bil-i-ty.
I-ras-ci-ble.
Ire.
Ire-ful.
I-ris.
I-rish.
Irk-some.
I-ron.
Iron-clad.
I-ron-ic-al.
I-ron-y.
Ir-ra-di-ate.
Ir-ra-di-a-tion.
Ir-ra-tion-al.
Ir-ra-tion-al-ly.
Ir-rec-on-cil-a-ble.
Ir-re-cov-er-a-ble.
Ir-re-cov-er-a-bly.
Ir-re-deem-a-ble.
Ir-re-du-ci-ble.
Ir-ref-ra-ga-ble.
Ir-ref-u-ta-ble.
Ir-reg-u-lar.
Ir-reg-u-lar-i-ty.
Ir-reg-u-lar-ly.
Ir-rel-a-tive.
Ir-rel-e-vant.

Ir-rel-e-van-cy.
Ir-re-lig-ion.
Ir-re-lig-ious.
Ir-re-me-di-a-ble.
Ir-rep-a-ra-ble.
Ir-rep-a-ra-bly.
Ir-re-peal-a-ble.
Ir-rep-re-hen-si-ble.
Ir-re-press-i-ble.
Ir-re-proach-a-ble.
Ir-re-sist-i-ble.
Ir-re-sist-i-bly.
Ir-res-o-lute.
Ir-res-o-lu-tion.
Ir-re-spect-ive.
Ir-re-spon-si-ble.
Ir-re-triev-a-ble.
Ir-rev-er-ence.
Ir-rev-er-ent.
Ir-re-ver-si-ble.
Ir-rev-o-ca-ble.
Ir-rev-o-ca-bly.
Ir-ri-gate.
Ir-ri-ga-tion.
Ir-rig-u-ous.
Ir-ri-ta-bil-i-ty.
Ir-ri-ta-ble.
Ir-ri-tant.
Ir-ri-tate.
Ir-ri-ta-tion.
Ir-rup-tion.
Ir-rup-tive.
Is.
I-sin-glass.
Is-land.
Isle.
Isl-et.
Is-o-late.
Is-o-la-tion.
I-so-therm-al.
Is-ra-el-ite.
Is-sue.
Isth-mus.
It.
I-tal-ian.
I-tal-ic.
I-tal-i-cize.
I-tal-ics.
Itch.
I-tem.
It-er-ate.
It-er-a-tion.
I-tin-er-ant.
I-tin-er-ate.
I-tin-er-a-ry.
It-self.
I-vo-ry.
I-vy.

J

JAB-BER.
Ja-cinth.
Jack.
Jack-al.
Jack-a-napes.
Jack-ass.
Jack-boots.
Jack-daw.
Jack-et.
Jack-knife.
Jac-o-bin.
Jac-o-bin-ic-al.
Jade.
Jag.
Jag-gy.
Jag-u-ar.
Jail.
Jail-er.
Jal-ap.
Jam.
Jamb.
Jan-gle.
Jan-i-tor.
Jan-i-za-ry.
Jant-y.
Jan-u-a-ry.
Ja-pan.
Jar.
Jar-gon.
Jas-mine.
Jas-per.
Jaun-dice.
Jaunt.
Jave-lin.
Jaw.
Jay.
Jeal-ous.
Jeal-ous-y.
Jean.
Jeer.
Je-ho-vah.
Je-june.
Je-june-ness.
Jel-ly.
Jen-ny.
Jeop-ard.
Jeop-ard-y.
Jerk.
Jerk-in.
Jes-sa-mine.
Jest.
Jes-u-it.
Jes-u-it-ic-al.
Jet.
Jew.

49

Jew-el.
Jew-el-er
Jew-el-ler.
Jew-el-ry.
Jew-ess.
Jew-ish.
Jews-harp.
Jib.
Jig.
Jilt.
Jin-gle.
Job.
Job-ber.
Jock-ey.
Jo-cose.
Joc-u-lar.
Joc-u-lar-i-ty.
Joc-und.
Jog.
Jog-gle.
Join
Join-er.
Join-er-y.
Joint.
Joint-ed.
Joint-ly.
Joint-ress.
Joint-stick.
Joint-ten-an-cy.
Joint-ten-ant.
Joint-ure.
Joist.
Joke.
Jole.
Jol-li-ty.
Jol-ly.
Jolt.
Jos-tle.
Jot.
Jour-nal.
Jour-nal-ist.
Jour-nal-ize.
Jour-ney
Jour-ney-man.
Joust.
Jo-vi-al.
Jowl.
Jowl-er.
Joy.
Joy-ful.
Joy-ful-ly.
Joy-less.
Joy-ous.
Ju-bi-lant.
Ju-bi-lee.
Ju-da-ic-al.
Ju-da-ism.
Ju-da-ize.
Judge.
Judg-ment.

Ju-di-ca-to-ry.
Ju-di-ca-ture.
Ju-di-cial.
Ju-di-cial-ly.
Ju-di-ci-a-ry.
Ju-di-cious.
Ju-di-cious-ly.
Jug.
Jug-gle.
Jug-gler
Jug-gler-y.
Ju-gu-lar.
Juice.
Jui-ci-ness.
Jui-cy.
Ju-lep.
Ju-ly.
Jum-ble.
Jump.
Junc-tion.
Junct-ure.
June.
Jun-gle.
Jun-ior.
Jun-ior-i-ty.
Ju-ni-per.
Junk.
Junk-et.
Jun-to.
Ju-rid-ic-al.
Ju-ris-dic-tion.
Ju-ris-pru-dence.
Ju-rist.
Ju-ror.
Ju-ry-man.
Ju-ry.
Just.
Jus-tice.
Jus-ti-ci-a-ry.
Jus-ti-fi-a-ble.
Jus-ti-fi-ca-tion.
Jus-ti-fy.
Just-ly.
Just-ness.
Jut.
Jut-ty.
Ju-ve-nes-cent.
Ju-ve-nile.
Ju-ve-nil-i-ty.
Jux-ta-po-si-tion.

K

Kale.
Ka-lei-do-scope.
Kan-ga-roo.
Kedge.
Keel.

Keel-haul.
Keel-son.
Keen.
Keen-ly.
Keep.
Keep-er.
Keep-ing.
Keep-sake.
Keg.
Kelp.
Ken.
Ken-nel.
Kept.
Ker-chief.
Ker-nel.
Ker-sey.
Ker-sey-mere.
Ket-tle.
Ket-tle-drum.
Key.
Key-stone.
Kick.
Kid.
Kid-nap.
Kid-ney.
Kill.
Kiln.
Kiln-dry.
Kilt.
Kin.
Ki-nate.
Kind.
Kin-der-gar-ten.
Kin-dle.
Kind-li-ness.
Kind-ly.
Kind-ness.
Kin-dred.
Kine.
King.
King-dom.
King-fish-er.
King-ly.
King's-e-vil.
Kink.
Kins-folk.
Kins-man.
Kip-skin.
Kirk.
Kir-tle.
Kiss.
Kit.
Kitch-en.
Kite.
Kit-ten.
Knack.
Knap-sack.
Knave.
Knav-er-y.
Knav-ish.

Knead.
Knee.
Knee-pan.
Kneel.
Knell.
Knew.
Knick-knack.
Knife.
Knight.
Knight-er-rant.
Knight-hood.
Knight-ly.
Knit.
Knit-ting-nee-dle.
Knob.
Knock.
Knock-er.
Knoll.
Knot.
Knot-ted.
Knot-ty.
Knout.
Know.
Knowl-edge.
Known.
Knuck-le.
Knurl.
Knurl-y.
Ko-ran.

L

La.
La-bel.
La-bi-al.
La-bor.
Lab-o-ra-to-ry.
La-bor-er.
La-bo-ri-ous.
Lab-y-rinth.
Lac.
Lace.
Lac-er-ate.
Lac-er-a-tion.
Lac-er-a-tive.
Lach-ry-mal.
Lach-ry-ma-to-ry.
Lack.
Lack-a-dai-sic-al.
Lack-ey.
La-con-ic.
La-con-ic-al.
La-con-ism.
La-con-i-cism.
Lac-quer.
Lac-te-al.

Lac-tif-er-ous.
Lad.
Lad-der.
Lade.
Lad-ing.
La-dle.
La-dy.
La-dy-ship.
Lag.
La-goon.
La-ic.
La-ic-al.
Laid.
Lain.
Lair.
Laird.
La-i-ty.
Lake.
Lamb.
Lam-bent.
Lamb-kin.
Lame.
Lam-el-lar.
Lam-el-late.
Lame-ness.
La-ment.
Lam-ent-a-ble.
Lam-ent-a-bly.
Lam-en-ta-tion.
Lam-i-na.
Lam-i-na-ted.
Lam-mas.
Lamp.
Lamp-black.
Lam-poon.
Lam-prey.
Lance.
Lan-cet.
Lanch.
Land.
Lan-dau.
Land-ed.
Land-hold-er.
Land-ing.
Land-la-dy.
Land-lock*e*d.
Land-lord.
Land-mark.
Land-of-fice.
Land-scape.
Land-slide.
Land-slip.
Lands-man.
Lane.
Lan-guage.
Lan-guid.
Lan-guish.
Lan-guish-ment.
Lan-guor.
Lank.

Lan-tern.
Lan-yard.
Lap.
Lap-dog.
La-pel.
Lap-i-da-ry.
Lap-pet.
Lapse.
Lap-stone.
Lar-board.
Lar-ce-ny.
Larch.
Lard.
Lard-er.
Large.
Large-ly.
Large-ness.
Lar-gess.
Lark.
Lark-spur.
Lar-va.
Lar-ynx.
Las-civ-i-ous.
Lash.
Lass.
Las-si-tude.
Las-so.
Last.
Last-ing.
Last-ly.
Latch.
Latch-et.
Late.
Late-ly.
La-tent.
Lat-er-al.
Lath.
Lathe.
Lath-er.
Lath-y.
Lat-in.
Lat-in-ism.
La-tin-i-ty.
Lat-in-ize.
Lat-i-tude.
Lat-i-tu-di-nal.
Lat-i-tu-di-na-ri-an.
Lat-ten.
Lat-ter.
Lat-ter-ly.
Lat-tice.
Laud.
Laud-a-ble.
Lau-da-num.
Laud-a-to-ry.
Laugh.
Laugh-a-ble.
Laugh-ter.
Launch.

Laun-dress.
Laun-dry.
Lau-re-ate.
Lau-rel.
La-va.
Lave.
Lav-en-der.
La-ver.
Lav-ish.
Law.
Law-ful.
Law-ful-ly.
Law-giv-er.
Law-less.
Lawn.
Law-suit.
Law-yer.
Lax.
Lax-a-tive.
Lax-i-ty.
Lay.
Lay-er.
Lay-man.
La-zar.
Laz-a-ret-to.
La-zi-ly.
La-zi-ness.
La-zy.
Lea.
Leach.
Lead.
Lead-*e*n.
Lead-er.
Leaf.
Leaf-let.
Leaf-y.
League.
Leak.
Leak-age.
Leak-y.
Lean.
Leap.
Leap-year.
Learn.
Learn-ed.
Learn-er.
Learn-ing.
Lease.
Leash.
Least.
Leath-er.
Leath-ern.
Leath-er-y.
Leave.
Leav-*e*n.
Leaves.
Leav-ings.
Lech-er.
Lech-er-ous.
Lech-er-y.

Lec-tion.
Lect-ure.
Lect-ur-er.
Led.
Ledge.
Ledg-er.
Lee.
Leech.
Leek.
Leer.
Lees.
Lee-shore.
Lee-ward.
Lee-way.
Left.
Left-hand-ed.
Leg.
Leg-a-cy.
Le-gal.
Le-gal-i-ty.
Le-gal-ize.
Le-gal-ly.
Leg-ate.
Leg-a-tee.
Le-ga-tion.
Leg-a-tor.
Leg-bail.
Le-gend.
Leg-end-a-ry.
Leg-er-de-main.
Leg-er-line.
Leg-gin.
Leg-ging.
Leg-i-bil-i-ty.
Leg-i-ble.
Leg-i-bly.
Le-gion.
Leg-is-late.
Leg-is-la-tion.
Leg-is-la-tive.
Leg-is-la-tor.
Leg-is-la-ture.
Le-git-i-ma-cy.
Le-git-i-mate.
Le-git-i-ma-tion.
Leg-ume.
Le-gu-mi-nous.
Leis-ure.
Leis-ure-ly.
Lem-on.
Lem-on-ade.
Lend.
Length.
Length-*e*n.
Length-wise.
Length-y.
Le-ni-en-cy.
Le-ni-ent.
Len-i-tive.
Len-i-ty.

Lens.
Lent.
Len-til.
Le-o-nine.
Leop-ard.
Lep-er.
Lep-ro-sy.
Lep-rous.
Le-sion.
Less.
Less-er.
Les-see.
Less-en.
Les-son.
Les-sor.
Lest.
Let.
Le-thar-gic.
Leth-ar-gy.
Le-the.
Le-the-an.
Let-ter
Let-ter-press.
Let-tuce.
Le-vant.
Le-van-tine.
Lev-ee.
Lev-el.
Le-ver.
Lev-er-et.
Le-vi-a-than.
Lev-i-gate.
Le-vite.
Le-vit-i-cal.
Lev-i-ty.
Lev-y.
Lewd.
Lewd-ness.
Lex-i-cog-ra-pher.
Lex-i-co-graph-ic-al.
Lex-i-cog-ra-phy.
Lex-i-con.
Li-a-ble.
Li-a-bil-i-ty.
Li-ar.
Li-ba-tion.
Li-bel.
Li-bel-ant.
Li-bel-lant.
Li-bel-ous.
Li-bel-lous
Lib-er-al.
Lib-er-al-i-ty.
Lib-er-al-ize.
Lib-er-al-ly.
Lib-er-ate.
Lib-er-a-tion.

Lib-er-a-tor.
Lib-er-tine.
Lib-er-ty.
Li-bid-i-nous.
Li-bra-ri-an.
Li-bra-ry.
Li-brate.
Li-bra-tion.
Lice.
Li-cense.
Li-cen-ti-ate.
Li-cen-tious.
Li-cen-tious-ness.
Li-chen.
Lick.
Lick-er-ish.
Lic-or-ice.
Lid.
Lie.
Lief.
Liege.
Li-en.
Lieu.
Lieu-ten-an-cy.
Lieu-ten-ant.
Lieve.
Life.
Life-blood.
Life-boat.
Life-guard.
Life-less.
Lift.
Lig-a-ment.
Li-ga-tion.
Lig-a-ture.
Light.
Light-en.
Light-er.
Light-head-ed.
Light-heart-ed.
Light-horse.
Light-house.
Light-ly.
Light-mind-ed.
Light-ness.
Light-ning.
Lights.
Lig-ne-ous.
Lig-num-vi-tæ.
Like.
Like-li-hood.
Like-ly.
Lik-en.
Like-ness.
Like-wise.
Lik-ing.
Li-lac.
Lil-i-pu-tian.
Lil-y.
Limb.

Lim-ber.
Lim-bo.
Lime.
Lime-kiln.
Lime-stone.
Lim-it.
Lim-it-a-tion.
Lim-it-less.
Limn.
Lim-ner.
Limp.
Lim-pet.
Lim-pid.
Limp-sy.
Linch-pin.
Lin-den.
Line.
Lin-e-age.
Lin-e-al.
Lin-e-al-ly.
Lin-e-a-ment.
Lin-e-ar.
Lin-en.
Lin-en-dra-per.
Lin-ger.
Lin-ger-ing.
Lin-gual.
Lin-guist.
Lin-guist-ic.
Lin-i-ment.
Lin-ing.
Link.
Lin-stock.
Lin-net.
Lin-seed.
Lint.
Lin-tel.
Li-on.
Li-on-ess.
Lip.
Lipped.
Liq-ue-fac-tion.
Liq-ue-fi-er.
Liq-ue-fy.
Li-ques-cent.
Liq-uid.
Liq-uid-ate.
Liq-uid-a-tion.
Li-quid-i-ty.
Liq-uid-ness.
Liq-uor.
Lisp.
List.
List-el
List-en.
List-en-er.
List-less.
Lit-a-ny.
Lit-er-al.
Lit-er-al-ly.

Lit-er-a-ry.
Lit-er-a-ti.
Lit-er-a-ture.
Lith-arge.
Lithe.
Lith-o-graph.
Li-thog-ra-pher.
Lith-o-graph-ic.
Li-thog-ra-phy.
Li-thot-o-my.
Lit-i-gant.
Lit-i-gate.
Lit-i-ga-tion.
Li-tig-ious.
Lit-ter.
Lit-tle.
Lit-tle-ness.
Li-tur-gic-al.
Lit-ur-gy.
Live.
Live-li-hood.
Live-li-ness.
Live-long.
Live-ly.
Liv-er.
Liv-er-y.
Lives.
Live-stock.
Liv-id.
Liv-ing.
Liz-ard.
Lo.
Load.
Load-star.
Load-stone
Loaf.
Loaf-er.
Loam.
Loam-y.
Loan.
Loath.
Loathe.
Loath-some.
Loaves.
Lob.
Lob-by.
Lobe.
Lob-ster.
Lo-cal.
Lo-cal-i-ty.
Lo-cal-ly.
Lo-cate.
Lo-ca-tion.
Loch.
Lock.
Lock-age.
Lock-er.
Lock-et.
Lock-smith.
Lo-co-mo-tion.

Lo-co-mo-tive.	Lose.	Lu-di-crous.	Lux-u-ri-ous-ly.
Lo-cust.	Loss.	Lu-di-crous-ly.	Lux-u-ry.
Lode.	Lost.	Luff.	Ly-ce-um.
Lodge.	Lot.	Lug.	Lye.
Lodg-er.	Loth.	Lug-gage.	Lymph.
Lodg-ing.	Lo-tion.	Lu-gu-bri-ous.	Lym-phat-ic.
Lodg-ment.	Lot-ter-y.	Luke-warm.	Lynx.
Loft.	Loud.	Luke-warm-ness.	Lyre.
Loft-i-ly.	Loud-ly.	Lull.	Lyr-ic.
Loft-i-ness.	Lough.	Lull-a-by.	Lyr-ic-al.
Loft-y.	Lounge.	Lum-ba-go.	
Log.	Loung-er.	Lum-bar.	
Log-a-rith-mic.	Louse.	Lum-ber.	
Log-a-rith-mic-al.	Lout.	Lum-ber-room.	**M**
Log-a-rithm.	Lov-a-ble.	Lu-mi-na-ry.	
Log-book.	Lov-age.	Lu-mi-nous.	Mac-ad-am-ize.
Log-ger-head.	Love.	Lump.	Mac-a-ro-ni.
Log-ic.	Love-feast.	Lump-ish.	Mac-a-ron-ic.
Log-ic-al.	Love-knot.	Lump-y.	Mac-ca-boy.
Log-ic-al-ly.	Love-let-ter.	Lu-na-cy.	Ma-caw.
Lo-gi-cian.	Love-li-ness.	Lu-nar.	Mace.
Lo-gom-a-chy.	Love-ly.	Lu-na-ry.	Mac-er-ate.
Log-wood.	Lov-er.	Lu-na-ri-an.	Mac-er-a-tion.
Loin.	Love-sick.	Lu-na-tic.	Mach-i-nate.
Loi-ter.	Love-song.	Lu-na-tion.	Mach-i-na-tion.
Loll.	Lov-ing.	Lunch.	Ma-chine.
Lone.	Lov-ing-kind-ness.	Lunch-eon.	Ma-chin-er-y.
Lone-li-ness.		Lu-nette.	Ma-chin-ist.
Lone-ly.	Low.	Lung.	Mack-er-el.
Lone-some.	Low-bred.	Lunge.	Ma-cro-cosm.
Long.	Low-er.	Lu-nu-lar.	Mad.
Longe.	Low-er-most.	Lu-nu-late.	Mad-am.
Lon-gev-i-ty.	Low-er-y.	Lu-pine.	Mad-cap.
Long-ing.	Low-land.	Lurch.	Mad-den.
Lon-gi-tude.	Low-li-ness.	Lure.	Mad-der.
Lon-gi-tu-di-nal.	Low-ly.	Lu-rid.	Made.
Long-suf-fer-ing.	Low-ness.	Lurk.	Ma-dei-ra.
Long-wind-ed.	Low-spir-it-ed.	Lurk-ing-place.	Mad-house.
Lob.	Low-wines.	Lus-cious.	Mad-ly.
Look.	Loy-al.	Lust.	Mad-man.
Look-ing-glass.	Loy-al-ly.	Lus-ter.	Mad-ness.
Loom.	Loy-al-ty.	Lus-tre.	Ma-don-na.
Loon.	Loz-enge.	Lust-ful.	Mad-re-pore.
Loop.	Lub-ber.	Lust-i-ly.	Mad-ri-gal.
Loop-hole.	Lub-ber-ly.	Lus-tral.	Mag-a-zine.
Loose.	Lu-bri-cate.	Lus-trate.	Mag-got.
Loose-ly.	Lu-bric-i-ty.	Lus-tra-tion.	Mag-got-y.
Loos-en.	Lu-bri-cous.	Lus-tring.	Ma-gi.
Loose-ness.	Lu-cid.	Lus-trous.	Ma-gi-an.
Lop.	Lu-cid-ness.	Lust-y.	Mag-ic.
Lo-qua-cious.	Lu-ci-fer.	Lute.	Mag-ic-al.
Lo-quac-i-ty.	Luck-less.	Lute-string.	Ma-gi-cian.
Lord.	Luck.	Lu-ther-an.	Mag-is-te-ri-al.
Lord-li-ness	Luck-i-ly.	Lu-thern.	Mag-is-te-ri-al-ly.
Lord-ling.	Luck-y.	Lux-ate.	
Lord-ly.	Lu-cra-tive.	Lux-a-tion.	Mag-is-tra-cy.
Lord-ship.	Lu-cre.	Lux-u-ri-ance.	Mag-is-trate.
Lore.	Lu-cu-brate.	Lux-u-ri-ant.	Mag-na Char-ta.
Lorgnette.	Lu-cu-bra-tion.	Lux-u-ri-ate.	Mag-na-nim-i-ty
	Lu-cu-lent.	Lux-u-ri-ous.	Mag-nan-i-mous.

Mag-nan-i-mous-
ly.
Mag-nate.
Mag-net.
Mag-net-ic.
Mag-net-ic-al.
Mag-net-ism.
Mag-net-ize.
Mag-nif-ic.
Mag-nif-i-cence.
Mag-nif-i-cent.
Mag-nif-i-cent-
ly.
Mag-ni-fi-er.
Mag-ni-fy.
Mag-nil-o-
quence.
Mag-nil-o-quent.
Mag-ni-tude.
Mag-no-li-a.
Mag-pie.
Ma-hog-a-ny.
Ma-hom-e-tan.
Maid.
Maid-en.
Maid-en-hair.
Maid-en-ly.
Maid-serv-ant.
Mail.
Mail-coach.
Maim.
Main.
Main-land.
Main-ly.
Main-mast.
Main-sail.
Main-tain.
Main-te-nance.
Maize.
Ma-jes-tic.
Ma-jes-tic-al.
Maj-es-ty.
Ma-jor.
Ma-jor-do-mo.
Ma-jor-i-ty.
Make.
Mak-er.
Mal-a-chite.
Mal-ad-min-is-
tra-tion.
Mal-a-dy.
Mal-a-pert.
Ma-la-ri-a.
Mal-con-tent.
Male.
Mal-e-dic-tion.
Mal-e-fac-tor.
Ma-lev-o-lence.
Ma-lev-o-lent.
Mal-fea-sance.

Mal-ice.
Ma-li-cious.
Ma-li-cious-ly.
Ma-lign.
Ma-lig-nan-cy.
Ma-lig-nant.
Ma-lig-ni-ty.
Mal-i-son.
Mall.
Mal-le-a-bil-i-ty.
Mal-le-a-ble.
Mal-let.
Mal-low.
Malm-sey.
Mal-prac-tice.
Malt.
Mal-treat
Mal-treat-ment.
Mal-ver-sa-tion.
Mam-ma.
Mam-mal.
Mam-mif-er-ous.
Mam-mil-la-ry.
Mam-mon.
Mam-moth.
Man.
Man-a-cle.
Man-a-cles.
Man-age.
Man-age-a-ble.
Man-age-ment.
Man-a-ger.
Man-da-mus.
Man-da-rin.
Man-date.
Man-da-to-ry.
Man-di-ble.
Man-drel.
Mane.
Ma-nege.
Ma-nes.
Ma-neu-ver.
Ma-nœu-vre.
Man-ful.
Man-ful-ly.
Man-ga-nese.
Mange.
Man-gel-wur-zel.
Man-ger.
Man-gle.
Man-go.
Man-grove.
Man-gy.
Man-hood.
Ma-ni-a.
Ma-ni-ac.
Ma-ni-ac-al.
Man-i-fest.
Man-i-fes-ta-tion.
Man-i-fest-ly.

Man-i-fes-to.
Man-i-fold.
Man-i-kin.
Ma-ni-oc.
Ma-nip-u-late.
Ma-nip-u-la-tion.
Man-kind.
Man-li-ness.
Man-ly.
Man-na.
Man-ner.
Man-ner-ism.
Man-ner-ly.
Man-of-war.
Man-or.
Ma-no-ri-al.
Manse.
Man-sion.
Man-slaugh-ter.
Man-tel.
Man-te-let.
Man-til-la.
Man-tle.
Man-tu-a.
Man-tua-mak-er.
Man-u-al.
Man-u-fac-to-ry.
Man-u-fact-ure.
Man-u-fact-ur-er.
Man-u-mis-sion.
Man-u-mit.
Ma-nure.
Man-u-script.
Ma-ny.
Map.
Ma-ple.
Mar.
Mar-a-nath-a.
Ma-ras-mus.
Ma-raud.
Ma-raud-er.
Mar-ble.
March.
March-es.
March-ion-ess.
Mare.
Mar-gin.
Mar-gin-al.
Mar-i-gold.
Ma-rine.
Mar-i-ner.
Mar-i-tal.
Mar-i-time.
Mar-jo-ram.
Mark.
Mark-et.
Mark-et-a-ble.
Marks-man.
Marl.
Mar-line.

Marl-y.
Mar-ma-lade.
Mar-mo-re-an.
Mar-mo-set.
Ma-roon.
Marque.
Mar-quee.
Mar-quet-ry.
Mar-quis.
Mar-quis-ate.
Mar-riage.
Mar-riage-a-ble.
Mar-row
Mar-row-fat.
Mar-ry.
Marsh.
Mar-shal.
Marsh-y.
Mart.
Mar-ten.
Mar-tial.
Mar-tin.
Mar-ti-net.
Mar-tin-mas.
Mar-tin-gal.
Mart-let.
Mar-tyr.
Mar-tyr-dom.
Mar-tyr-ol-o-gist.
Mar-tyr-ol-o-gy.
Mar-vel.
Mar-vel-ous.
Mas-cu-line.
Mash.
Mask.
Mas-lin.
Ma-son.
Ma-son-ic.
Ma-son-ry.
Mas-quer-ade.
Mass.
Mas-sa-cre.
Mass-i-ness.
Mass-ive-ness.
Mass-ive.
Mass-y.
Mast.
Mas-ter.
Mas-ter-key.
Mas-ter-ly.
Mas-ter-piece.
Mas-ter-y.
Mas-ti-cate.
Mas-ti-ca-tion.
Mas-tic.
Mas-tiff.
Mas-to-don.
Mat.
Match.
Match-less.

Match-lock.
Mate.
Ma-te-ri-al.
Ma-te-ri-al-ism.
Ma-te-ri-al-ist.
Ma-te-ri-al-i-ty.
Ma-te-ri-al-ly.
Ma-ter-nal.
Ma-ter-ni-ty.
Math-e-mat-ic.
Math-e-mat-ic-al.
Math-e-mat-ic-al-ly.
Math-**e-ma-ti**-cian.
Math-e-mat-ics.
Mat-in.
Mat-ins.
Mat-rass.
Ma-trice.
Ma-trix.
Mat-ri-cide.
Ma-tric-u-late.
Ma-tric-u-la-tion.
Mat-ri-mo-ni-al.
Mat-ri-mo-ny.
Ma-tron.
Mat-ron-al.
Ma-tron-ly.
Mat-ter.
Mat-ting.
Mat-tock.
Mat-tress.
Mat-u-rate.
Mat-u-ra-tion.
Ma-ture.
Ma-ture-ly.
Ma-tu-ri-ty.
Maud-lin.
Maul.
Maund-er.
Mau-so-le-um.
Ma-vis.
Maw.
Mawk-ish.
Max-il-lar.
Max-il-la-ry.
Max-im.
Max-i-mum.
May.
May-day.
May-or.
May-or-al-ty.
May-or-ess.
Maz-a-rine.
Maz-ard.
Maze.
Ma-zy.
Me.
Mead.

Mead-ow.
Mea-ger.
Mea-gre.
Meal.
Meal-y.
Mean.
Means.
Me-an-der.
Mean-ing.
Mean-ly.
Mean-ness.
Meant.
Mean-time.
Mean-while.
Mea-sly.
Mea-sles.
Meas-ur-a-ble.
Meas-ure.
Meas-ure-ment.
Meat.
Me-chan-ic.
Me-chan-ic-al.
Me-chan-ic-al-ly.
Mech-a-ni-cian.
Me-chan-ics.
Mech-an-ism.
Mech-an-ist.
Med-al.
Med-al-ist.
Med-al-list.
Me-dal-lion.
Med-dle.
Med-dler.
Med-dle-some.
Me-di-æ-val.
Me-di-al.
Me-di-ate.
Me-di-ate-ly.
Me-di-a-tion.
Me-di-a-tor.
Me-di-a-to-ri-al.
Med-ic-al.
Med-ic-al-ly.
Med-i-ca-ment.
Med-i-cate.
Me-dic-i-nal.
Me-dic-i-nal-ly.
Med-i-cine.
Me-di-oc-ri-ty.
Med-i-tate.
Med-i-ta-tion.
Med-i-ta-tive.
Me-di-um.
Med-lar.
Med-ley.
Me-dul-lar.
Med-ul-la-ry.
Meed.
Meek.
Meer-schaum.

Meet.
Meet-ing.
Meet-ing-house.
Meet-ly.
Mel-an-chol-ic.
Mel-an-chol-y.
Mel-ior-ate.
Mel-ior-a-tion.
Mel-lif-lu-ence.
Mel-lif-lu-ent.
Mel-lif-lu-ous.
Mel-low.
Mel-low-ness.
Me-lo-di-ous.
Mel-o-drame.
Mel-o-dra-**mat**-ic.
Mel-o-dy.
Mel-on.
Melt.
Mem-ber.
Mem-ber-ship.
Mem-bra-na-ceous.
Mem-brane.
Mem-bra-nous.
Me-men-to.
Mem-oir.
Mem-o-ra-ble.
Mem-o-ran-dum.
Me-mo-ri-al.
Me-mo-ri-al-ist.
Me-mo-ri-al-ize.
Mem-o-rize.
Mem-o-ry.
Men.
Men-ace.
Men-ag-er-ie.
Mend.
Men-da-cious.
Men-dac-i-ty.
Men-di-can-cy.
Men-dic-i-ty.
Men-di-cant.
Me-ni-al.
Men-stru-al.
Men-stru-um.
Men-su-ra-ble.
Men-su-ra-tion.
Men-tal.
Men-tal-ly.
Men-tion.
Me-phit-ic.
Me-phi-tis.
Mer-can-tile.
Mer-ce-na-ry.
Me,-cer.
Mer-chan-dise.
Mer-chant.
Mer-chant-a-ble.

Mer-chant-man.
Mer-ci-ful.
Mer-ci-less.
Mer-cu-ri-al
Mer-cu-ry.
Mer-cy.
Mere.
Mere-ly.
Mer-e-tri-cious.
Merge.
Me-rid-i-an.
Me-rid-i-on-al.
Me-ri-no.
Mer-it.
Mer-i-to-ri-ous.
Mer-maid.
Mer-man.
Mer-ri-ly.
Mer-ri-ment.
Mer-ry.
Mer-ry-An-drew.
Mer-ry-mak-ing.
Mesh.
Mes-mer-ic.
Mes-mer-ism.
Mes-mer-ize.
Mess.
Mes-sage.
Mes-sen-ger.
Mes-si-ah.
Mes-suage.
Met.
Met-al.
Me-tal-lic.
Met-al-lif-er-ous.
Met-al-line.
Met-al-lur-gy.
Met-a-mor-phose.
Met-a-mor-pho-sis.
Met-a-phor.
Met-a-phor-ic-al.
Met-a-phor-ic-al-ly.
Met-a-phys-ic-al.
Met-a-phy-si-cian.
Met-a-phys-ics.
Mete.
Me-te-or.
Me-te-or-ic.
Me-te-or-o-lite.
Me-te-or-ite.
Me-te-or-o-log-ic-al.
Me-te-or-ol-o-gist.
Me-te-or-ol-o-gy.
Me-ter.
Me-tre.

Me-theg-lin.
Me-thinks.
Meth-od.
Me-thod-ic.
Me-thod-ic-al.
Me-thod-ic-al-ly.
Meth-od-ism.
Meth-od-ist.
Meth-od-ize.
Me-ton-o-my.
Met-ric-al.
Me-trop-o-lis.
Met-ro-pol-i-tan.
Met-tle.
Met-tle-some.
Mew.
Mewl.
Mez-zo-tin-to.
Mi-asm.
Mi-as-ma.
Mi-ca.
Mi-ca-ceous.
Mice.
Mich-ael-mas.
Mi-cro-cosm.
Mi-cro-scope.
Mi-cro-scop-ic.
Mi-cro-scop-ic-al.
Mid.
Mid-day.
Mid-dle.
Mid-dling.
Midge.
Mid-land.
Mid-night.
Mid-riff.
Mid-ship-man.
Midst.
Mid-sum-mer.
Mid-way.
Mid-wife.
Mid-wife-ry.
Mien.
Miff
Might.
Might-i-ly.
Might-i-ness.
Might-y.
Mign-on-ette.
Mi-grate.
Mi-gra-tion.
Mi-gra-to-ry.
Milch.
Mild.
Mil-dew.
Mild-ly.
Mild-ness.
Mile.
Mile-age.
Mil-i-tant.

Mil-i-ta-ry.
Mil-i-tate.
Mi-li-tia.
Milk.
Milk-i-ness.
Milk-maid.
Milk-man.
Milk-y.
Milk-y-way.
Mill.
Mill-dam.
Mil-le-na-ri-an.
Mil-len-ni-al.
Mil-len-ni-um.
Mill-er.
Mil-let.
Mil-li-ner.
Mil-li-**ner-y.**
Mill-ion.
Mill-ion-aire.
Mill-race.
Mill-stone.
Milt.
Mime.
Mim-ic.
Mim-ic-al.
Mim-ick-er.
Mim-ic-ry.
Min-a-ret.
Mince.
Mind.
Mind-ed.
Mind-ful.
Mine.
Min-er.
Min-er-al.
Min-er-al-ize.
Min-er-al-o-gist.
Min-er-al-og-ic-al.
Min-er-al-o-gy.
Min-gle.
Min-i-a-ture.
Min-im.
Min-i-mum.
Min-ion.
Min-is-ter.
Min-is-te-ri-al.
Min-is-tra-tion.
Min-is-try.
Mink.
Min-now.
Mi-nor.
Mi-nor-i-ty.
Min-o-taur.
Min-ster.
Min-strel.
Min-strel-sy.
Mint.
Min-u-end.

Min-u-et.
Mi-nus.
Min-ute.
Mi-nute.
Min-ute-gun.
Mi-nute-ly.
Minx.
Mir-a-cle.
Mi-rac-u-lous.
Mire.
Mir-ror.
Mirth.
Mirth-ful.
Mir-y.
Mis-an-thrope.
Mis-an-thro-pist.
Mis-an-throp-ic.
Mis-an-throp-ic-al.
Mis-an-thro-py.
Mis-ap - pli - ca - tion.
Mis-ap-ply.
Mis-ap-pre-hend.
Mis-ap-pre - hen - sion.
Mis-be-come.
Mis-be-have.
Mis-be-hav-ior.
Mis-be-lieve.
Mis-be-lief.
Mis-cal-cu-late.
Mis-cal - cu - la - tion.
Mis-call.
Mis-car-riage.
Mis-car-ry.
Mis-cel - la - **ne** - ous.
Mis-cel-la-ny.
Mis-chance.
Mis-chief.
Mis-chiev-ous.
Mis-choose.
Mis-cite.
Mis-con-ceive.
Mis-con-cep-tion.
Mis-con-duct.
Mis-con-ject-ure.
Mis - con - **struc-**tion.
Mis-con-strue.
Mis-count.
Mis-cre-ant.
Mis-date.
Mis-deed.
Mis-deem.
Mis-de-mean.
Mis-de-mean-or.
Mis-di-rect.

Mis-do-ing.
Mis-em-ploy.
Mis - em - ploy - ment.
Mi-ser.
Mis-er-a-ble.
Mis-er-a-bly.
Mi-ser-ly.
Mis-er-y.
Mis-fort-une.
Mis-give.
Mis-giv-ing.
Mis-gov-ern.
Mis - gov - **ern** - ment.
Mis-guid-ance.
Mis-guide.
Mis-hap.
Mis-im-prove.
Mis-in-form.
Mis-in - for - ma - tion.
Mis-in-ter-pret.
Mis-in-ter - pret-a-tion.
Mis-judge.
Mis-lay.
Mis-lead.
Mis-le.
Mis-led.
Mis-man-age.
Mis - man - age - ment.
Mis-match.
Mis-name.
Mis-no-mer.
Mis-place.
Mis-print.
Mis-pro-nounce.
Mis-pro-nun-ci-a-tion.
Mis-pro-por-tion.
Mis-quo-ta-tion.
Mis-quote.
Mis-re-port.
Mis-rep-re-sent.
Mis-rep-re-sent-a-tion.
Mis-rule.
Miss.
Mis-sal.
Mis-shape.
Mis-sile.
Mis-sion.
Mis-sion-a-ry.
Mis-sive.
Mis-spell.
Mis-spend.
Mis-state.
Mis-state-ment.

Mist.
Mis-take.
Mis-tak-en.
Mist-i-ness.
Mis-tle.
Mis-tle-toe.
Mis-le-toe.
Mis-took.
Mis-trans-late.
Mis-trans-la-tion.
Mis-tress.
Mis-trust.
Mis-trust-ful.
Mist-y.
Mis - un - der - stand.
Mis - un - der - stand-ing.
Mis-us-age.
Mis-use.
Mite.
Mi-ter
Mi-tre.
Mit-i-ga-ble.
Mit-i-gate.
Mit-i-ga-tion.
Mit-ten.
Mix.
Mixt-ure.
Miz-zen.
Miz-zle.
Mne-mon-ic.
Mne-mon-ics.
Moan.
Moat.
Mob.
Mo-bil-i-ty.
Moc-ca-sin.
Mock.
Mock-er-y.
Mo-dal.
Mode.
Mod-el.
Mod-er-ate.
Mod-er-ate-ly.
Mod-er-a-tion.
Mod-er-a-tor.
Mod-ern.
Mod-ern-ize.
Mod-erns.
Mod-est.
Mod-est-y.
Mod-i-cum.
Mod-i-fi-ca-tion.
Mod-i-fi-er.
Mod-i-fy.
Mo-dill-ion.
Mod-ish.
Mo-diste.
Mod-u-late.

Mod-u-la-tion.
Mo-hair.
Mo-ham-med-an.
Moi-e-ty.
Moil.
Moist.
Moist-en.
Moist-ness.
Moist-ure.
Mo-lar.
Mo-las-ses.
Mold.
Mold-er.
Mold-y.
Mole.
Mo-lec-u-lar.
Mol-e-cule.
Mole-hill.
Mo-lest.
Mol-es-ta-tion.
Mol-li-fi-ca-tion.
Mol-li-fy.
Molt.
Molt-en.
Mo-ment.
Mo-ment-a-ri-ly.
Mo-ment-a-ry
Mo-ment-ly.
Mo-ment-ous.
Mo-men-tum.
Mon-a-chism.
Mon-ad.
Mon-arch.
Mo-narch-ic.
Mo-narch-ic-al.
Mon-arch-ist.
Mon-arch-y.
Mon-as-ter-y.
Mo-nas-tic.
Mo-nas-ti-cism.
Mon-day.
Mon-e-ta-ry.
Mon-ey.
Mon-eyed.
Mon-grel.
Mo-ni-tior.
Mon-i-tor.
Mon-i-to-ri-al.
Mon-i-to-ry.
Mon-i-tress.
Monk.
Monk-er-y.
Monk-ey.
Monk-ish.
Mon-o-dy
Mo-nog-a-mist.
Mo-nog-a-my.
Mon-o-gram.
Mon-o-graph.
Mon-o-logue.

Mon-o-ma-nt-a.
Mon-o-ma-ni-ac.
Mo-nop-o-list.
Mo-nop-o-liz-er.
Mo-nop-o-lize.
Mo-nop-o-ly.
Mon-o-syl-lab-ic.
Mon-o-syl-lab-ic-al.
Mon-o-syl-la-ble.
Mon-o-the-ism.
Mon-o-tone.
Mo-not-o-nous.
Mo-not-o-ny.
Mon-soon.
Mon-ster.
Mon-stros-i-ty.
Mon-strous.
Mon-strous-ly.
Month.
Month-ly.
Mon-u-ment.
Mon-u-ment-al.
Mood.
Mood-i-ness.
Mood-y.
Moon.
Moon-light.
Moon-shine.
Moon-struck.
Moor.
Moor-ings.
Moor-ish.
Moor-land.
Moose.
Moot.
Moot-case.
Mop.
Mope.
Mop-ish.
Mor-al.
Mor-al-ist.
Mo-ral-i-ty.
Mor-al-ize.
Mor-al-ly.
Mor-als.
Mo-rass.
Mor-bid.
Mor-bid-ness.
Mor-dant.
More.
Mo-reen.
More-o-ver.
Mo-resque.
Morn.
Morn-ing.
Mo-roc-co.
Mo-rose.
Mo-rose-ly.
Mor-ris.

Mor-row.
Morse.
Mor-sel.
Mor-tal.
Mor-tal-i-ty.
Mor-tal-ly.
Mor-tar.
Mort-gage.
Mort-ga-gee.
Mort-ga-ger.
Mor-ti-fi-ca-tion.
Mor-ti-fy.
Mor-tise.
Mort-main.
Mo-sa-ic.
Mosque.
Mos-qui-to.
Moss.
Moss-y.
Most.
Most-ly.
Mote.
Moth.
Moth-er.
Moth-er-hood.
Moth-er-in-law.
Moth-er-less.
Moth-er-ly.
Moth-er-wit.
Mo-tion.
Mo-tion-less.
Mo-tive.
Mot-ley.
Mo-tor.
Mot-to.
Mould.
Moul-der.
Moult.
Mound.
Mount.
Mount-ain.
Mount-ain-eer.
Mount-ain-ous.
Mount-e-bank.
Mourn.
Mourn-er.
Mourn-ful.
Mourn-ful-ly.
Mourn-ing.
Mouse.
Mous-er.
Mouth.
Mouth-ful.
Mouth-piece.
Mov-a-ble.
Mov-a-bles.
Move.
Move-ment.
Mov-ing
Mow.

Mown.
Much.
Mu-ci-lage.
Mu-ci-lag-i-nous.
Muck.
Mu-cous.
Mu-cus.
Mud.
Mud-dle.
Mud-dy.
Muff.
Muf-fin.
Muf-fle.
Muf-fler.
Muf-ti.
Mug.
Mug-gy.
Mu-lat-to.
Mul-ber-ry.
Mulch.
Mulct.
Mule.
Mu-let-eer.
Mul-ish.
Mull.
Mul-ler.
Mull-ion.
Mul-ti-fa-ri-ous.
Mul-ti-form.
Mul-ti-form-i-ty.
Mul-ti-no-mi-al.
Mul-tip-ar-tite.
Mul-ti-ped.
Mul-ti-ple.
Mul-ti-pli-cand.
Mul-ti-pli-ca-tion.
Mul-ti-plic-i-ty.
Mul-ti-pli-er.
Mul-ti-ply.
Mul-ti-tude.
Mul-ti-tu-di-nous.
Mum.
Mum-ble.
Mum-mer.
Mum-mer-y.
Mum-my.
Mump-ish.
Mumps.
Munch.
Mun-dane.
Mu-nic-i-pal.
Mu-nic-i-pal-i-ty.
Mu-nif-i-cence.
Mu-nif-i-cent.
Mu-ni-ment.
Mu-ni-tion.
Mu-ral.
Mur-der.

Mur-der-er.
Mur-der-ous.
Mu-ri-at-ic.
Murk-y.
Mur-mur.
Mur-rain.
Mus-cle.
Mus-co-va-do.
Mus-cu-lar.
Muse.
Mu-se-um.
Mush.
Mush-room.
Mu-sic.
Mu-sic-al.
Mu-sic-al-ly.
Mu-si-cian.
Musk.
Mus-ket.
Mus-ket-ry.
Musk-mel-on.
Musk-ox.
Musk-y.
Mus-lin.
Mus-qui-to.
Mus-sul-man.
Must.
Mus-tache.
Mus-ta-ches.
Mus-tard.
Mus-ter.
Mus-ti-ness.
Mus-ty
Mu-ta-bil-i-ty.
Mu-ta-ble.
Mu-ta-tion.
Mute.
Mute-ly.
Mute-ness.
Mu-ti-late.
Mu-ti-la-tion.
Mu-ti-neer.
Mu-ti-nous.
Mu-ti-ny.
Mut-ter.
Mut-ton.
Mut-u-al.
Mut-u-al-i-ty.
Mut-u-al-ly.
Muz-zle.
My.
Myr-i-ad.
Myr-mi-don.
Myrrh.
Myr-tle.
My-self.
Mys-te-ri-ous.
Mys-ter-y.
Mys-tic.
Mys-tic-al.

Mys-tic-al-ly.
Mys-ti-cism.
Mys-ti-fy.
Myth.
Myth-ic.
Myth-o-log-ic.
Myth-o-log-ic-al.
My-thol-o-gist.
My-thol-o-gy.

N

Nab.
Na-bob.
Na-cre.
Na-dir.
Nag.
Na-iad.
Nail.
Na-ked.
Na-ked-ly.
Na-ked-ness.
Name.
Name-less.
Name-ly.
Name-sake.
Nan-keen.
Nap.
Nape.
Naph-tha.
Nap-kin.
Nap-py.
Nar-cot-ic.
Nard.
Nar-rate.
Nar-ra-tion.
Nar-ra-tive.
Nar-row.
Nar-row-ly.
Nar-rows.
Nar-whal.
Na-sal.
Nas-cent.
Nas-ty.
Na-tal.
Na-tion.
Na-tion-al.
Na-tion-al-i-ty.
Na-tive.
Na-tiv-i-ty.
Nat-u-ral.
Nat-u-ral-ist.
Nat-u-ral-i-za-tion.
Nat-u-ral-ize.
Nat-u-ral-ly.
Nat-ure.
Naught.

Naught-i-ly.
Naught-i-ness.
Naught-y.
Nau-se-a.
Nau-se-ate.
Nau-seous.
Nau-tic-al.
Nau-ti-lus.
Na-val.
Nave.
Na-vel.
Nav-i-ga-ble.
Nav-i-gate.
Nav-i-ga-tion.
Nav-i-ga-tor.
Na-vy.
Nay.
Neap.
Near.
Near-ly.
Near-ness.
Near-sight-ed.
Neat.
Neat-cat-tle.
Neat-ly.
Neat-ness.
Neb-u-la.
Neb-u-los-i-ty.
Neb-u-lous.
Nec-es-sa-ries.
Nec-es-sa-ri-ly.
Nec-es-sa-ry.
Ne-ces-si-tate.
Ne-ces-si-tous.
Ne-ces-si-ty.
Neck.
Neck-cloth.
Neck-er-chief.
Neck-lace.
Ne-crol-o-gy.
Nec-ro-man-cer.
Nec-ro-man-cy.
Nec-tar.
Nec-ta-re-an.
Nec-tar-ine.
Nec-tar-y.
Need.
Need-ful.
Nee-dle.
Need-less.
Need-less-ly.
Needs.
Need-y.
Ne'er.
Ne-fa-ri-ous.
Ne-ga-tion.
Neg-a-tive.
Neg-a-tive-ly.
Neg-lect.
Neg-lect-ful.

Neg-li-gence.	Nice-ly.	Nod-dy.	Nose-gay.
Neg-li-gent.	Ni-ce-ty.	Node.	No-sol-o-gy.
Ne-go-ti-a-ble.	Niche.	Nod-u-lar.	Nos-tril.
Ne-go-ti-ate.	Nick.	Nod-ule.	Nos-trum.
Ne-go-ti-a-tion.	Nick-el.	Nog-gin.	Not.
Ne-gress.	Nick-nacks.	Noise.	Not-a-ble.
Ne-gro.	Nick-name.	Noise-less.	Not-a-bly.
Ne-gus.	Nic-tate.	Noi-si-ly.	No-ta-ri-al.
Neigh.	Nic-ti-tate.	Noi-si-ness.	No-ta-ry.
Neigh-bor.	Nic-ta-tion.	Noi-some.	No-ta-tion.
Neigh-bor-ing.	Nic-ti-ta-tion.	Noi-sy.	Notch.
Neigh-bor-hood.	Niece.	Nom-ad.	Note.
Neigh-bor-ly.	Nig-gard.	No-mad-ic.	Note-book.
Nei-ther.	Nig-gard-ly.	No-men-clat-ure.	Not-ed.
Ne-ol-o-gism.	Nigh.	Nom-i-nal.	Note-ing.
Ne-ol-o-gist.	Night.	Nom-i-nal-ly.	Noth-ing-ness.
Ne-ol-o-gy.	Night-cap.	Nom-i-nate.	No-tice.
Ne-o-phyte.	Night-fall.	Nom-i-na-tion.	No-tice-a-ble.
Neph-ew.	Night-gown.	Nom-i-na-tive.	No-ti-fi-ca-tion.
Ne-phrit-ic.	Night-hawk.	Nom-i-nee.	No-ti-fy.
Nep-o-tism.	Night-in-gale.	Non-age.	No-tion.
Ne-re-id.	Night-ly.	Non – at - tend - ance.	No-tion-al.
Nerve.	Night-mare.		No-to-ri-e-ty.
Nerve-less.	Night-shade.	Non-con-duct-or.	No-to-ri-ous.
Nerv-ine.	Night-watch.	Non-con - form - ist.	Not - with-stand - ing.
Nerv-ous.	Ni-hil-i-ty.		
Nerv-ous-ly.	Nim-ble.	Non-con-form-i- ty.	Nought.
Nerv-ous-ness.	**Nim-bly.**		Noun.
Nes-cience.	**Nim-bus.**	Non-de-script.	Nour-ish.
Nest.	**Nine.**	None.	Nour-ish-ment.
Nes-tle.	**Nine-pins.**	Non-en-ti-ty.	Nov-el.
Nest-ling.	**Nine-teen.**	Nones.	Nov-el-ist.
Net.	**Nine-ti-eth.**	None-such.	Nov-el-ty.
Neth-er.	**Nine-ty.**	Non-ex-ist-ence.	No-vem-ber.
Neth-er-most.	**Nin-ny.**	Non-ju-ror.	Nov-ice.
Net-ting.	**Ninth.**	Non-pa-reil.	No-vi-ti-ate.
Net-tle.	**Nip.**	Non-plus.	Now.
Net-work.	**Nip-pers.**	Non-res-i-dent.	Now-a-days.
Neu-ral-gi-a.	**Nip-ple.**	Non-re-sist-ance.	No-where.
Neu-ral-gic.	**Nit.**	Non-re-sist-ant.	No-wise.
Neu-ter.	**Nit-id.**	Non-sense.	Nox-ious.
Neu-tral.	**Ni-ter.**	Non-sens-ic-al.	Noz-zle.
Neu-tral-i-ty.	**Ni-tre.**	Non-suit.	Nu-cle-us.
Neu-tral - i - za - tion.	**Ni-trate.**	Nook.	Nude.
	Ni-tric.	Noon.	Nu-di-ty.
Neu-tral-ize.	**Ni-tro-gen.**	Noon-day.	Nu-ga-to-ry.
Nev-er.	**Ni-tro-glyc - er - ine.**	Noon-tide.	Nug-get.
Nev-er-the-less.		Noon-ing.	Nui-sance.
New.	Ni-trous.	Noose.	Null.
New-fan-gled.	No.	Nor.	Nul-li-**fi-ca-tion.**
New-ly.	No-bil-i-ty.	Nor-mal.	Nul-li-fy.
New-ness.	No-ble.	North.	Nul-li-ty.
News.	No-ble-man.	North-east.	Numb.
News-mon-ger.	No-ble-ness.	North-east-ern.	Num-ber.
News-pa-per.	No-bly.	North-er-ly.	Num-ber-less.
Newt.	No-bod-y.	North-ern.	Nu-mer-al.
Next.	Noc-tam-bu-list.	North-ward.	Nu-mer-a-tion.
Nib.	Noc-tur-nal.	North-west.	Nu-mer-a-tor.
Nib-ble.	Nod.	North-west-ern.	Nu-mer-ic-al.
Nice.	Nod-dle.	Nose.	Nu-mer-ic-al-ly.

Nu-mer-ous.
Nu-mis-mat-ics.
Num-skull.
Nun.
Nun-ci-o.
Nun-cu-pa-tive.
Nun-ner-y.
Nup-tial.
Nup-tials.
Nurse.
Nurs-er-y.
Nurs-ling.
Nurt-ure.
Nut.
Nu-ta-tion.
Nut-gall.
Nut-meg.
Nu-tri-ment.
Nu-tri-ment-al.
Nu-tri-tious.
Nu-tri-tion.
Nu-tri-tive.
Nymph.

O

O.
Oaf.
Oak.
Oak-en.
Oak-um.
Oar.
O-a-sis.
Oat.
Oat-en.
Oath.
Ob-du-ra-cy.
Ob-du-rate.
O-be-di-ence.
O-be-di-ent.
O-bei-sance.
Ob-e-lisk.
O-bese.
O-bese-ness.
O-bes-i-ty.
O-bey.
Ob-fus-ca-tion.
O-bit.
O-bit-u-a-ry.
Ob-ject.
Ob-jec-tion.
Ob-jec-tion-a-ble.
Ob-ject-ive.
Ob-ject-or.
Ob-jur-ga-to-ry.
Ob-late.
Ob-la-tion.
Ob-li-gate.

Ob-li-ga-tion.
Ob-li-ga-to-ry.
O-blige.
O-blig-ing.
Ob-lique.
Ob-lique-ly.
Ob-liq-ui-ty.
Ob-lit-er-ate.
Ob-lit-er-a-tion.
Ob-liv-i-on.
Ob-liv-i-ous.
Ob-long.
Ob-lo-quy.
Ob-nox-ious.
O-bo-e.
Ob-o-vate.
Ob-scene.
Ob-scen-i-ty.
Ob-scu-ra-tion.
Ob scure.
Ob-scur-ly.
Ob-scu-ri-ty.
Ob-se-quies.
Ob-se-qui-ous.
Ob-se-qui-ous-ly.
Ob-se-qui-ous-ness.
Ob-serv-a-ble.
Ob-serv-ance.
Ob-serv-ant.
Ob-ser-va-tion.
Ob-serv-a-to-ry.
Ob-serve.
Ob-serv-er.
Ob-ses-sion.
Ob-so-les-cent.
Ob-so-lete.
Ob-sta-cle.
Ob-stet-ric.
Ob-stet-rics.
Ob-sti-na-cy.
Ob-sti-nate.
Ob-sti-nate-ly.
Ob-strep-er-ous.
Ob-struct.
Ob-struc-tion.
Ob-struct-ive.
Ob-tain.
Ob-tain-a-ble.
Ob-test.
Ob-tes-ta-tion.
Ob-trude.
Ob-tru-sion.
Ob-tru-sive.
Ob-tuse.
Ob-tuse-ly.
Ob-tuse-ness.
Ob-verse.
Ob-vert.
Ob-vi-ate.

Ob-vi-ous.
Ob-vi-ous-ly.
Oc-ca-sion.
Oc-ca-sion-al.
Oc-ca-sion-al-ly.
Oc-ci-dent.
Oc-ci-dent-al.
Oc-cip-i-tal.
Oc-ci-put.
Oc-clu-sion.
Oc-cult.
Oc-cul-ta-tion.
Oc-cu-pan-cy.
Oc-cu-pant.
Oc-cu-pa-tion.
Oc-cu-py.
Oc-cur.
Oc-cur-rence.
O-cean.
O-ce-an-ic.
O-cher.
O-chre.
Oc-ta-chord.
Oc-ta-gon.
Oc-tag-o-nal.
Oc-ta-he-dral.
Oc-ta-he-dron.
Oc-tan-gu-lar.
Oc-tave.
Oc-ta-vo.
Oc-ten-ni-al.
Oc-to-ber.
Oc-to-ge-na-ri-an.
Oc-u-lar.
Oc-u-list.
Odd.
Odd-i-ty.
Odd-ly.
Odds.
Ode.
O-de-on.
O-di-ous.
O-di-um.
O-dor.
O-dor-if-er-ous.
O-dor-ous.
O'er.
Of.
Off.
Of-fal.
Of-fence.
Of-fend.
Of-fend-er.
Of-fense.
Of-fen-sive.
Of-fer.
Of-fer-ing.
Off-hand.
Of-fice.

Of-fi-cer.
Of-fi-cial.
Of-fi-cial-ly.
Of-fi-ci-ate.
Of-fi-cious.
Off-ing.
Off-scour-ing.
Off-set.
Off-spring.
Oft.
Oft-en.
Oft-en-times.
O-gee.
O-gle.
O-gre.
Oh.
Oil.
Oil-cloth.
Oil-i-ness.
Oil-y.
Oint.
Oint-ment.
Old.
Old-en.
O-le-ag-i-nous.
O-le-o-mar-ga-rine.
Ol-fac-to-ry.
O-lib-a-num.
Ol-i-garch-y.
Ol-ive.
O-lym-pi-ad.
O-lym-pic.
O-me-ga.
Om-e-let.
O-men.
Om-i-nous.
O-mis-sion.
Om-ni-bus.
O-mit.
Om-nip-o-tence.
Om-nip-o-tent.
Om-ni-pres-ence.
Om-ni-pres-ent.
Om-nis-cience.
Om-nis-cient.
Om-niv-o-rous.
On.
Once.
One.
One-ness.
On-er-a-ry
On-er-ous.
On-ion.
On-ly.
On-set.
On-slaught.
On-to-log-ic-al.
On-tol-o-gy.
On-ward.

On-wards.
O-nyx.
Ooze.
Ooz-y.
O-pac-i-ty.
O-paque.
O-pal.
O-pal-es-cent.
O-pal-ine.
Ope.
O-pen.
O-pen-ing.
O-pen-ly.
O-pen-ness.
Op-e-ra.
Op-er-ate.
Op-er-at-ic.
Op-er-a-tion.
Op-er-a-tive.
Op-er-a-tor.
Op-er-ose.
Oph-i-cleide.
Oph-thal-mic.
Oph-thal-my.
O-pi-ate.
O-pin-ion.
O-pin-ion-a-ted.
O-pin-ion-a-tive.
O-pi-um.
O-po-del-doc.
Op-po-nent.
Op-por-tune.
Op-por-tune-ly.
Op-por-tu-ni-ty.
Op-pose.
Op-po-site.
Op-po-si-tion.
Op-po-si-tion-ist.
O-pos-sum.
Op-press.
Op-pres-sion.
Op-press-ive.
Op-press-ive-ly.
Op - press - ive - ness.
Op-press-or.
Op-pro-bri-ous.
Op - pro - bri-ous ly.
Op-pro-bri-um.
Op-pugn.
Op-ta-tive.
Op-tic.
Op-tic-al.
Op-ti-cian.
Op-tics.
Op-ti-mism.
Op-ti-mist.
Op-tion.
Op-tion-al.

Op-u-lence.
Op-u-lent.
Or.
Or-a-cle.
O-rac-u-lar.
O-ral.
O-ral-ly.
Or-ange.
O-rang-ou-tang.
O-ra-tion.
Or-a-tor.
Or-a-tor-ic-al.
Or-a-to-ri-o.
Or-a-to-ry.
Orb.
Or-bic-u-lar.
Orb-it.
Or-bit-al.
Or-chard.
Or-ches-tra.
Or-chis.
Or-dain.
Or-de-al.
Or-der.
Or-der-ly.
Or-di-nal.
Or-di-nance.
Or-di-na-ri-ly.
Or-di-na-ry.
Or-di-na-tion.
Ord-nance.
Ore.
Or-gan.
Or-gan-ic.
Or-gan-ic-al.
Or-gan-ism.
Or-gan-ist.
Or-gan-i-za-tion.
Or-gan-ize.
Or-gasm.
Or-gies.
O-ri-el.
O-ri-ent.
O-ri-ent-al.
O-ri-en-tal-ist.
Or-i-fice.
Or-i-gin.
O-rig-i-nal.
O-rig-i-nal-i-ty.
O-rig-i-nal-ly.
O-rig-i-nate.
O-rig-i-na-tion.
O-rig-i-na-tor.
O-ri-ole.
O-ri-on.
Or i-son.
Or-lop.
Or-mo-lu.
Or-na-ment.
Or-na-ment-al.

Or-nate.
Or-ni-thol-o-gist.
Or-ni-tho-log-ic-al.
Or-ni-thol-o-gy.
O-rol-o-gy.
Or-phan.
Or-phan-age.
Or-phan-ism.
Or-phe-an.
Or-phic.
Or-re-ry.
Or-tho-dox.
Or-tho-dox-y.
Or-tho-ep-ic-al.
Or-tho-e-pist.
Or-tho-e-py.
Or-thog-ra-pher.
Or-tho-graph-ic.
Or-tho - graph-ic al.
Or-thog-ra-phy.
Or-to-lan.
Os-cil-late.
Os-cil-la-tion.
Os-cil-la-to-ry.
Os-cu-late.
O-sier.
Os-prey.
Os-se-ous.
Os-si-fi-ca-tion.
Os-si-fy.
Os-siv-o-rous.
Os-ten-si-ble.
Os-ten-si-bly.
Os-ten-ta-tion.
Os-ten-ta-tious.
Os-ten- ta - tious-ly.
Os-te-ol-o-gist.
Os-te-ol-o-gy.
Os-ti-a-ry.
Os-tra-cism.
Os-tra-cize.
Os-trich.
Oth-er.
Oth-er-wise.
Ot-ter.
Ot-to-man.
Ouch.
Ought
Ounce.
Ours.
Our.
Our-selves.
Ou-sel.
Oust.
Out.
Out-bal-ance.
Out-bid.

Out-bound.
Out-break.
Out-burst.
Out-cast.
Out-cry.
Out-do.
Out-er.
Out-er-most.
Out-face.
Out-fit.
Out-gen-er-al.
Out-go.
Out-go-ing.
Out-grow.
Out-Her-od.
Out-house.
Out-land-ish.
Out-last.
Out-law.
Out-law-ry.
Out-lay.
Out-let.
Out-line.
Out-live.
Out-look.
Out-num-ber.
Out-post.
Out-rage.
Out-rage-ous.
Out-reach.
Out-rid-er.
Out-right.
Out-run.
Out-sail.
Out-sell.
Out-set.
Out-side.
Out-skirt.
Out-spread.
Out-stand-ing.
Out-stretch.
Out-strip.
Out-walk.
Out-ward.
Out-wards.
Out-ward-ly.
Out-wear.
Out-weigh.
Out wit.
Out-work.
O-val.
O-va-ry.
O-vate.
O-va-tion.
Ov-en.
O-ver.
O-ver-act.
O-ver-alls.
O-ver-arch.
O-ver-awe.

O-ver-bal-ance.
O-ver-bear-ing.
O-ver-board.
O-ver-bur-den.
O-ver-cast.
O-ver-charge.
O-ver-coat.
O-ver-come.
O-ver-do.
O-ver-dose.
O-ver-draw.
O-ver-flow.
O-ver-grow.
O-ver-hang.
O-ver-haul.
O-ver-head.
O-ver-hear.
O-ver-joy.
O-ver-land.
O-ver-lay.
O-ver-leap.
O-ver-load.
O-ver-look.
O-ver-lie.
O-ver-match.
O-ver-much.
O-ver-pass.
O-ver-plus
O-ver-poise.
O-ver-pow-er.
O-ver-rate.
O-ver-reach.
O-ver-rule.
O-ver-run.
O-ver-see.
O-ver-seer.
O-ver-set.
O-ver-shad-ow.
O-ver-shoot.
O-ver-shot.
O-ver-sight.
O-ver-sleep.
O-ver-spread.
O-ver-state.
O-ver-step.
O-ver-stock.
O-vert.
O-ver-take.
O-ver-task.
O-ver-throw.
O-ver-top.
O-ver-trade.
O-vert-ure.
O-ver-turn.
O-ver-ween-ing.
O-ver-weight.
O-ver-whelm.
O-ver-work.
O-vi-form.
O-vip-er-ous.

O-void.
Owe.
Ow-ing.
Owl.
Owl-ish.
Own.
Own-er.
Own-er-ship.
Ox.
Ox-ide.
Ox-id-ate.
Ox-id-ize.
Ox-id-a-tion.
Ox-y-gen.
Ox-y-gen-ate.
Ox-y-gen-ize.
O-yer.
Oys-ter.

P

PACE.
Pa-cer.
Pa-cha.
Pa-cif-ic.
Pa-cif-i-ca-tion.
Pa-cif-i-ca-tor.
Pa-cif-i-ca-to-ry.
Pac-i-fy.
Pack.
Pack-age.
Pack-et.
Pack-horse.
Pack-thread.
Pact.
Pad.
rad-dle.
Pad-dock.
Pad-lock.
Pad-ua-soy.
Pæ-an.
Pa-gan.
Pa-gan-ism.
Pa-gan-ize.
Page.
Pag-eant.
Pag-eant-ry.
Pa-go-da.
Paid.
Pail.
Pain.
Pain-ful.
Pain-less.
Pains.
Paint.
Paint-er.
Paint-ing.
Pair.

Pal-ace.
Pal-a-din.
Pal-an-quin.
Pal-a-ta-ble.
Pal-a-tal.
Pal-ate.
Pa-la-tial.
Pal-a-tine.
Pa-la-ver.
Pale.
Pale-ness.
Pa-le-og-ra-phy.
Pa-le-ol-o-gy.
Pa-le-on-tol-o-gy.
Pal-ette.
Pal-frey.
Pal-ing.
Pal-i-sade.
Pall.
Pal-la-di-um.
Pal-let.
Pal-li-ate.
Pal-li-a-tion.
Pal-li-a-tive.
Pal-lid.
Palm.
Pal-ma-ted.
Pal-met-to.
Pal-mis-try.
Palm-y.
Pal-pa-ble.
Pal-pa-bly.
Pal-pi-tate.
Pal-pi-ta-tion.
Pal-sied.
Pal-sy.
Pal-ter.
Pal-try.
Pam-per.
Pam-phlet.
Pam-phlet-eer.
Pan.
Pan-a-ce-a.
Pan-cake.
Pan-cre-as.
Pan-cre-at-ic.
Pan-dect.
Pan-de-mo-ni-um.
Pan-der.
Pane.
Pan-e-gyr-ic.
Pan-e-gyr-ist.
Pan-e-gy-rize.
Pan-el.
Pang.
Pan-ic.
Pan-nier.
Pan-o-ply.

Pan-o-ra-ma.
Pan-sy.
Pant.
Pan-ta-lets.
Pan-ta-loons.
Pan-the-ism.
Pan-the-ist.
Pan-the-ist-ic.
Pan-the-on.
Pan-ther.
Pan-to-graph.
Pan-tog-ra-phy.
Pan-to-mime.
Pan-to-mim-ic.
Pan-to-mim-ic-al.
Pan-try.
Pap.
Pa-pa.
Pa-pa-cy.
Pa-pal.
Pa-paw.
Pa-per.
Pa-pil-io-na-ceous.
Pap-il-la-ry.
Pa-pist.
Pa-pist-ic.
Pa-pist-ic-al.
Pap-poose.
Pap-py.
Pa-py-rus.
Par.
Par-a-ble.
Pa-rab-o-la.
Par-a-bol-ic.
Par-a-bol-ic-al.
Par-a-chute.
Par-a-clete.
Pa-rade.
Par-a-digm.
Par-a-dise.
Par-a-di-si-ac-al.
Par-a-dox.
Par-a-dox-ic-al.
Par-a-gog-ic.
Par-a-gog-ic-al.
Par-a-gon.
Par-a-graph.
Par-al-lax.
Par-al-lel.
Par-al-lel-ism.
Par-al-lel-o-gram.
Par-al-lel-o-biped.
Pa-ral-y-sis.
Par-a-lyt-ic.
Par-a-lyze.
Par-a-mount.
Par-a-mour.

Par-a-pet.
Par-a-pher-na-li-a.
Par-a-phrase.
Par-a-phrast-ic.
Par-a-site.
Par-a-sit-ic.
Par-a-sit-ic-al.
Par-a-sol.
Par-boil.
Par-cel.
Parch.
Parch-ment.
Pard.
Par-don.
Par-don-a-ble.
Pare.
Par-e-gor-ic.
Par-ent.
Par-ent-age.
Pa-rent-al.
Pa-ren-the-sis.
Par-en-thet-ic.
Par-en-thet-ic-al.
Par-hel-ion.
Pa-ri-ah.
Par-ing.
Par-ish.
Pa-rish-ion-er.
Par-i-ty.
Park.
Par-lance.
Par-ley.
Par-lia-ment.
Par-lia-ment-a-ry.
Par-lor.
Pa-ro-chi-al.
Par-o-dy.
Pa-rol.
Pa-role.
Par-o-nym.
Par-o-nyme.
Pa-ron-y-mous.
Par-o-quet.
Pa-rot-id.
Par-ox-ysm.
Par-quet.
Par-quet-ry.
Par-ri-ci-dal.
Par-ri-cide.
Par-rot.
Par-ry.
Parse.
Par-si-mo-ni-ous.
Par-si-mo-ny.
Pars-ley.
Pars-nip.
Par-son.
Par-son-age.

Part.
Par-take.
Par-terre.
Par-tial.
Par-ti-al-i-ty.
Par-tial-ly.
Par-tic-i-pant.
Par-tic-i-pate.
Par-tic-i-pa-tion.
Par-ti-cip-i-al.
Par-ti-ci-ple.
Par-ti-cle.
Par-tic-u-lar.
Par-tic-u-lar-i-ty.
Par-tic-u-lar-ize.
Par-tic-u-lar-ly.
Par-ti-san.
Par-ti-tion.
Part-i-tive.
Part-ly.
Part-ner.
Part-ner-ship.
Par-took.
Par-tridge.
Par-tu-ri-tion.
Par-ty.
Par-ty-col-ored.
Pas-chal.
Pa-sha.
Pa-sha-lic.
Pas-quin-ade.
Pass.
Pass-a-ble.
Pass-a-bly.
Pas-sage.
Pass-book.
Pas-sen-ger.
Pass-ing.
Pas-sion.
Pas-sion-ate.
Pas-sion-ate-ly.
Pas-sion-less.
Pas-sive.
Pas-sive-ly.
Pass-o-ver.
Pass-port.
Pass-word.
Past.
Paste.
Paste-board.
Pas-tern.
Pas-tile.
Pas-time.
Pas-tor.
Pas-tor-al.
Pas-tor-ate.
Pas-try.
Past-ur-a-ble.
Past-ur-age.
Past-ure.

Pas-ty.
Pat.
Patch.
Patch-work.
Pate.
Pa-tent.
Pa-tent-ee.
Pa-ter-nal.
Pa-ter-ni-ty.
Pa-ter-nos-ter
Path.
Pa-thet-ic
Path-less.
Path-o-log-ic.
Path-o-log-ic-al.
Pa-thol-o-gist.
Pa-thol-o-gy.
Pa-thos.
Path-way.
Pa-tience.
Pa-tient.
Pa-tient-ly.
Pa-tri-arch.
Pa-tri-arch-al.
Pa-tri-cian.
Pat-ri-mo-ni-al.
Pat-ri-mo-ny.
Pa-tri-ot.
Pa-tri-ot-ic.
Pa-tri-ot-ism.
Pa-tris-tic.
Pa-trol.
Pa-tron.
Pat-ron-age.
Pat-ron-al.
Pa-tron-ess.
Pat-ron-ize.
Pat-ro-nym-ic.
Pat-ten.
Pat-ter.
Pat-tern.
Pat-ty.
Pau-ci-ty.
Paunch.
Pau-per.
Pau-per-ism.
Pause.
Pave.
Pave-ment.
Pav-er.
Pav-ier.
Pa-vil-ion.
Paw.
Pawn.
Pawn-bro-ker.
Pay.
Pay-a-ble.
Pay-day.
Pay-ee.
Pay-mas-ter.

Pay-ment.
Pea.
Peace.
Peace-a-ble.
Peace-ful.
Peace-mak-er.
Peach.
Pea-cock.
Pea-hen.
Peak.
Peal.
Pe-an.
Pear.
Pearl.
Pearl-ash.
Pearl-y.
Peas-ant.
Peas-ant-ry.
Pease.
Peat.
Peb-ble.
Peb-bly.
Pe-can.
Pec-ca-bil-i-ty.
Pec-ca-ble.
Pec-ca-dil-lo.
Peck.
Pec-to-ral.
Pec-u-late.
Pec-u-la-tion.
Pec-u-la-tor.
Pe-cul-iar.
Pe-cul-iar-i-ty.
Pe-cul-iar-ly.
Pe-cun-ia-ry.
Ped-a-gog-ic.
Ped-a-gog-ic-al.
Ped-a-gog-ism.
Ped-a-gogue.
Ped-al.
Ped-ant.
Pe-dant-ic.
Ped-ant-ry.
Ped-dle.
Ped-dler.
Ped-es-tal.
Pe-des-tri-an.
Pe-des-tri-an-ism.
Ped-i-gree.
Ped-i-ment.
Pe-do-bap-tist.
Pe-dun-cle.
Peel.
Peep.
Peer.
Peer-age.
Peer-ess.
Peer-less.
Pee-vish.

Peg.
Pelf.
Pel-i-can.
Pe-lisse.
Pell.
Pel-let.
Pel-li-cle.
Pell-mell.
Pel-lu-cid
Pelt.
Pelt-ry.
Pel-vis.
Pem-mi-can
Pen.
Pe-nal.
Pen-al-ty.
Pen-ance.
Pence.
Pen-cil.
Pend-ant.
Pend-en-cy.
Pend-ent.
Pend-ing.
Pend-u-lous.
Pend-u-lum.
Pen-e-tra-bil-i-ty.
Pen-e-tra-ble.
Pen-e-trate.
Pen-e-tra-tion.
Pen-e-tra-tive.
Pen-e-tra-ting.
Pen-guin.
Pen-in-su-la.
Pen-in-su-lar.
Pen-i-tence.
Pen-i-tent.
Pen-i-ten-tial.
Pen-i-ten-ti-a-ry.
Pen-knife.
Pen-man.
Pen-man-ship.
Pen-nant.
Pen-non.
Pen-nate.
Pen-ni-less.
Pen-ny.
Pen-ny-roy-al.
Pen-ny-weight.
Pen-ny-wise.
Pen-ny-worth.
Pen-sile.
Pen-sion.
Pen-sion-a-ry.
Pen-sion-er.
Pen-sive.
Pent.
Pen-ta-gon.
Pen-tag-o-nal.
Pen-ta-graph.

Pen-ta-he-dral.
Pen-ta-he-dron.
Pen-tam-e-ter.
Pen-tan-gu-lar.
Pen-ta-teuch.
Pen-te-cost.
Pent-house.
Pe-nult.
Pe-nul-ti-ma.
Pe-nul-ti-mate.
Pe-num-bra.
Pe-nu-ri-ous.
Pen-u-ry.
Pe-on.
Pe-on-age.
Pe-o-ny.
Peo-ple.
Pep-per.
Pep-per-mint.
Pep-per-y.
Per-ad-vent-ure.
Per-am-bu-late.
Per-am-bu-la-tion.
Per-am-bu-la-tor.
Per-ceiv-a-ble.
Per-ceive.
Per-cent-age.
Per-cep-ti-ble.
Per-cep-ti-bly.
Per-cep-tion.
Per-cep tive.
Perch.
Per-chance.
Per-cip-i-ent.
Per-co-late.
Per-co-la-tion.
Per-cus-sion.
Per-di-tion.
Per-du.
Per-e-gri-na-tion.
Per-emp-to-ri-ly.
Per-emp-to-ri-ness.
Per-emp-to-ry.
Per-en-ni-al.
Per-fect.
Per-fec-tion.
Per-fect-ive.
Per-fid-i-ous.
Per-fi-dy.
Per-for-ate.
Per-fo-ra-tion.
Per-force.
Per-form.
Per-form-ance.
Per-form-er.
Per-fume.
Per-fum-er-y.
Per-func-to-ry.

Per-haps.
Pe-ri.
Per-i-car-di-um.
Per-i-carp.
Per-i-gee.
Per-i-hel-ion.
Per-il.
Per-il-ous.
Pe-rim-e-ter.
Pe-ri-od.
Pe-ri-od-ic-al.
Pe-ri-od-ic-al-ly.
Pe-riph-er-y.
Per-i-phrase.
Pe-riph-ra-sis.
Per-i-phras-tic.
Per-ish.
Per-ish-a-ble.
Per-i-stal-tic.
Per-i-style.
Per-i-wig.
Per-i-wink-le.
Per-jure.
Per-ju-ry.
Perk.
Per-ma-nence.
Per-ma-nen-cy.
Per-ma-nent.
Per-me-a-ble.
Per-me-ate.
Per-me-a-tion.
Per-mis-si-ble.
Per-mis-sion.
Per-mis-sive.
Per-mit.
Per-mu-ta-tion.
Per-ni-cious.
Per-o-ra-tion.
Per-pen-dic-u-lar.
Per-pen-dic-u-lar-ly.
Per-pe-trate.
Per-pe-tra-tion.
Per-pe-tra-tor.
Per-pet-u-al.
Per-pet-u-ate.
Per-pet-u-a-tion.
Per-pe-tu-i-ty.
Per-plex.
Per-plex-ing.
Per-plex-i-ty.
Per-qui-site.
Per-se-cute.
Per-se-cu-tion.
Per-se-cu-tor.
Per-se-ver-ance.
Per-se-vere.
Per-sim-mon.
Per-sist.

Per-sist-ence.
Per-son.
Per-son-a-ble.
Per-son-age.
Per-son-al.
Per-son-al-i-ty.
Per-son-al-ly.
Per-son-al-ty.
Per-son-ate.
Per-son-a-tion.
Per-son-i-fi-ca-tion.
Per-son-i-fy.
Per-spec-tive.
Per-spi-ca-cious.
Per-spi-cac-i-ty.
Per-spi-cu-i-ty.
Per-spic-u-ous.
Per-spi-ra-tion.
Per-spire.
Per-suade.
Per-sua-sion.
Per-sua-sive.
Pert.
Per-tain.
Per-ti-na-cious.
Per-ti-nac-i-ty.
Per-ti-nence.
Per-ti-nen-cy.
Per-ti-nent.
Per-ti-nent-ly.
Pert-ly.
Pert-ness.
Per-turb.
Per-tur-ba-tion.
Per-uke.
Pe-ru-sal.
Pe-ruse.
Per-vade.
Per-va-sion.
Per-va-sive.
Per-verse.
Per-ver-sion.
Per-ver-si-ty.
Per-ver-sive.
Per-vert.
Per-vi-ous.
Per-vi-ous-ness.
Pest.
Pes-ter.
Pest-house.
Pes-tif-er-ous.
Pes-ti-lence.
Pes-ti-lent.
Pes-ti-len-tial.
Pes-tle.
Pet.
Pet-al.
Pe-tard.
Pet-i-ole.

Pet-it.
Pe-ti-tion.
Pet-rel.
Pet-ri-fac-tion.
Pet-ri-fact-ive.
Pe-trif-ic.
Pet-ri-fy.
Pe-tro-le-um.
Pet-ti-coat.
Pet-ti-fog-ger.
Pet-ti-fog-ger-y.
Pet-tish.
Pet-ti-toes.
Pet-ty.
Pet-u-lance.
Pet-u-lant.
Pew
Pe-wit.
Pew-ter.
Pha-e-ton.
Phal-anx.
Phal-an-ster-y.
Phan-tasm.
Phan-tas-ma-**go**-ri-a.
Phan-tom.
Phar-a-sa-ic.
Phar-a-sa-ic-al.
Phar-i-sa-ism.
Phar-i-see.
Phar-ma-ceu-tic.
Phar-ma-cy.
Pha-ros.
Phar-ynx.
Phase.
Pheas-ant.
Phe-nix.
Phe-nom-e-non.
Phi-al.
Phil-an-throp-ic.
Phil-an-throp-ic-al.
Phi-lan-thro-pist.
Phi-lan-thro-py.
Phi-lip-pic.
Phil-o-log-ic-al.
Phi-lol-o-ger.
Phi-lol-o-gist.
Phi-lol-o-gy.
Phil-o-mel.
Phi-lo-pro-gen-i-tive-ness.
Phi-los-o-pher.
Phil-o-soph-ic.
Phil-o-soph-ic-al.
Phil-o-soph-ic-al-ly.
Phi-los-o-phize.
Phi-los-o-phy.
Phil-ter.

Phiz.
Phle-bot-o-mist.
Phle-bot-o-my.
Phlegm.
Phleg-mat-ic.
Phœ-nix.
Pho-net-ic.
Pho-net-ics.
Pho-nog-ra-phy.
Pho-nol-o-gy.
Phos - **pho** - res - cence.
Phos - **pho** - res - cent.
Phos-phor-ic.
Phos-pho-rus.
Pho-to-graph.
Pho-tog-ra-phy.
Phrase.
Phra-se-ol-o-gy.
Phre-nol-o-gist.
Phre-nol-o-gy.
Phren-sy.
Phthis-ic.
Phthis-ic-al.
Phthi-sis.
Phy-lac-ter-y.
Phys-ic.
Phys-ic-al.
Phy-si-cian.
Phys-ics.
Phys - i - og - **no** - mist.
Phys-i-og-no-my.
Phys-i-o-log-ic.
Phys-i-o - log - ic-al.
Phys-i-ol-o-gist.
Phys-i-ol-o-gy.
Pi-a-no-for-te.
Pi-az-za.
Pi-ca.
Pick.
Pick-ax.
Pick-axe.
Pick-ed.
Pick-et.
Pick-le.
Pick-pock-et.
Pic-nic.
Pic-to-ri-al.
Pict-ure.
Pict-ur-esque.
Pie.
Pie-bald.
Piece.
Piece-meal.
Pied.
Pier.
Pier-glass.

Pierce.
Pierc-ing.
Pi-e-tism.
Pi-e-ty.
Pig.
Pig-eon.
Pig-eon-hole.
Pig-ment.
Pig-my.
Pike.
Pik-ed.
Pi-las-ter.
Pil-chard.
Pile.
Piles.
Pil-fer.
Pil-grim.
Pil-grim-age.
Pill.
Pil-lage.
Pil-lar.
Pill-ion.
Pil-lo-ry.
Pil-low.
Pil-low-case.
Pi-lot.
Pi-lot-age.
Pimp.
Pim-per-nel.
Pim-ple.
Pim-pled.
Pin.
Pin-a-fore.
Pinch.
Pinch-beck.
Pin-cers.
Pinch-ers.
Pin-cush-ion.
Pine.
Pine-ap-ple.
Pin-feath-er.
Pin-fold.
Pin-ion.
Pink.
Pin-mon-ey.
Pin-nace.
Pin-na-cle.
Pint.
Pin-tle.
Pin-y.
Pi-o-neer.
Pi-o-ny.
Pi-ous.
Pip.
Pipe.
Pip-kin.
Pip-pin.
Piq-uan-cy.
Piq-uant.
Pique.

Pi-quet.
Pi-ra-cy.
Pi-rate.
Pi-rat-ic-al.
Pis-ca-to-ri-al.
Pis-ca-to-ry.
Pish.
Pis-mire.
Pis-ta-chio.
Pis-ta-reen.
Pis-til.
Pis-tol.
Pis-tole.
Pis-ton.
Pit.
Pitch.
Pitch-er.
Pitch-fork.
Pitch-pipe.
Pitch-y.
Pit-e-ous.
Pit-fall.
Pith.
Pith-y.
Pit-i-a-ble.
Pit-i-ful.
Pit-i-ful-ly.
Pit-i-less.
Pit-**man**.
Pit-saw.
Pit-tance.
Pi-tu-i-tous.
Pi-tu-i-ta-ry.
Pit-y.
Piv-ot.
Pla-ca-bil-i-ty.
Pla-ca-ble.
Pla-card.
Place.
Place-man.
Plac-id.
Pla-cid-i-ty.
Plac-id-ness.
Pla-gia-rism.
Pla-gia-rist.
Pla-gia-ry.
Pla-gia-rize.
Plague.
Plagu-y.
Plaice.
Plaid.
Plain.
Plain-ly.
Plain-ness.
Plaint.
Plaint-iff.
Plaint-ive.
Plait.
Plan.
Plane.

Plan-et.
Plan-et-a-ry.
Plane-tree.
Plan-ish.
Plank.
Plant.
Plant-ain.
Plan-ta-tion.
Plant-er.
Plan-ti-grade.
Plash.
Plas-ter.
Plas-ter-ing.
Plas-tic.
Plas-tic-i-ty.
Plat.
Plate.
Plat-ed.
Pla-teau.
Plate-ful.
Plat-en.
Plat-form.
Plat-i-num.
Plat-i-tude.
Pla-ton-ic.
Pla-to-nism.
Pla-to-nist.
Pla-toon.
Plat-ter.
Plau-dit.
Plau-si-bil-i-ty.
Plau-si-ble.
Plau-si-bly.
Play.
Play-bill.
Play-er.
Play-fel-low.
Play-ful.
Play-house.
Play-mate.
Play-thing.
Plea.
Plead.
Plead-ing.
Pleas-ant.
Pleas-ant-ry.
Please.
Pleas-ing.
Pleas-ur-a-ble.
Pleas-ure.
Ple-be-ian.
Pledge.
Pledg-et.
Ple-ia-des.
Ple-iads.
Ple-na-ry.
Ple-nip-o-tence.
Ple-nip-o-tent.
Plen-i-po-ten-ti-

Plen-i-tude.
Plen-te-ous.
Plen-ti-ful.
Plen-ty.
Ple-o-nasm.
Ple-o-nas-tic.
Pleth-o-ra.
Ple-thor-ic.
Pleu-ra.
Pleu-ri-sy.
Pleu-ro-pneu-mo-
  ni-a.
Plex-i-form.
Pli-a-bil-i-ty.
Pli-a-ble.
Pli-an-cy.
Pli-ant.
Pli-ers.
Plight.
Plinth.
Plod.
Plot.
Plot-ter.
Plov-er.
Plow.
Plough.
Plow-man.
Plough-man.
Plow-share.
Plough-share.
Pluck.
Plug.
Plum.
Plu-mage.
Plumb.
Plum-ba-go.
Plumb-er.
Plumb-line.
Plumb-cake.
Plume.
Plum-met.
Plump.
Plump-ly.
Plump-ness.
Plum-pud-ding.
Plun-der.
Plunge.
Plu-ral.
Plu-ral-ist.
Plu-ral-i-ty.
Plu-ral-ly.
Plus.
Plush.
Plu-vi-al.
Ply.
Pneu-mat-ic.
Pneu-mat-ics.
Pneu-ma-tol-o-
  gy.
Pneu-mo-nia.

Pneu-mon-ic.
Pneu-mo-ni-tus.
Poach.
Poach-er.
Pock.
Pock-et.
Pock-et-book.
Pock-y.
Pod.
Po-em.
Po-e-sy.
Po-et.
Po-et-as-ter.
Po-et-ess.
Po-et-ic.
Po-et-ic-al.
Po-et Lau-re-ate.
Po-et-ry.
Poh.
Poign-an-cy.
Poign-ant.
Point.
Point-blank.
Point-ed.
Point-er.
Point-less.
Poise.
Poi-son.
Poi-son-ous.
Poke.
Pok-er.
Po-lar.
Po-lar-i-ty.
Po-lar-i-za-tion.
Po-lar-ize.
Pole.
Pole-ax.
Pole-axe.
Pole-cat.
Po-lem-ic.
Po-lem-ic-al.
Pole-star.
Po-lice.
Pol-i-cy.
Pol-ish.
Po-lite.
Po-lite-ness.
Pol-i-tic.
Po-lit-ic-al.
Po-lit-ic-al-ly.
Pol-i-ti-cian.
Pol-i-tics.
Pol-i-ty.
Pol-ka.
Poll.
Pol-lard.
Pol-len.
Pol-lock.
Poll-tax.
Pol-lute.

Pol-lu-tion.
Pol-troon.
Pol-troon-er-y.
Pol-y-an-thus.
Po-lyg-a-mist.
Po-lyg-a-my.
Pol-y-glot.
Pol-y-gon.
Po-lyg-o-naf.
Pol-y-graph.
Pol-y-he-dron.
Pol-y-no-mi-al.
Pol-yp.
Pol-y-pus.
Pol-y-scope.
Pol-y-syl-lab-ic.
Pol-y-syl-lab-ic-
  al.
Pol-y-syl-la-ble.
Pol-y-tech-nic.
Pol-y-the-ism.
Pol-y-the-ist.
Pol-y-the-ist-ic.
Pom-ace.
Po-made.
Po-ma-tum.
Pome-gran-ate.
Pom-mel.
Pom-mel-ion.
Po-mol-o-gist.
Po-mol-o-gy.
Pomp.
Pom-pos-i-ty.
Pomp-ous.
Pond.
Pon-der.
Pon-der-a-ble.
Pon-der-os-i-ty.
Pon-der-ous.
Pon-gee.
Pon-iard.
Pon-tiff.
Pon-tif-ic.
Pon-tif-ic-al.
Pon-tif-ic-ate.
Pon-toon.
Po-ny.
Poo-dle.
Pool.
Poop.
Poor.
Poor-ly.
Pop.
Pope.
Pope-dom.
Pop-er-y.
Pop-gun.
Pop-in-jay.
Pop-lar.
Pop-lin.

Pop-ish.
Pop-py.
Pop-u-lace.
Pop-u-lar.
Pop-u-lar-i-ty.
Pop-u-late.
Pop-u-la-tion.
Pop-u-lous.
Por-ce-lain.
Porch.
Por-cine.
Por-cu-pine.
Pore.
Pork.
Pork-er.
Po-ros-i-ty.
Po-rous.
Por-phy-ry.
Por-poise.
Por-ridge.
Por-rin-ger.
Port.
Port-a-ble.
Port-age.
Port-al.
Port-cul-lis.
Porte.
Porte-mon-naie.
Por-tend.
Por-tent.
Por-tent-ous.
Por-ter.
Port-fol-io.
Port-hole.
Por-ti-co.
Por-tion.
Port-li-ness.
Port-ly.
Port-man-teau.
Por-trait.
Por-trait-ure.
Por-tray.
Por-tray-al.
Pose.
Pos-er.
Po-si-tion.
Pos-i-tive.
Pos-i-tive-ly.
Pos-sess.
Pos-ses-sion.
Pos-sess-ive.
Pos-sess-or.
Pos-set.
Pos-si-bil-i-ty.
Pos-si-ble.
Pos-si-bly.
Post.
Post-age.
Post-al.
Post-chaise.

Post-date.
Pos-te-ri-or.
Pos-te-ri-ors.
Pos-ter-i-ty.
Post-ern.
Post-fix.
Post-haste.
Post-hu-mous.
Pos-till-ion.
Post-man.
Post-mark.
Post-mas-ter.
Post-of-fice.
Post-paid.
Post-pone.
Post-pone-ment.
Post-script.
Post-u-late.
Post-u-la-tion.
Post-ure.
Po-sy.
Pot.
Po-ta-ble.
Pot-ash.
Po-ta-tion.
Po-ta-to.
Po-ten-cy.
Po-tent.
Po-tent-ate.
Po-ten-tial.
Po-ten-tial-ly.
Po-tent-ly.
Pot-hang-er.
Poth-er
Pot-house.
Po-tion.
Pot-sherd.
Pot-tage.
Pot-ter.
Pot-ter-y.
Pot-tle.
Pouch.
Poul-ter-er.
Poul-tice.
Poul-try.
Pounce.
Pound.
Pound-er.
Pour.
Pout.
Pov-er-ty.
Pow-der.
Pow-der-y.
Pow-er.
Pow-er-ful.
Pow-er-less.
Pow-er-loom.
Pox.
Prac-ti-ca-bil-i-ty.

Prac-ti-ca-ble.
Prac-ti-cal.
Prac-ti-cal-ly.
Prac-tice.
Prac-ti-tion-er.
Prag-mat-ic.
Prag-mat-ic-al.
Prai-rie.
Praise.
Praise-wor-thy.
Prance.
Prank.
Prate.
Prat-tle.
Prat-tler.
Prawn.
Pray.
Pray-er.
Prayer.
Prayer-book.
Prayer-ful.
Preach.
Preach-er.
Pre-am-ble.
Preb-end.
Preb-end-a-ry.
Pre-ca-ri-ous.
Pre-ca-ri-ous-ly.
Pre-cau-tion.
Pre-cau-tion-al.
Pre-cau-tion-a-ry.
Pre-ced.
Pre-ced-ence.
Pre-ced-en-cy.
Pre-ced-ent.
Prec-e-dent.
Prec-e-dent-ed.
Pre-ced-ing.
Pre-cen-tor.
Pre-cept.
Pre-cept-ive.
Pre-cept-or.
Pre-cep-tress.
Pre-ces-sion.
Pre-cinct.
Pre-cious.
Pre-cious-ly.
Prec-i-pice.
Pre-cip-i-tance.
Pre-cip-i-tan-cy.
Pre-cip-i-tant.
Pre-cip-i-tate.
Pre-cip-i-ta-tion.
Pre-cip-i-tous.
Pre-cip-i-tous-ly.
Pre-cise.
Pre-cise-ly.
Pre-cis-ian.
Pre-cis-ion.

Pre-clude.
Pre-clu-sion.
Pre-co-cious.
Pre-coc-i-ty.
Pre-con-ceive.
Pre-con-cep-tion.
Pre-con-cert.
Pre-con-cert-ed.
Pre-con-tract.
Pre-cur-sor.
Pre-da-ceous.
Pred-a-to-ry.
Pred-e-ces-sor.
Pre-des-ti-na-ri-an.
Pre-des-ti-nate.
Pre-des-tine.
Pre-des-ti-na-tion.
'e-de-ter-mi-nate.
re-de-ter-mi-na-tion.
Pre-de-ter-mine.
Pre-di-al.
Pred-i-ca-bil-i-ty.
Pred-i-ca-ble.
Pre-dic-a-ment.
Pred-i-cate.
Pred-i-ca-tion.
Pre-dict.
Pre-dic-tion.
Pre-dict-ive.
Pre-di-lec-tion.
Pre-dis-pose.
Pre-dis-po-si-tion.
Pre-dom-i-nance.
Pre-dom-i-nan-cy.
Pre-dom-i-nant.
Pre-dom-i-nate.
Pre-em-i-nence.
Pre-em-i-nent.
Pre-em-i-nent-ly
Pre-emp-tion.
Pre-en-gage.
Pre-en-gage-ment.
Pre-es-tab-lish.
Pre-ex-ist.
Pre-ex-ist-ence.
Pre-ex-ist-ent.
Pre-ex-ist-ing
Pref-ace.
Pref-a-to-ry.
Pre-fect.
Pref-ect-ure.
Pre-fer.
Pref-er-a-ble.

Pref-er-ence.
Pre-fer-ment.
Pre-fig-u-ra-tion.
Pre-fig-u-ra-tive.
Pre-fig-ure.
Pre-fix.
Preg-nan-cy.
Preg-nant.
Pre-hen-sile.
Pre-hen-sion.
Pre-judge.
Pre-judg-ment.
Prej-u-dice.
Prej-u-di-cial.
Prel-a-cy.
Prel-ate.
Pre-lat-ic.
Pre-lat-ic-al.
Pre-lec-tion.
Pre-li-ba-tion.
Pre-lim-i-na-ry.
Pre-lude.
Pre-lu-sive.
Pre-lu-so-ry.'
Pre-ma-ture.
Pre-med-i-tate.
Pre-med-i-ta-ted.
Pre-med-i-ta-tion.
Pre-mi-er.
Pre-mise.
Prem-is-es.
Pre-mi-um.
Pre-mon-ish.
Pre-mo-ni-tion.
Pre-mon-i-to-ry.
Pre-oc-cu-pa-tion.
Pre-oc-cu-py.
Pre-or-dain.
Pre-or-di-na-tion.
Prep-a-ra-tion.
Pre-par-a-tive.
Pre-par-a-to-ry.
Pre-pare.
Pre-pay.
Pre-pense.
Pre-pon-der-ance.
Pre-pon-der-ant.
Pre-pon-der-ate.
Pre-pon-der-a-tion.
Prep-o-si-tion.
Pre-pos-sess.
Pre-pos-sess-ing.
Pre-pos-ses-sion.
Pre-pos-ter-ous.
Pre-req-ui-site.

Pre-rog-a-tive.
Pre-sage.
Pres-by-ter.
Pres-by-te-ri-an.
Pres-by-te-ri-an-ism.
Pres-by-ter-y.
Pre-sci-ence.
Pre-sci-ent.
Pre-scribe.
Pre-script.
Pre-scrip-tion.
Pre-scrip-tive.
Pres-ence.
Pres-ent.
Pre-sent.
Pre-sent-a-ble.
Pres-en-ta-tion.
Pre-sen-ti-ment.
Pres-ent-ly.
Pre-sent-ment.
Pres-er-va-tion.
Pre-serv-a-tive.
Pre-serve.
Pre-side.
Pres-i-den-cy.
Pres-i-dent.
Pres-i-den-tial.
Press.
Press-gang.
Press-ing.
Press-ure.
Pre-sum-a-ble.
Pre-sume.
Pre-sump-tion.
Pre-sump-tive.
Pre-sumpt-u-ous.
Pre-sup-pose.
Pre-tence.
Pre-tend.
Pre-tend-ed.
Pre-tend-er.
Pre-tense.
Pre-ten-sion.
Pre-ten-tious.
Pret-er-it.
Pre-ter-i-tion.
Pre-ter-mis-sion.
Pre-ter-mit.
Pre-ter-nat-u-ral.
Pre-text.
Pre-tor.
Pre-to-ri-an.
Pret-ti-ly.
Pret-ty.
Pre-vail.
Prev-a-lence.
Prev-a-lent.
Pre-var-i-cate.
Pre-var-i-ca-tion.

Pre-ven-i-ent.
Pre-vent.
Pre-ven-tion.
Pre-vent-ive.
Pre-vi-ous.
Pre-vis-ion.
Prey.
Price.
Price-cur-rent.
Price-less.
Prick.
Prick-le.
Prick-ly.
Pride.
Priest.
Priest-craft.
Priest-ess.
Priest-hood.
Priest-ly.
Prig.
Prig-gish.
Prim.
Pri-ma-cy.
Prim-age.
Pri-ma-ri-ly.
Pri-ma-ry.
Pri-mate.
Prime.
Prim-er.
Pri-me-val.
Prim-ing.
Prim-i-tive.
Prim-ness.
Pri-mo-gen-i-ture.
Pri-mor-di-al.
Prim-rose.
Prince.
Prince-dom.
Prince-ly
Prin-cess.
Prin-ci-pal.
Prin-ci-pal-i-ty.
Prin-ci-pal-ly.
Prin-ci-ple.
Prink.
Print.
Print-er.
Print-ing.
Pri-or.
Pri-or-ess.
Pri-or-i-ty.
Pri-or-y.
Prism.
Pris-mat-ic.
Pris-on.
Pris-on-er.
Pris-tine.
Prith-ee.
Pri-va-cy.

Pri-vate.
Pri-va-teer.
Pri-vate-ly.
Pri-va-tion.
Priv-a-tive.
Priv-et.
Priv-i-lege.
Priv-i-ly.
Priv-i-ty.
Priv-y.
Prize.
Prob-a-bil-i-ty.
Prob-a-ble.
Prob-a-bly.
Pro-bate.
Pro-ba-tion.
Pro-ba-tion-a-ry
Pro-ba-tion-er.
Probe.
Prob-i-ty.
Prob-lem.
Prob-lem-at-ic-al.
Pro-bos-cis.
Pro-ced-ure.
Pro-ceed.
Pro-ceed-ing.
Pro-ceeds.
Proc-ess.
Pro-ces-sion.
Pro-claim.
Proc-la-ma-tion.
Pro-cliv-i-ty.
Pro-con-sul.
Pro-con-su-lar.
Pro-cras-ti-nate.
Pro-cras-ti-na-tion.
Pro-cre-ate.
Pro-cre-a-tion.
Pro-cre-a-tive.
Pro-cre-a-tor.
Proc-tor.
Pro-cum-bent.
Pro-cur-a-ble.
Proc-u-ra-tion.
Proc-u-ra-tor.
Pro-cure.
Pro-cure-ment.
Prod-i-gal.
Prod-i-gal-i-ty.
Prod-i-gal-ly.
Pro-dig-ious.
Pro-dig-ious-ly
Prod-i-gy.
Pro-duce.
Prod-uce.
Pro-du-cer.
Pro-du-ci-ble.
Prod-uct.

68

Pro-duc-tion.
Pro-duct-ive.
Pro - duct - ive - ness.
Pro-em.
Prof-a-na-tion.
Pro-fane.
Pro-fane-ly.
Pro-fane-ness.
Pro-fan-i-ty.
Pro-fess.
Pro-fess-ed-ly.
Pro-fes-sion.
Pro-fes-sion-al.
Pro-fess-or.
Pro-fess-or-ship.
Prof-fer.
Pro-fi-cien-cy.
Pro-fi-cient.
Pro-file.
Prof-it.
Prof-it-a-ble.
Prof-it-a-bly.
Prof-li-ga-cy.
Prof-li-gate.
Pro-found.
Pro-found-ness.
Pro-fund-i-ty.
Pro-fuse.
Pro-fu-sion.
Prog.
Pro-gen-i-tor.
Prog-e-ny.
Prog-no-sis.
Prog-nos-tic.
Prog-nos-tic-ate.
Prog-**nos**-ti-ca-tion.
Pro-gram.
Pro-gramme.
Prog-ress.
Pro-gress.
Pro-gres-sion.
Pro-gress-ive.
Pro-hib-it.
Pro-hi-bi-tion.
Pro-hib-it-ive.
Pro-hib-it-o-ry.
Pro-ject.
Proj-ect.
Pro-ject-ile.
Pro-jec-tion.
Pro-ject-or.
Pro-late.
Prol-i-cide.
Pro-lif-ic.
Pro-lix.
Pro-lix-i-ty.
Pro-lix-ness.
Prol-o-cu-tor.

Pro-logue.
Pro-long.
Pro-lon-ga-tion.
Prom-e-nade.
Prom-i-nence.
Prom-i-nent.
Prom-i-nent-ly.
Pro-mis-cu-ous.
Prom-ise.
Prom-is-so-ry.
Prom-on-to-ry.
Pro-mote.
Pro-mo-tion.
Pro-mo-tive.
Prompt.
Prompt-er.
Prompt-ly.
Prompt-ness.
Prompt-i-tude.
Pro-mul-gate.
Pro-mul-ga-tion.
Pro-mul-ga-tor.
Prone.
Prong.
Pro-nom-i-nal.
Pro-noun.
Pro-nounce.
Pro - nounce - **a** - ble.
Pro - nun - ci - a - men-to.
Pro - nun - ci - a - tion.
Proof.
Proof-sheet.
Prop.
Prop-a-gan-dist.
Prop-a-gate.
Prop-a-ga-tion.
Prop-a-ga-tor.
Pro-pel.
Pro-pel-ler.
Pro-pense.
Pro-pen-si-ty.
Prop-er.
Prop-er-ty.
Proph-e-cy.
Proph-e-sy.
Proph-et.
Proph-et-ess.
Pro-phet-ic.
Pro-phet-ic-al.
Pro-pin-qui-ty.
Pro-pi-ti-ate.
Pro-pi-ti-a-tion.
Pro-pi-ti-a-tor.
Pro-pi-ti-a-to-ry.
Pro-pi-tious.
Pro-po-lis.
Pro-por-tion.

Pro - por - tion-a - ble.
Pro - por - tion-a - bly.
Pro-por-tion-al.
Pro-por-tion-ate.
Pro - por - tion-al-ly.
Pro-pos-al.
Pro-pose.
Prop-o-si-tion.
Pro-pound.
Pro-pri-e-ta-ry.
Pro-pri-e-tor.
Pro-pri-e-ty.
Pro-pul-sion.
Pro-ro-ga-tion.
Pro-rogue.
Pro-sa-ic.
Pro-sce-ni-um.
Pro-scribe.
Pro-scrip-tion.
Pro-scrip-tive.
Prose.
Pros-e-cute.
Pros-e-cu-tion.
Pros-e-cu-tor.
Pros-e-lyte.
Pros-e-lyt-ism.
Pros-o-dist.
Pros-o-dy.
Pros-pect.
Pro-spect-ive.
Pro-spec-tus.
Pros-per.
Pros-per-i-ty.
Pros-per-ous.
Pros-ti-tute.
Pros-ti-tu-tion.
Pros-trate.
Pros-tra-tion.
Pro-style.
Pro-sy.
Pro-tect.
Pro-tec-tion.
Pro-tect-ive.
Pro-tect-or.
Pro-tec-tor-ate.
Protege.
Pro-test.
Prot-est-ant.
Prot-est-ant-ism.
Prot-es-ta-tion.
Pro-thon-o-ta-ry.
Pro-to-col.
Pro-to-mar-tyr.
Pro-to-type.
Pro-tract.
Pro-trac-tion.
Pro-trude.

Pro-tru-sion.
Pro-tru-sive.
Pro-tu-ber-ance.
Pro-tu-ber-ant.
Pro-tu-ber-ate.
Proud.
Prove.
Prov-en-der.
Prov-erb.
Pro-verb-i-al.
Pro-verb-i-al-ly.
Pro-vide.
Prov-i-dence.
Prov-i-dent.
Prov-i-den-tial.
Prov-i - den -tial-ly.
Prov-i-dent-ly.
Prov-ince.
Pro-vin-cial.
Pro-vin-cial-ism.
Pro-vi-sion.
Pro-vi-sion-al.
Pro-vi-sion-a-ry.
Pro-vi-sion-al-ly.
Pro-vi-so.
Prov-o-ca-tion.
Pro-vo-ca-tive.
Pro-voke.
Prov-ost.
Pro - **vost** - **mar**. shal.
Prow.
Prow-ess.
Prowl.
Prox-i-mate.
Prox-im-i-ty.
Prox-i-mo.
Proxy.
Prude.
Pru-dence.
Pru-dent.
Pru-den-tial.
Pru-der-y.
Pru-dish.
Prune.
Pru-nel-la.
Pru-nel-lo.
Pru-ri-ence.
Pru-ri-ent.
Prus-sic.
Pry.
Psalm.
Psalm-ist.
Psalm-o-dist.
Psalm-o-dy.
Psal-ter.
Psal-ter-y.
Pshaw.
Psy-cho-log-ic.

Psy-chol-ogy.
Ptol-e-ma-ic.
Pu-ber-ty.
Pu-bes-cence.
Pu-bes-cent.
Pub-lic.
Pub-li-can.
Pub-li-ca-tion.
Pub-lic-i-ty.
Pub-lic-ly.
Pub-lish.
Pub-lish-er.
Pub-lish-ment.
Puck-er.
Pud-ding.
Pud-dle.
Pu-er-ile.
Pu-er-il-i-ty.
Pu-er-per-al.
Puff.
Puff-y.
Pug.
Pu-gil-ism.
Pu-gil-ist.
Pu-gil-ist-ic.
Pug-na-cious.
Pug-nac-i-ty.
Puis-ne.
Pu-is-sance.
Pu-is-sant.
Puke.
Pule.
Pull.
Pul-let.
Pul-ley.
Pul-mo-na-ry.
Pul-mon-ic.
Pulp.
Pul-pit.
Pulp-ous.
Pulp-y.
Pul-sate.
Pul-sa-tion.
Pulse.
Pul-ver-i-za-tion.
Pul-ver-ize.
Pul-ver-u-lent.
Pum-ice.
Pump.
Pump-kin.
Pun.
Punch.
Punch-eon.
Pun-chi-nel-lo.
Punc-til-io.
Punc-til-ious.
Punc-to.
Punct-u-al.
Punct-u-al-i-ty.
Punct-u-ate.

Punct-u-a-tion.
Punct-ure.
Pun-dit.
Pun-gen-cy.
Pun-gent.
Pu-nic.
Pun-ish.
Pun-ish-ment.
Pu-ni-tive.
Punk.
Pun-ster.
Punt.
Pu-ny.
Pup.
Pu-pa.
Pu-pil.
Pu-pil-age.
Pup-pet.
Pup-py.
Pup-py-ism.
Pur.
Pur-blind.
Pur-chas-a-ble.
Pur-chase.
Pur-cha-ser.
Pure.
Pure-ly.
Pur-ga-tion.
Pur-ga-tive.
Pur-ga-to-ry.
Purge.
Pu-ri-fi-ca-tion.
Pu-ri-fy.
Pu-rism.
Pu-rist.
Pu-ri-tan.
Pu-ri-tan-ic.
Pu-ri-tan-ic-al.
Pu-ri-tan-ism.
Pu-ri-ty.
Purl.
Pur-lieu.
Pur-lin.
Pur-loin.
Pur-ple.
Pur-port.
Pur-pose.
Pur-pose-ly.
Purr.
Purse.
Purse-proud.
Purs-er.
Pur-su-ance.
Pur-su-ant.
Pur-sue.
Pur-su-er.
Pur-suit.
Pur-sui-vant.
Purs-y.
Pu-ru-lence.

Pu-ru-lent.
Pur-vey.
Pur-vey-or.
Pur-view.
Pus.
Push.
Pu-sil-la-nim-i-ty.
Pu-sil-lan-i-mous.
Puss.
Pust-ule.
Put.
Pu-ta-tive.
Put-log.
Put-off.
Pu-tre-fac-tion.
Pu-tre-fac-tive.
Pu-tre-fy.
Pu-tres-cence.
Pu-tres-cent.
Pu-trid.
Pu-trid-i-ty.
Pu-trid-ness.
Put-ty.
Puz-zle.
Pyg-me-an.
Pyg-my.
Pyr-a-mid.
Pyr-a-mid-al.
Pyr-a-mid-ic-al.
Pyre.
Pyr-i-form.
Py-ri-tes.
Pyr-o-lig-ne-ous.
Pyr-o-lig-nic.
Py-rom-e-ter.
Pyr-o-tech-nics.
Pyr-o-tech-ny.
Pyr-o-tech-nist.
Pyx.

Q

Quack.
Quack-er-y.
Qaud-ra-ges-i-ma.
Quad-ran-gle.
Quad-ran-gu-lar.
Quad-rant.
Quad-rat.
Quad-rate.
Quad-rat-ic.
Quad-ra-ture.
Quad-ren-ni-al.
Quad-ri-lat-er-al.
Qua-drille.

Quad-rill-ion.
Quad-rip-ar-tite.
Quad-ri-syl-la-ble.
Quad-ri-valve.
Quad-ru-ma-nous.
Quad-ru-ped.
Quad-ru-ple.
Quad-ru-pli-cate.
Quad-ru-pli-ca-tion.
Quaff.
Quag-mire.
Quag-gy.
Quail.
Quaint.
Quaint-ly.
Quaint-ness.
Quake.
Quak-er.
Quak-er-ism.
Qual-i-fi-a-ble.
Qual-i-fi-ca-tion.
Qual-i-fy.
Qual-i-ty.
Qualm.
Qualm-ish.
Quan-da-ry.
Quan-ti-ty.
Quar-an-tine.
Quar-rel.
Quar-rel-some.
Quar-ry.
Quart.
Quar-tan.
Quar-ter.
Quar-ter-day.
Quar-ter-deck.
Quar-ter-ly.
Quar-ter-mas-ter.
Quar-tern.
Quar-ter-staff.
Quar-tette.
Quar-tet.
Quar-to.
Quartz.
Quash.
Quas-sa-tion.
Quas-si-a.
Qua-ter-ni-on.
Qua-ver.
Quay.
Quean.
Quea-sy.
Queen.
Queen-dow-a-ger.
Queer.

Queer-ness.
Quell.
Quench.
Quench-a-ble.
Quer-cit-ron.
Que-rist.
Quern.
Quer-u-lous.
Quer-u-lous-ness.
Que-ry.
Quest.
Ques-tion.
Ques-tion-a-ble.
Ques-tion-er.
Quib-ble.
Quib-bler.
Quick.
Quick-en.
Quick-lime.
Quick-ly.
Quick-ness.
Quick-sand.
Quick-set.
Quick-sil-ver.
Quid.
Quid-di-ty.
Quid-dle.
Quid-nunc.
Qui-es-cence.
Qui-es-cent.
Qui-et.
Qui-et-ism.
Qui-et-ly.
Qui-et-ness.
Qui-e-tude.
Qui-e-tus.
Quill.
Quilt.
Qui-na-ry.
Quince.
Qui-nine.
Quin - qua - ges-i-ma.
Quin - quan - gu - lar.
Quin-quen-ni-al.
Quin-sy.
Quint-al.
Quin-tan.
Quin-tes-sence.
Quin-tu-ple.
Quip.
Quire.
Quirk.
Quit.
Quit-claim.
Quite.
Quit-rent.
Quit-tance.
Quiv-er.

Quix-ot-ic.
Quix-ot-ism.
Quiz.
Quoin.
Quoit.
Quon-dam.
Quo-rum.
Quo-ta.
Quo-ta-ble.
Quo-ta-tion.
Quote.
Quoth.
Quo-tid-i-an.
Quo-tient.

R

Rab-bet.
Rab-bi.
Rab-bin-ic.
Rab-bin-ic-al.
Rab-bit.
Rab-ble.
Rab-id.
Rac-coon.
Race.
Race-horse.
Rac-er.
Ra-ceme.
Ra-ci-ness.
Rack.
Rack-et.
Rack-rent.
Ra-cy.
Ra-di-ance.
Ra-di-ant.
Ra-di-ate.
Ra-di-a-tion.
Ra-di-a-tor.
Rad-i-cal.
Rad-i-cal-ly.
Rad-i-cle.
Rad-ish.
Ra-di-us.
Ra-dix.
Raff.
Raf-fle.
Raft.
Raft-er.
Rag.
Rag-a-muf-fin.
Rage.
Rag-ged.
Rag-ing.
Ra-gout.
Rail.
Rail-ing.
Rail-ler-y.

Rag.-road.
Rail-way.
Rai-ment.
Rain.
Rain-bow.
Rain-y.
Raise.
Rai-sin.
Rake.
Rak-ish.
Ral-ly.
Ram.
Ram-ble.
Ram-bling.
Ram-i-fi-ca-tion.
Ram-i-fy.
Ram-mer.
Ra-mose.
Ra-mous.
Ramp-an-cy.
Ramp-ant.
Ram-part.
Ram-rod.
Ran.
Ran-cho.
Ranch.
Ran-che-ro.
Ran-cid.
Ran-cid-i-ty.
Ran-cid-ness.
Ran-cor.
Ran-cor-ous.
Ran-dom.
Rang.
Range.
Rank.
Rank-le.
Ran-sack.
Ran-som.
Rant.
Rant-er.
Rap.
Ra-pa-cious.
Ra-pac-i-ty.
Rape.
Rap-id.
Ra-pid-i-ty.
Rap-id-ly.
Rap-ids.
Ra-pi-er.
Rap-ine.
Rap-pee.
Rap-per.
Rapt.
Rapt-ure.
Rapt-ur-ous.
Rare.
Rar-e-fac-tion.
Rar-e-fy.
Rare-ly.

Rare-ness.
Rar-i-ty.
Rare-ripe.
Ras-cal.
Ras-cal-lion.
Ras-cal-i-ty.
Ras-cal-ly.
Rase.
Rash.
Rash-er.
Rash-ly.
Rash-ness.
Rasp.
Rasp-ber-ry.
Ras-ure.
Rat.
Rat-a-fi-a.
Ratch-et.
Ratch-et-wheel.
Rate.
Rath-er.
Rat-i-fi-ca-tion.
Rat-i-fy.
Ra-ti-o.
Ra-ti-oc - i - na tion.
Ra-tion.
Ra-tion-al.
Ra-tion-a-ble.
Ra-tion-al-ist.
Ra-tion-al-i-ty.
Rats-bane.
Rat-tan.
Rat-ting.
Rat-tle.
Rat-tle-snake.
Rau-ci-ty.
Rav-age.
Rave.
Rav-el.
Rave-lin.
Rav-en.
Rav-en.
Rav-en-ous.
Ra-vine.
Rav-ing.
Rav-ish.
Rav-ish-ment.
Raw.
Raw-boned.
Ray.
Ray-less.
Raze.
Ra-zee.
Ra-zor.
Reach.
Re-act.
Re-ac-tion.
Re-act-ive.
Re-ac-tion-a-ry.

Read.
Read-a-ble.
Read-er.
Read-i-ly.
Read-i-ness.
Read-ing.
Re-ad-mis-sion.
Re-ad-mit.
Read-y.
Re-al.
Re-al-i-ty.
Re-al-i-za-tion.
Re-al-ize.
Re-al-ly.
Realm.
Ream.
Re-an-i-mate.
Reap.
Reap-er.
Re-ap-pear.
Re-ap-point.
Rear.
Rear-ad-mi-ral.
Rear-guard.
Rear-ward.
Rea-son.
Rea-son-a-ble.
Rea-son-a-bly.
Rea-son-er.
Rea-son-ing.
Re-as-sume.
Re-as-sure.
Re-bate.
Re-bec.
Reb-el.
Re-bel.
Re-bell-ion.
Re-bell-ious.
Re-bound.
Re-buff.
Re-buke.
Re-bus.
Re-but.
Re-but-ter.
Re-call.
Re-cant.
Re-can-ta-tion.
Re-ca-pit-u-late.
Re-ca-pit-u-la-tion.
Re-ca-pit-u-la-to-ry.
Re-cap-tion.
Re-capt-ure
Re-cast.
Re-cede.
Re-ceipt.
Re-ceiv-a-ble.
Re-ceive.
Re-ceiv-er.

Re-cen-cy.
Re-cen-sion.
Re-cent.
Re-cent-ly.
Re-cep-ta-cle.
Re-cep-tion.
Re-cep-tive.
Re-cess.
Re-ces-sion.
Re-charge.
Recherche.
Rec-i-pe.
Re-cip-i-ent.
Re-cip-ro-cal.
Re-cip-ro-cal-ly
Re-cip-ro-cate.
Re-cip-ro-ca-tion.
Rec-i-proc-i-ty.
Re-cit-al.
Rec-i-ta-tion.
Rec-i-ta-tive.
Re-cite.
Reck-less.
Reck-on.
Reck-on-ing.
Re-claim.
Re-claim-ant.
Rec-la-ma-tion.
Rec-li-na-tion.
Re-cline.
Re-cluse.
Re-clu-sion.
Rec-og-ni-tion.
Rec-og-niz-a-ble.
Rec-og-ni-zance.
Rec-og-nize.
Re-coil.
Rec-ol-lect.
Rec-ol-lect.
Rec-ol-lec-tion.
Re-com-mence.
Rec-om-mend.
Rec-om-mend-a-tion.
Rec-om-mend-a-to-ry.
Re-com-mit.
Re-com-mit-ment.
Re-com-mit-al.
Rec-om-pense.
Re-com-pose.
Rec-on-cil-a-ble.
Rec-on-cile.
Rec-on-cil-i-a-tion.
Rec-on-dite.
Re-con-nais-sance.

Re-con-nois-sance.
Re-con-noi-ter.
Re-con-quer.
Re-con-sid-er.
Re-con-sid-er-a-tion.
Re-cord.
Rec-ord.
Re-cord-er.
Re-count.
Re-course.
Re-cov-er.
Re-cov-er-a-ble.
Re-cov-er-y.
Rec-re-ant.
Re-cre-ate.
Rec-re-a-tion.
Rec-re-ment.
Rec-re-men-tal.
Rec-re-men-ti-tious.
Re-crim-i-nate.
Re-crim-i-na-tion.
Re-crim-i-na-to-ry.
Re-cruit.
Rect-an-gle.
Rect-an-gu-lar.
Rec-ti-fi-ca-tion.
Rec-ti-fy.
Rec-ti-lin-e-al.
Rec-ti-lin-e-ar.
Rec-ti-tude.
Rec-tor.
Rec-tor-ship.
Rec-tor-y.
Rec-tum.
Re-cum-ben-cy
Re-cum-bent.
Re-cup-er-ate.
Re-cup-er-a-tive.
Re-cur.
Re-cur-rence.
Re-cur-rent.
Re-cu-sant.
Red.
Re-dan.
Red-den.
Red-dish.
Re-deem.
Re-deem-er.
Re-demp-tion.
Red-gum.
Red-hot.
Re-din-te-grate.
Red-ness.
Red-o-lence.
Red-o-lent.

Re-doub-le.
Re-doubt.
Re-doubt-a-ble.
Re-dound.
Re-dress.
Red-top.
Re-duce.
Re-du-ci-ble.
Re-duc-tion.
Re-duc-tive.
Re-dun-dance.
Re-dun-dant.
Re-du-pli-cate.
Re-du-pli-ca-tion.
Re-ech-o.
Reed.
Reed-y.
Reef.
Reek.
Reek-ter.
Reek-y.
Reel.
Re-e-lect.
Re-e-lec-tion.
Re-em-bark.
Re-en-act.
Re-en-act-ment.
Re-en-force.
Re-en-force-ment.
Re-en-gage.
Re-en-list.
Re-en-ter.
Re-en-trance.
Re-es-tab-lish.
Reeve.
Re-ex-am-ine.
Re-fec-tion.
Re-fec-to-ry.
Re-fer.
Ref-er-a-ble.
Ref-er-ee.
Ref-er-ence.
Ref-er-en-tial.
Ref-er-ri-ble.
Re-fine.
Re-fined.
Re-fine-ment.
Re-fin-er.
Re-fin-ery.
Re-fit.
Re-flect.
Re-flec-tion.
Re-flect-ive.
Re-flect-or.
Re-flux.
Ref-lu-ence.
Re-form.
Ref-or-ma-tion.
Re-for-ma-tion.

Re-form-a-to-ry.
Re-form-er.
Re-fract.
Re-frac-tion.
Re-fract-ive.
Re-frac-to-ri-ness.
Re-frac-to-ry.
Ref-ra-ga-ble.
Re-frain.
Re-fran-gi-bil-i-ty.
Re-fran-gi-ble.
Re-fresh.
Re-fresh-ing.
Re-fresh-ment.
Re-frig-er-ate.
Re-frig-er-a-tion.
Re-frig-er-a-tor.
Re-frig-er-a-to-ry.
Ref-uge.
Ref-u-gee.
Re-ful-gence.
Re-ful-gen-cy.
Re-ful-gent.
Re-fund.
Re-fu-sal.
Re-fuse.
Ref-use.
Ref-u-ta-tion.
Re-fute.
Re-gain.
Re-gal.
Re-gale.
Re-ga-li-a.
Re-gal-i-ty.
Re-gal-ly.
Re-gard.
Re-gard-less.
Re-gat-ta.
Re-gen-cy.
Re-gen-er-ate.
Re-gen-er-a-tion.
Re-gen-er-a-tive.
Re-gent.
Reg-i-cide.
Regime.
Reg-i-men.
Reg-i-ment.
Reg-i-ment-al.
Reg-i-ment-als.
Re-gion.
Reg-is-ter.
Reg-is-trar.
Reg-is-tra-tion.
Reg-is-try.
Reg-nant.
Re-gress.
Re-gres-sion.

Re-gret.
Reg-u-lar.
Reg-u-lar-i-ty.
Reg-u-lar-ly.
Reg-u-late.
Reg-u-la-tion.
Reg-u-la-tor.
Re-gur-gi-tate.
Re-ha-bil-i-tate.
Re-ha-bil-i-ta-tion.
Re-hears-al.
Re-hearse.
Reign.
Re-im-burse.
Re-im-**burse**-ment.
Rein.
Rein-deer.
Reins.
Re-in-state.
Re-in-sure.
Re-it-er-ate.
Re-it-er-a-tion.
Re-ject.
Re-jec-tion.
Re-joice.
Re-joic-ing.
Re-join.
Re-join-der.
Re-ju-ve-nate.
Re-ju-ve-nes-cence.
Re-kin-dle.
Re-lapse.
Re-late.
Re-la-tion.
Re-la-tion-ship.
Rel-a-tive.
Rel-a-tive-ly.
Re-lax.
Re-lax-a-tion.
Re-lay.
Re-lease.
Rel-e-gate.
Rel-e-ga-tion.
Re-lent.
Re-lent-less.
Rel-e-vance.
Rel-e-van-cy.
Rel-e-vant.
Re-li-a-ble.
Re-li-ance.
Rel-ic.
Rel-ict.
Re-lief.
Re-lieve.
Re-lie-vo.
Re-lig-ion.
Re-lig-ion-ist.

Re-lig-ious.
Re-lig-ious-ly.
Re-lin-quish.
Re-lin-quish-ment.
Rel-i-qua-ry.
Rel-ish.
Re-luc-tance.
Re-luc-tant.
Re-luc-tant-ly.
Re-ly.
Re-made.
Re-main.
Re-main-der.
Re-mains.
Re-mand.
Re-mark.
Re-mark-a-ble.
Re-mark-a-bly.
Re-me-di-a-ble.
Re-me-di-al.
Re-med-i-less.
Rem-e-dy.
Re-mem-ber.
Re-mem-brance.
Re-mem-**bran**-cer.
Re-mind.
Rem-i-nis-cence.
Re-miss.
Re-mis-si-ble.
Re-mis-sion.
Re-miss-ly.
Re-miss-ness.
Re-mit.
Re-mit-tal.
Re-mit-tance.
Re-mit-tent.
Rem-nant.
Re-mod-el.
Re-mon-strance.
Re-mon-strant.
Re-mon-strate.
Re-morse.
Re-morse-ful.
Re-morse-less.
Re-mote.
Re-mote-ly.
Re-mote-ness.
Re-mount.
Re-mov-a-ble.
Re-mov-al.
Re-move.
Re-mu-ner-ate.
Re-mu-ner-**a**-tion.
Re-mu-**ner-a**-tive.
Re-nal.
Ren-ard.

Re-nas-cent.
Ren-coun-ter.
Rend.
Ren-der.
Ren-der-ing.
Ren-dez-vous.
Ren-di-tion.
Ren-e-gade.
Ren-e-ga-do.
Re-new.
Re-new-a-ble.
Re-new-al.
Re-new-ed-ly.
Ren-net.
Re-nounce.
Re-nounce-ment.
Ren-o-vate.
Ren-o-va-tion.
Re-nown.
Re-nowned.
Rent.
Rent-al.
Re-nun-ci-a-tion.
Re-or-gan-i-za-tion.
Re-or-gan-ize.
Re-paid.
Re-pair.
Rep-a-ra-tion.
Rep-ar-tee.
Re-pass.
Re-past.
Re-pay.
Re-pay-ment.
Re-peal.
Re-peal-er.
Re-peat.
Re-peat-ed-ly.
Re-peat-er.
Re-pel.
Re-pel-len-cy.
Re-pel-lent.
Re-pent.
Re-pent-ance.
Re-pent-ant.
Re-peo-ple.
Re-per-cus-sion.
Rep-er-to-ry.
Rep-e-tend.
Rep-e-ti-tion.
Rep-e-ti-tious.
Re-pine.
Re-place.
Re-plen-ish.
Re-plete.
Re-ple-tion.
Re-plev-i-a-ble.
Re-plev-i-sa-ble.
Re-plev-in.
Re-plev-y.

73

Rep-li-cant.
Rep-li-ca-tion.
Re-ply
Re-port.
Re-port-er.
Re-pose.
Re-pos-it.
Re-pos-i-to-ry.
Re-pos-sess.
Re-pos-ses-sion.
Rep-re-hend.
Rep - re - hen - si-
 ble.
Rep-re-hen-sion.
Rep-re-hen-sive.
Rep-re-sent.
Rep - re - sen - ta-
 tion.
Rep - re - sent - a-
 tive.
Re-press.
Re-pres-sion.
Re-press-ive.
Re-prieve.
Rep-ri-mand.
Re-print.
Re-pri-sal.
Re-proach.
Re-proach-ful.
Rep-ro-bate.
Rep-ro-ba-tion.
Re-pro-duce.
Re-pro-duc-tion.
Re-pro-duc-tive.
Re-proof.
Re-prov-al.
Re-prove.
Rep-tile.
Re-pub-lic.
Re-pub-lic-an.
Re - pub - lic - an-
 ism.
Re-pub-li-ca-tion.
Re-pub-lish.
Re-pu-di-ate.
Re-pu-di-a-tion.
Re-pu-di-a-tor.
Re-pug-nance.
Re-pug-nan-cy.
Re-pug-nant.
Re-pulse.
Re-pul-sion.
Re-pul-sive.
Rep-u-ta-ble.
Rep-u-ta-tion.
Re-pute.
Re-put-ed.
Re-quest.
Re-qui-em.
Re-quire.

Re-quire-ment.
Req-ui-site.
Req-ui-si-tion.
Re-quit-al.
Re-quite.
Re-scind.
Re-scis-sion.
Re-script.
Res-cue.
Re-search.
Re-sem-blance.
Re-sem-ble.
Re-sent.
Re-sent-ful.
Re-sent-ment.
Res-er-va-tion.
Re-serve.
Re-served.
Re-serv-ed-ly.
Res-er-voir.
Re-set.
Re-set-tle.
Re-set-tle-ment.
Re-ship.
Re-ship-ment.
Re-side.
Res-i-dence.
Res-i-dent.
Res-i-den-ti-a-ry.
Re-sid-u-al.
Re-sid-u-a-ry.
Res-i-due.
Re-sid-u-um.
Re-sign.
Res-ig-na-tion.
Re-signed.
Re-sil-i-ence.
Re-sil-i-ent.
Res-in.
Res-in-ous.
Re-sist.
Re-sist-ance.
Re-sist-less.
Res-o-lu-ble.
Res-o-lute.
Res-o-lute-ly.
Res-o-lu-tion.
Re-solv-a-ble.
Re-solve.
Re-solv-ent.
Res-o-nance.
Res-o-nant.
Re-sort.
Re-sound.
Re-source.
Re-spect.
Re-spect-a - bil - i-
 ty.
Re-spect-a-ble.
Re-spect-a-bly.

Re-spect-ed.
Re-spect-ful.
Re-spect-ful-ly.
Re-spect-ive.
Re-spect-ive-ly.
Re-spir-a-ble.
Re-spi-ra-tion.
Re-spir-a-to-ry.
Re-spire.
Re-spite.
Re-splen-dence.
Re-splen-dent.
Re-spond.
Re-spond-ent.
Re-sponse.
Re-spon - si-bil-i -
 ty.
Re-spon-si-ble.
Re-spon-sive.
Rest.
Res-tau-rant.
Res-tau-ra-teur.
Rest-iff.
Rest-ive.
Res-ti-tu-tion.
Rest-ive-ness.
Rest-less.
Re-stor-a-ble.
Res-to-ra-tion.
Re-stor-a-tive.
Re-store.
Re-strain.
Re-straint.
Re-strict.
Re-stric-tion.
Re-strict-ive.
Re-sult.
Re-sume.
Re-sump-tion.
Res-ur-rec-tion.
Re-sus-ci-tate.
Re-sus-ci-ta-tion.
Re-tail.
Re-tail-er.
Re-tain.
Re-tain-er.
Re-take.
Re-tal-i-ate.
Re-tal-i-a-tion.
Re-tal-i-a-tive.
Re-tal-i-a-to-ry.
Re-tard.
Retch.
Re-ten-tion.
Re-ten-tive.
Re-ten-tive-ness.
Re-tic-u-lar.
Re-tic-u-late.
Re-tic-u-lat-ed.
Re-tic-u-la-tion.

Ret-i-cule.
Re-ti-na.
Ret-i-nue.
Re-tire.
Re-tired.
Re-tire-ment.
Re-tort.
Re-touch.
Re-trace.
Re-tract.
Re-tract-ile.
Re-trac-tion.
Re-treat.
Re-trench.
Re-trench-ment.
Ret-ri-bu-tion.
Re-trib-u-tive.
Re-trib-u-to-ry.
Re-triev-a-ble.
Re-trieve.
Re-tro-ac-tion.
Re-tro-cede.
Re-tro-ces-sion.
Ret-ro-grade.
Re-tro-gres-sion.
Re-tro-spect.
Re-tro-spec-tion.
Re-tro-spect-ive.
Re-turn.
Re-turn-a-ble.
Re-un-ion.
Re-u-nite.
Re-veal.
Re-veil-le.
Rev-el.
Rev-e-la-tion.
Rev-el-ry.
Re-venge.
Re-venge-ful.
Rev-e-nue.
Re-ver-ber-ant.
Re-ver-ber-ate.
Re - ver - ber - a-
 tion.
Re-ver-ber - a-to-
 ry.
Re-vere.
Rev-er-ence.
Rev-er-end.
Rev-er-ent.
Rev-er-en-tial.
Rev-er-ie.
Rev-er-y.
Re-ver-sal.
Re-verse.
Re-ver-si-ble.
Re-ver-sion.
Re-ver-sion-a-ry.
Re-vert.
Re-view.

Re-view-er.
Re-vile.
Re-vi-sal.
Re-vis-ion.
Re-vise.
Re-vis-it.
Re-vi-so-ry.
Re-vi-val.
Re-vi-val-ist.
Re-vive.
Re-viv-i-fi-ca'-tion.
Re-viv-i-fy.
Rev-o-ca-ble.
Rev-o-ca-tion.
Re-voke.
Re-volt.
Rev-o-lu-tion.
Rev-o-lu-tion-a-ry.
Rev-o-lu-tion-ist.
Rev-o-lu-tion-ize.
Re-volve.
Re-vul-sion.
Re-vul-sive.
Re-ward.
Re-write.
Rhap-sod-ic-al.
Rhap-so-dist.
Rhap-so-dy.
Rhen-ish.
Rhet-o-ric.
Rhe-tor-ic-al.
Rhet-o-ri-cian.
Rheum.
Rheu-mat-ic.
Rheu-ma-tism.
Rheum-y.
Rhi-noc-er-os.
Rhomb.
Rhom-bus.
Rhom-bic.
Rhom-boid.
Rhu-barb.
Rhyme.
Rhym-er.
Rhythm.
Rib.
Rib-ald.
Rib-ald-ry.
Ribbed.
Rib-bon.
Rice.
Rich.
Rich-es.
Rich-ly.
Rich-ness.
Rick.
Rick-ets.

Rick-et-y.
Ric-o-chet.
Rid.
Rid-dance.
Rid-dle.
Ride.
Rid-er.
Ridge.
Rid-i-cule.
Ri-dic-u-lous.
Rife.
Riff-raff.
Ri-fle.
Ri-fle-man.
Rift.
Rig.
Rig-ger.
Rig-ging.
Right.
Right-an-gled.
Right-eous.
Right-eous-ly.
Right-eous-ness.
Right-ful.
Right-hand-ed.
Rig-id.
Ri-gid-i-ty.
Rig-id-ness.
Rig-id-ly.
Rig-or.
Rig-or-ous.
Rill.
Rim.
Rime.
Rind.
Ring.
Ring-bolt.
Ring-dove.
Ring-lead-er.
Ring-let.
Ring-worm.
Rinse.
Ri-ot.
Ri-ot-er.
Ri-ot-ous.
Rip.
Ripe.
Ripe-ly.
Rip-en.
Ripe-ness.
Rip-ple.
Rise.
Ris-en.
Ris-i-bil-i-ty.
Ris-i-ble.
Ris-ing.
Risk.
Rite.
Rit-u-al.
Rit-u-al-ism.

Rit-u-al-ist.
Ri-val.
Ri-val-ry.
Rive.
Riv-en.
Riv-er.
Riv-et.
Riv-u-let.
Rix-dol-lar.
Roach.
Road.
Road-stead.
Roam.
Roan.
Roar.
Roast.
Rob.
Rob-ber.
Rob-ber-y.
Robe.
Rob-in.
Ro-bust.
Ro-bust-ness.
Roch-et.
Rock.
Rock-er.
Rock-et.
Rock-i-ness.
Rock-salt.
Rock-y.
Rod.
Rode.
Ro-dent.
Rod-o-mont-ade.
Roe.
Roe-buck.
Ro-ga-tion.
Rogue.
Rogu-er-y.
Rogu-ish.
Roil.
Roll.
Roll-er.
Roll-ing-pin.
Ro-man.
Ro-mance.
Ro-man-cer.
Ro-man-ism.
Ro-man-ist.
Ro-man-tic.
Ro-man-ti-cism.
Rom-ish.
Romp.
Rood.
Roof.
Rook.
Rook-er-y.
Room.
Room-i-ness.
Room-y.

Roost.
Roost-er.
Root.
Rope.
Rope-dan-cer.
Rope-walk.
Rope-yarn.
Rop-i-ness.
Rop-y.
Roq-ue-laur.
Ro-sa-ry.
Rose.
Ro-se-ate.
Rose-bug.
Rose-ma-ry.
Ro-sette.
Rose-wa-ter.
Rose-wood.
Ros-in.
Ros-ter.
Ros-tral.
Ros-trum.
Ro-sy.
Rot.
Ro-ta-ry.
Ro-ta-to-ry.
Ro-tate.
Ro-ta-tion.
Rote.
Rot-ten.
Rot-ten-ness.
Ro-tund.
Ro-tun-da.
Ro-tun-do.
Ro-tund-i-ty.
Rouge.
Rough.
Rough-cast.
Rough-en.
Rough-hew.
Rough-ly.
Rough-ness.
Rough-shod.
Rou-lette.
Rounce.
Round.
Round-a-bout.
Round-e-lay.
Round-head.
Round-ing.
Round-ish.
Round-ly.
Round-ness.
Round-rob-in.
Rouse.
Rout.
Route.
Rou-tine.
Rove.
Rov-er.

Row.
Row-el.
Row-en.
Roy-al.
Roy-al-ist
Roy-al-ly.
Roy-al-ty.
Rub.
Rub-ber.
Rub-bish.
Ru-bi-cund.
Ru-ble.
Ru-bric.
Ru-bric-al.
Ru-bric-ate.
Ru-by.
Rud-der.
Rud-di-ness
Rud-dy.
Rude.
Rude-ly.
Rude-ness.
Ru-di-ment.
Ru-di-ment-al.
Rue.
Rue-ful.
Ruff.
Ruf-fian.
Ruf-fian-ism.
Ruf-fle.
Ru-fous.
Rug.
Rug-ged.
Rug-ged-ness.
Ru-in.
Ru-in-ous.
Rul-a-ble.
Rule.
Rul-er.
Rum.
Rum-ble.
Rum-bling.
Ru-mi-nant.
Ru-mi-nate.
Ru-mi-na-tion.
Rum-mage.
Ru-mor.
Rump.
Rum-ple.
Run.
Run-a-gate.
Run-a-way.
Run-dle.
Rung.
Run-let.
Run-ner.
Run-net.
Runt.
Ru-pee.
Rupt-ure.

Ru-ral.
Ruse.
Rush.
Rush-light.
Rush-y.
Rusk.
Russ.
Rus-set.
Rus-set-ing.
Rus-sian.
Rust.
Rus-tic.
Rus-tic-ate.
Rus-ti-ca-tion.
Rus-tic-i-ty.
Rust-i-ness.
Rus-tle.
Rust-y.
Rut.
Ru-ta-ba-ga.
Ruth.
Ruth-less.
Rye.

S

Sab-a-oth.
Sab-ba-ta-ri-an.
Sab-bath.
Sab-bat-ic.
Sab-bat-ic-al.
Sa-ber.
Sa-bre.
Sa-ble.
Sac.
Sac-cha-rine.
Sac-er-do-tal.
Sa-chem.
Sack.
Sack-but.
Sack-cloth.
Sac-ra-ment.
Sac-ra-ment-al.
Sa-cred.
Sa-cred-ly.
Sa-cred-ness.
Sac-ri-fice.
Sac-ri-fi-cial.
Sac-ri-lege.
Sac-ri-le-gious.
Sac-ri-le-gious-ly.
Sac-ris-tan.
Sac-ris-ty.
Sad.
Sad-den.
Sad-dle.
Sad-dler.

Sad-dler-y.
Sad-dle-tree.
Sad-du-cee.
Sad-i-ron.
Sad-ly.
Sad-ness.
Safe.
Safe-con-duct.
Safe-guard.
Safe-ly.
Safe-ty.
Safe-ty-valve.
Saf-fron.
Sag.
Sa-ga-cious.
Sa-ga-cious-ly.
Sa-gac-i-ty.
Sag-a-more.
Sage.
Sage-ly.
Sag-it-tal.
Sa-go.
Said.
Sail.
Sail-cloth.
Sail-loft.
Sai-lor.
Sail-yard.
Saint.
Saint-ed.
Saint-ly.
Sake.
Sal-a-ble.
Sa-la-cious.
Sal-ad.
Sal-a-man-der.
Sal-a-ried.
Sal-a-ry.
Sale.
Sal-e-ra-tus.
Sales-man.
Sal-ic.
Sa-li-ent.
Sal-i-fi-a-ble.
Sal-i-fy.
Sa-line.
Sa-li-va.
Sal-i-va-ry.
Sal-i-vate.
Sal-i-va-tion.
Sal-low.
Sal-low-ness.
Sal-ly.
Sal-ly-port.
Sal-ma-gun-di.
Sal-mon.
Sa-loon.
Sal-si-fy.
Salt.
Sal-ta-tion.

Sal-ta-to-ry.
Salt-cel-lar.
Salt-ness.
Salt-pe-ter.
Salt-pe-tre.
Salt-rheum.
Sa-lu-bri-ous.
Sa-lu-bri-ty
Sal-u-ta-ry.
Sal-u-ta-tion.
Sa-lu-ta-to-ri-an
Sa-lu-ta-to-ry.
Sa-lute.
Sal-va-ble.
Sal-vage.
Sal-va-tion.
Salve.
Sal-ver.
Sal-vo.
Same.
Same-ness.
Sa-mi-el.
Samp.
Sam-phire.
Sam-ple.
Sam-pler.
San-a-tive.
San-a-to-ry.
Sanc-ti-fi-ca-tion
Sanc-ti-fy.
Sanc-ti- mo - ni - ous.
Sanc-ti-mo-ny.
Sanc-tion.
Sanc-ti-ty.
Sanct-u-a-ry.
Sanc-tum.
Sand.
San-dal.
San-dal-wood.
San-di-ver.
Sand-stone.
Sand-wich.
San-dy.
Sane.
Sang.
San-ga-ree.
Sang-froid.
San-guif-er-ous.
San-gui-na-ry.
San-guine.
San-guin-e-ous.
San-he-drim.
Sa-ni-ous.
San-i-ta-ry.
San-i-ty.
Sank.
San-scrit.
San-skrit.
Sap.

Sap-id.
Sa-pid-i-ty.
Sa-pi-ence.
Sa-pi-ent.
Sap-less.
Sap-ling.
Sap-o-na-ceous.
Sa-pon-i-fy.
Sa-por.
Sap-phic.
Sap-phire.
Sap-phir-ine.
Sap-py.
Sar-a-band.
Sar-casm.
Sar-cas-tic.
Sar-cas-tic-al.
Sarce-net.
Sar-coph-a-gus.
Sar-di-us.
Sar-don-ic.
Sar-do-nyx.
Sar-sa-pa-ril-la.
Sash.
Sas-sa-fras.
Sat.
Sa-tan.
Sa-tan-ic.
Sa-tan-ic-al.
Satch-el.
Sate.
Sat-el-lite.
Sa-ti-ate.
Sa-ti-e-ty.
Sat-in.
Sat-in-et.
Sat-ire.
Sa-tir-ic.
Sa-tir-ic-al.
Sa-tir-ic-al-ly.
Sat-ir-ist.
Sat-ir-ize.
Sat-is-fac-tion.
Sat-is-fac-to-ri-ly.
Sat-is-fac-to-ry.
Sat-is-fy.
Sa-trap.
Sat-u-rate.
Sat-u-ra-tion.
Sat-ur-day.
Sat-urn.
Sat-ur-na-li-a.
Sat-ur-na-li-an.
Sat-ur-nine.
Sa-tyr.
Sauce.
Sauce-box.
Sau-cer.
Sau-ci-ly.

Sau-cy.
Saun-ter.
Sau-ri-an.
Sau-sage.
Sav-a-ble.
Sav-age.
Sav-age-ly.
Sav-age-ness.
Sav-age-ry.
Sa-van-na.
Savant.
Save.
Sav-ing.
Sav-ior.
Sav-iour.
Sa-vor.
Sa-vor-y.
Sa-voy.
Saw.
Saw-pit.
Saw-yer.
Sax-i-frage.
Sax-on.
Say.
Say-ing.
Scab.
Scab-bard.
Scab-bed.
Scab-by.
Sca-brous.
Scaf-fold.
Scaf-fold-ing.
Scagl-io-la.
Sca-lade.
Scald.
Scald-head.
Scale.
Sca-lene.
Sca-li-ness.
Scall-ion.
Scal-lop.
Scalp.
Scalp-el.
Scal-y.
Scam-mo-ny.
Scamp.
Scamp-er.
Scan.
Scan-dal.
Scan-dal-ize.
Scan-dal-ous.
Scan-ning.
Scan-sion.
Scan-so-ri-al.
Scant.
Scant-i-ly.
Scant-ly.
Scant-i-ness.
Scant-ness.
Scant-ling.

Scant-y.
Scape.
Scape-goat.
Scape-grace.
Scap-u-la.
Scap-u-lar.
Scap-u-la-ry.
Scar.
Scarce.
Scarce-ly.
Scar-ci-ty.
Scare.
Scare-crow.
Scarf.
Scarf-skin.
Scar-i-fi-ca-tion.
Scar-i-fy.
Scar-la-ti-na.
Scar-lat-i-nous.
Scar-let.
Scar-let **Fe-ver.**
Scarp.
Scath.
Scathe.
Scath-less.
Scat-ter.
Scav-en-ger.
Scene.
Scen-er-y.
Scen-ic.
Scen-ic-al.
Sce-nog-ra-phy.
Scent.
Scent-less.
Scep-ter.
Scep-tre.
Scep-tic.
Sched-ule.
Scheme.
Schem-er.
Schism.
Schis-mat-ic.
Schis-mat-ic-al.
Schol-ar.
Schol-ar-like.
Schol-ar-ly.
Schol-ar-ship.
Scho-las-tic.
Scho-las-ti-cism.
Scho-li-ast.
Scho-li-um.
School.
School-fel-low.
School-house.
School-ing.
School-man.
School-mas-ter.
Schoon-er.
Sci-at-ic.
Sci-at-ic-a.

Sci-ence.
Sci-en-tif-ic.
Sci-en-tif-ic-al.
Scin-til-la-tion.
Scin-til-late.
Sci-o-lism.
Sci-o-list.
Sci-on.
Scir-rhos-i-ty.
Scir-rhous.
Scir-rhus.
Scis-sion.
Scis-sors.
Scle-rot-ic.
Scoff.
Scold.
Scold-ing.
Sconce.
Scoop.
Scope.
Scor-bu-tic.
Scorch.
Score.
Sco-ri-a.
Scorn.
Scorn-er.
Scorn-ful.
Scor-pi-on.
Scot.
Scotch.
Scotch-col-lops.
Scot-free.
Scot-ti-cism.
Scot-tish.
Scoun-drel.
Scoun-drel-ism.
Scour.
Scourge.
Scout.
Scow.
Scowl.
Scrab-ble.
Scrag.
Scrag-ged.
Scrag-gy.
Scrag-gi-ness.
Scram-ble.
Scrap.
Scrap-book.
Scrape.
Scrap-er.
Scratch.
Scrawl.
Scraw-ny.
Screak.
Scream.
Screech.
Screed.
Screen.
Screw.

Scrib-ble.
Scrib-bler.
Scribe.
Scrimp.
Scrip.
Script.
Script-ur-al.
Script-ure.
Scrive-ner.
Scrof-u-la.
Scrof-u-lous.
Scroll.
Scrub.
Scrub-by.
Scru-ple.
Scru-pu-los-i-ty.
Scru-pu-lous.
Scru-ti-nize.
Scru-ti-ny.
Scru-toire.
Scud.
Scuf-fle.
Scull.
Scull-er-y.
Scull-ion.
Sculpt-or.
Sculpt-ure.
Scum.
Scup-per.
Scurf.
Scurf-i-ness.
Scurf-y.
Scur-rile.
Scur-ril-ous.
Scur-ril-i-ty.
Scur-vy.
Scutch-eon.
Scu-ti-form.
Scut-tle.
Scym-e-tar.
Scythe.
Sea.
Sea-board.
Sea-breeze.
Sea-coast.
Sea-el-e-phant.
Sea-far-er.
Sea-far-ing.
Sea-fight.
Sea-green.
Sea-horse.
Seal.
Seal-ing-wax.
Seam.
Sea-man.
Sea-man-ship.
Seam-less.
Sea-mew.
Seam-stress.
Sea-port.

Sear.
Search.
Search-er.
Search-ing.
Sea-room.
Sea-shell.
Sea-shore.
Sea-sick.
Sea-side.
Sea-son.
Sea-son-a-ble.
Sea-son-a-bly.
Sea-son-ing.
Sea-weed.
Sea-wor-thi-ness.
Sea-wor-thy.
Seat.
Sea-ward.
Se-ba-ceous.
Se-cant.
Se-cede.
Se-ced-er.
Se-ces-sion.
Seck-el.
Se-clude.
Se-clu-sion.
Sec-ond.
Sec-ond-a-ri-ly.
Sec-ond-a-ry.
Sec-ond-hand.
Sec-ond-ly.
Sec-onds.
Se-cre-cy.
Se-cret.
Sec-re-ta-ry.
Sec-re-ta-ry-ship.
Se-crete.
Se-cre-tion.
Se-cret-ly.
Se-cre-to-ry.
Sect.
Sec-ta-ri-an.
Sec-ta-ri-an-ism.
Sec-ta-rist.
Sect-a-ry.
Sec-tile.
Sec-tion.
Sec-tion-al.
Sect-or.
Sec-u-lar.
Sec-u-lar-ize.
Sec-u-lar-i-ty.
Se-cure.
Se-cure-ly.
Se-cur-i-ty.
Se-dan.
Se-date.
Sed-a-tive.
Sed-en-ta-ry.
Sedge.

Sedg-y.
Sed-i-ment.
Sed-i-ment-a-ry.
Se-di-tion.
Se-di-tious.
Se-duce.
Se-du-cer.
Se-duc-tion.
Se-duc-tive.
Se-du-li-ty.
Sed-u-lous.
Sed-u-lous-ly.
See.
Seed.
Seed-cake.
Seed-ling.
Seeds-man.
Seed-time.
Seed-ves-sel.
Seed-y.
Seek.
Seek-er.
Seem.
Seem-ing.
Seem-ing-ly.
Seem-ly.
Seen.
Seer.
See-saw.
Seethe.
Seg-ment.
Seg-re-gate.
Seg-re-ga-tion.
Seign-eu-ri-al.
Seign-ior.
Seign-ior-age.
Seign-ior-y.
Seine.
Seize.
Sei-zin.
Seiz-ure.
Sel-dom.
Se-lect.
Se-lec-tion.
Se-lect-man.
Sel-e-nog-ra-phy.
Self.
Self-con-ceit.
Self-de-ni-al.
Self-es-teem.
Self-ev-i-dent.
Self-ex-ist-ent.
Self-in-ter-est.
Self-ish.
Self-ish-ly.
Self-ish-ness.
Self-love.
Self-same.
Self-will.
Sell.

Sell-er.
Sel-vage.
Sel-vedge.
Selves.
Sem-blance.
Sem-i-an-nu-al.
Sem-i-breve.
Sem-i-cir-cle.
Sem-i-co-lon.
Sem-i-di-am-e-ter.
Sem-i-lu-nar.
Sem-i-nal.
Sem-i-na-ry.
Sem-i-qua-ver.
Sem-i-tone.
Sem-i-vow-el.
Sem-pi-ter-nal.
Semp-stress.
Sen-ate.
Sen-a-tor.
Sen-a-to-ri-al.
Sen-a-tor-ship.
Send.
Se-nes-cence.
Sen-es-chal.
Se-nile.
Se-nil-i-ty.
Sen-ior.
Sen-ior-i-ty.
Sen-na.
Sen-night.
Sen-sa-tion.
Sen-sa-tion-al.
Sense.
Sense-less.
Sen-si-bil-i-ty.
Sen-si-ble.
Sen-si-bly.
Sen-si-tive.
Sen-si-tive-ness.
Sen-su-al.
Sen-su-al-ism.
Sen-su-al-ist.
Sen-su-al-i-ty.
Sent.
Sen-tence.
Sen-ten-tial.
Sen-ten-tious.
Sen-tient.
Sen-ti-ment.
Sen-ti-ment-al.
Sen-ti-ment-al-ist.
Sen-ti-men-tal-i-ty.
Sen-ti-nel.
Sen-try.
Sen-try-box.
Sep-a-ra-ble.

Sep-a-rate.
Sep-a-rate-ly.
Sep-a-ra-tion.
Sep-a-ra-tist.
Se-poy.
Sept-an-gu-lar.
Sep-tem-ber.
Sep-ten-a-ry.
Sep-ten-ni-al.
Sep-tic.
Sep-tic-al.
Sep-tu-a-ge-na-ri-an.
Sep-tu-a-gint.
Sep-tu-ple.
Sep-ul-cher.
Sep-ul-chre.
Se-pul-chral.
Sep-ul-ture.
Se-qua-cious.
Se-quel.
Se-quence.
Se-quent.
Se-ques-ter.
Se-ques-trate.
Seq-ues-tra-tion.
Seq-ues-tra-tor.
Se-quin.
Se-ragl-io.
Ser-aph.
Se-raph-ic.
Ser-a-phine.
Ser-a-phim.
Ser-e-nade.
Se-rene.
Se-ren-i-ty.
Serf.
Serge.
Ser-geant.
Se-ri-al.
Se-ries.
Se-ri-ous.
Ser-mon.
Ser-mon-ize.
Se-roon.
Se-ros-i-ty.
Se-rous.
Ser-pent.
Ser-pent-ine.
Ser-rate.
Se-rum.
Serv-ant.
Serve.
Serv-ice.
Serv-ice-a-ble.
Serv-ile.
Ser-vil-i-ty.
Serv-i-tor.
Serv-i-tude.
Ses-sion.

Sess-pool.
Set.
Se-ta-ceous.
Set-off.
Se-ton.
Se-tose.
Se-tous.
Set-tee.
Set-ter.
Set-tle.
Set-tle-ment.
Set-tler.
Set-to.
Sev-en.
Sev-en-night.
Sev-enth.
Sev-en-teen.
Sev-en-ty.
Sev-er.
Sev-er-al.
Sev-er-al-ly.
Sev-er-al-ty.
Sev-er-ance.
Se-vere.
Se-ver-i-ty.
Sew.
Sew-er.
Sex.
Sex-a-ge-na-ri-an.
Sex-ag-e-na-ry.
Sex-a-ges-i-ma.
Sex-an-gu-lar.
Sex-en-ni-al.
Sex-tant.
Sex-tile.
Sex-ton.
Sex-tu-ple.
Sex-u-al.
Shab.
Shab-bi-ly.
Shab-bi-ness.
Shab-by.
Shack-le.
Shack-les.
Shad.
Shad-dock.
Shade.
Sha-di-ness.
Shad-ow.
Shad-ow-y.
Sha-dy.
Shaft.
Shag.
Shag-ged.
Shag-gy.
Shag-gi-ness.
Sha-green.
Snah.
Shake.

Shak-er.
Shale.
Shall.
Shal-loon.
Shal-lop.
Shal-low.
Shalt.
Sham.
Sham-ble.
Sham-bles.
Sham-bling.
Shame.
Shame-faced.
Shame-ful.
Shame-less.
Sham-my.
Sham-poo.
Sham-rock.
Shank.
Shan-ty.
Shape.
Shape-less.
Shape-ly.
Shard.
Share.
Share-hold-er.
Shark.
Sharp.
Sharp-en.
Sharp-er.
Sharp-ie.
Sharp-ly.
Sharp-ness.
Sharp-set.
Shat-ter.
Shave.
Shav-er.
Shav-ing.
Shawl.
Shawm.
She.
Sheaf.
Shear.
Shears.
Sheath.
Sheathe.
Sheath-ing.
Sheave.
Shed.
Sheen.
Sheen-y.
Sheep.
Sheep-cot.
Sheep-fold.
Sheep-ish.
Sheep's-eye.
Sheer.
Sheet.
Sheet-an-chor.
Sheet-ing.

Shek-el.
Shel-drake.
Shelf.
Shelf-y.
Shell.
Shell-fish.
Shel-ter.
Shelve.
Shelv-y.
Shep-herd.
Shep-herd-ess.
Sher-bet.
Sher-iff.
Sher-ry.
Shew.
Shewn.
Shib-bo-leth.
Shield.
Shift.
Shift-less.
Shil-ling.
Shim-mer.
Shin.
Shine.
Shin-gle.
Shin-ing.
Shin-y.
Ship.
Ship-board.
Ship-mas-ter.
Ship-ment.
Ship-ping.
Ship-shape.
Ship-wreck.
Ship-wright.
Shire.
Shirk.
Shirt.
Shive.
Shiv-er.
Shiv-er-ing.
Shiv-er-y.
Shoal.
Shoal-y.
Shock.
Shock-ing.
Shod.
Shoe.
Shoe-black.
Shoe-boy.
Shoe-mak-er.
Shone.
Shook.
Shoot.
Shoot-er.
Shop.
Shop-keep-er.
Shop-lift-er.
Shop-lift-ing.
Shop-ping.

Shore.
Shorn.
Short.
Short-en.
Short-en-ing.
Short-hand.
Short-lived.
Short-ly.
Short-ness.
Shorts.
Short-sight-ed.
Shot.
Shote.
Shot-ten.
Should.
Shoul-der.
Shoul-der-blade.
Shout.
Shove.
Shov-el.
Show.
Shew-bread.
Show-er.
Show-er-y.
Show-i-ly.
Shown.
Show-y.
Shred.
Shrew.
Shrewd.
Shrew-ish.
Shriek.
Shrike.
Shrill.
Shrill-y.
Shrill-ness.
Shrimp.
Shrine.
Shrink.
Shrink-age.
Shriv-el.
Shroud.
Shrove-tide.
Shrub.
Shrub-ber-y.
Shrub-by.
Shrug.
Shrunk.
Shuck.
Shud-der.
Shuf-fle.
Shuf-fling.
Shun.
Shunt.
Shut.
Shut-ter.
Shut-tle.
Shut-tle-cock.
Shy.
Shy-ly.

Shy-ness.
Sib-i-lant.
Sib-i-la-tion.
Sib-yl.
Sib-yl-line.
Sick.
Sick-en.
Sick-ish.
Sick-le.
Sick-li-ness.
Sick-ly.
Sick-ness.
Side.
Side-board.
Side-long.
Sid-er-al.
Si-de-re-al.
Side-sad-dle.
Side-wise.
Si-dle.
Siege.
Si-e-nite.
Si-es-ta.
Sieve.
Sift.
Sift-er.
Sigh.
Sight.
Sight-less.
Sight-ly.
Sign.
Sig-nal.
Sig-nal-ize.
Sig-nal-ly.
Sig-na-ture.
Sign-er.
Sig-net.
Sig-nif-i-cance.
Sig-nif-i-can-cy.
Sig-nif-i-cant.
Sig-ni-fi-ca-tion.
Sig-nif-i-ca-tive.
Sig ni-fy.
Sign-post.
Si-lence.
Si-lent.
Si-lex.
Sil-i-ca.
Si-lic-ic.
Si-li-cious.
Silk.
Silk-en.
Silk-worm.
Silk-y.
Sill.
Sil-la-bub.
Sil-li-ness.
Sil-ly.
Silt.
Sil-ver.

Sil-ver-smith.
Sil-ver-y.
Sim-i-lar.
Sim-i-lar-i-ty.
Sim-i-lar-ly.
Sim-i-le.
Si-mil-i-tude.
Sim-mer.
Sim-o-ni-ac-al.
Sim-o-ny.
Si-moom.
Sim-per.
Sim-ple.
Sim-ple-ton.
Sim-plic-i-ty
Sim-pli-fi-ca-tion.
Sim-pli-fy.
Sim-ply.
Sim-u-late.
Sim-u-la-tion.
Si-mul-ta-ne-ous.
Si-mul-ta-ne-ous-ly.
Sin.
Sin-a-pism.
Since.
Sin-cere.
Sin-cer-i-ty.
Sine.
Si-ne-cure.
Sin-ew.
Sin-ew-y.
Sin-ful.
Sin-ful-ness.
Sing.
Singe.
Sing-er.
Sing-ing.
Sin-gle.
Sin-gle-ness.
Sin-gly.
Sing-song.
Sin-gu-lar.
Sin-gu-lar-i-ty.
Sin-gu-lar-ly.
Sin-is-ter.
Sin-is-trous.
Sink.
Sink-ing-fund.
Sin-less.
Sin-ner.
Sin-of-fer-ing.
Sin-u-a-tion.
Sin-u-os-i-ty.
Sin-u-ous.
Sip.
Si-phon.
Sir.
Sire.
Si-ren.

Sir-loin.
Si-roc-co.
Sir-rah.
Sir-up.
Sis-ter.
Sis-ter-hood.
Sis-ter-ly.
Sit.
Site.
Sit-ting.
Sit-u-ate.
Sit-u-a-ted.
Sit-u-a-tion.
Six.
Six-pence.
Six-teen.
Six-teenth.
Sixth.
Six-ty.
Siz-a-ble.
Si-zar.
Size.
Siz-y.
Skate.
Skein.
Skel-e-ton.
Skep-tic.
Skep-tic-al.
Skep-ti-cism.
Sketch.
Sketch-y.
Skew-er
Skid.
Skiff.
Skill.
Skilled.
Skil-let.
Skill-ful.
Skil-ful.
Skill-ful-ly.
Skil-ful-ly.
Skim.
Skim-mer.
Skim-milk.
Skin.
Skin-flint.
Skin-ny.
Skip.
Skip-per.
Skir-mish.
Skirt.
Skit-tish.
Skit-tles.
Skulk.
Skull.
Skull-cap.
Skunk.
Sky.
Sky-light.
Sky-sail.

Slab.	Sling.	Smil-ing.	Snow-shoe.
Slab-ber.	Slink.	Smirch.	Snow-y.
Slack.	Slip.	Smirk.	Snub.
Slack-en.	Slip-knot.	Smite.	Snuff.
Slack-ness.	Slip-per.	Smith.	Snuff-box.
Slag.	Slip-per-i-ness.	Smith-er-y.	Snuff-ers.
Slain.	Slip-per-y.	Smit-ten.	Snuf-fle.
Slake.	Slip-shod.	Smock.	Snug.
Slam.	Slit.	Smoke.	Snug-gle.
Slan-der.	Slit-ting-mill.	Smok-er.	Snug-ly.
Slan-der-ous.	Sliv-er.	Smok-y.	So.
Slang.	Slob-ber.	Smol-der.	Soak.
Slant.	Sloe.	Smoul-der.	Soap.
Slant-ing.	Sloop.	Smooth.	Soap-boil-er.
Slap.	Slop.	Smooth-ly.	Soap-stone.
Slash.	Slope.	Smooth-ness.	Soap-suds.
Slat.	Slop-py.	Smote.	Soap-y.
Slate.	Slot.	Smoth-er.	Soar.
Slat-tern.	Sloth.	Smug-gle.	Sob.
Slat-tern-ly.	Sloth-ful.	Smut.	So-ber.
Slat-y.	Slouch.	Smutch.	So-ber-ly.
Slaugh-ter.	Slough.	Smut-ti-ness	So-bri-e-ty.
Slaugh-ter-house.	Slov-en.	Smut-ty.	So-bri-quet.
Slaugh-ter-ous.	Slov-en-li-ness.	Snack.	So-cia-bil-i-ty
Slave.	Slov-en-ly.	Snaf-fle.	So-cia-ble.
Slav-er.	Slow.	Snag.	So-cia-bly.
Slav-er-y.	Slow-ly.	Snag-ged.	So-cial.
Slav-ish.	Slow-ness.	Snag-gy.	So-cial-ism.
Slay.	Slue.	Snail.	So-ci-e-ty.
Slay-er.	Slug.	Snake.	So-cin-i-an.
Slea-zy.	Slug-gard.	Snake-root.	Sock.
Sled.	Slug-gish.	Snap.	Sock-et.
Sled-ding.	Sluice.	Snap-drag-on.	Sod.
Sledge.	Slum-ber.	Snap-pish.	So-da.
Sleek.	Slump.	Snare.	Sod-den.
Sleek-ness.	Slung.	Snarl.	Sod-er.
Sleep.	Slunk.	Snatch.	So-fa.
Sleep-er.	Slur.	Snath.	Sof-fit.
Sleep-i-ness.	Slut.	Sneak.	Soft.
Sleep-less.	Slut-tish.	Sneak-ing.	Soft-en.
Sleep-less-ness.	Sly.	Sneer.	Soft-ly.
Sleep-y.	Sly-boots.	Sneeze.	Soft-ness.
Sleet.	Sly-ly.	Sniff.	Sog-gy.
Sleeve.	Sly-ness.	Snick-er.	Soil.
Sleigh.	Smack.	Snig-ger.	Soiree.
Sleigh-ing.	Small.	Snip.	So-journ.
Sleight.	Small-arms.	Snipe.	So-journ-er.
Slen-der.	Small-beer.	Sniv-el.	Sol.
Slen-der-ness.	Small-pox.	Snob.	Sol-ace.
Slept.	Smalt.	Snob-bish.	So-lar.
Slew.	Smart.	Snooze.	Sold.
Sley.	Smart-ly.	Snore.	Sol-der.
Slice.	Smart-ness.	Snor-ing.	Sol-dier.
Slide.	Smash.	Snort.	Sol-dier-ly.
Slight.	Smat-ter.	Snot.	Sol-dier-y.
Slight-ly.	Smat-ter-ing.	Snout.	Sole.
Sli-ly.	Smear.	Snow.	Sol-e-cism.
Slim.	Smell.	Snow-ball.	Sole-ly.
Slime.	Smelt.	Snow-ber-ry.	Sol-emn.
Slim-y.	Smile.	Snow-drop.	So-lem-ni-ty.

Sol-em-ni-za-tion.	Soot.	South-west.	Spec-ter.
Sol-em-nize.	Sooth.	Souvenir.	Spec-tre.
Sol-emn-ly.	Soothe.	Sov-er-eign.	Spec-tral.
So-lic-it.	Sooth-say.	Sov-er-eign-ty.	Spec-trum.
So-lic-it-a-tion.	Sooth-say-er.	Sow.	Spec-u-lar.
So-lic-it-er.	Soot-y.	Sown.	Spec-u-late.
So-lic-it-ous.	Sop.	Soy.	Spec-u-la-tion.
So-lic-i-tude.	Soph-ism.	Spa.	Spec-u-la-tive.
Sol-id.	Soph-ist.	Space.	Spec-u-la-tor.
Sol-i-dar-i-ty.	Soph-ist-er.	Spa-cious.	Spec-u-lum.
So-lid-i-fy.	So-phist-ic-al.	Spade.	Sped.
So-lid-i-ty.	So-phist-ic-al-ly.	Span.	Speech.
Sol-id-ly.	So-phist-ic-ate.	Span-gle.	Speech-less.
So-lil-o-quize.	Soph-ist-ry.	Span-iard.	Speed.
So-lil-o-quy.	Soph-o-more.	Span-iel.	Speed-i-ly.
Sol-i-ta-ri-ness.	Soph-o-mor-ic.	Span-ish.	Speed-y.
Sol-i-ta-ry.	Soph-o-mor-ic-al.	Spank.	Spell.
Sol-i-tude.	Sop-o-rif-er-ous.	Spank-er.	Spell-er.
So-lo.	Sop-o-rif-ic.	Spar.	Spelt.
Sol-stice.	So-pra-no.	Spar-deck	Spel-ter.
Sol-sti-tial.	Sor-cer-er.	Spare.	Spen-cer.
Sol-u-bil-i-ty.	Sor-cer-ess.	Spare-rib.	Spend.
Sol-u-ble.	Sor-cer-ous.	Spar-ing.	Spend-thrift.
So-lu-tion.	Sor-cer-y.	Spark.	Sperm.
Solv-a-bil-i-ty.	Sor-did.	Spark-le.	Sper-ma-ce-ti.
Solv-a-ble.	Sor-did-ly.	Spar-row.	Spew.
Solve.	Sore.	Spar-ry.	Sphere.
Solv-en-cy.	Sore-ness.	Sparse.	Spher-ic.
Solv-ent.	Sor-rel.	Sparse-ly.	Spher-ic-al.
Som-ber.	Sor-ri-ly.	Spar-tan.	Sphe-ric-i-ty.
Som-bre.	Sor-row.	Spasm.	Spher-ics.
Som-brous.	Sor-row-ful.	Spas-mod-ic.	Sphe-roid.
Some.	Sor-ry.	Spat-ter.	Sphe-roid-al
Some-bod-y.	Sort.	Spat-u-la.	Spher-ule.
Som-er-set.	Sot.	Spav-in.	Sphinx.
Some-how.	Sot-tish.	Spawn.	Spice.
Some-thing.	Sou.	Spay.	Spic-u-lar.
Some-times.	Sou-chong.	Speak.	Spi-cy.
Some-what.	Sough.	Speak-er.	Spi-der.
Som-nam-bu-lism.	Sought.	Spear.	Spig-ot.
Som-nam-bu-list.	Soul.	Spear-man.	Spike.
Som-nif-er-ous.	Soul-less.	Spear-mint.	Spike-nard.
Som-nif-ic.	Sound.	Spe-cial.	Spik-y.
Som-nil-o-quence.	Sound-ings.	Spe-cial-ly.	Spile.
Som-nil-o-quist.	Sound-ly.	Spe-cial-ty.	Spill.
Som-no-lence.	Sound-ness.	Spe-cie.	Spin.
Som-no-lent.	Soup.	Spe-cies.	Spin-ach.
Son.	Sour.	Spe-cif-ic.	Spin-age.
So-na-ta.	Source.	Spe-cif-ic-al-ly.	Spi-nal.
Song.	Sour-ish.	Spec-i-fi-ca-tion.	Spin-dle.
Song-ster.	Sour-ly.	Spec-i-fy.	Spine.
Song-stress.	Sour-ness.	Spec-i-men.	Spi-nel.
Son-net.	Souse.	Spe-cious.	Spin-et.
Son-net-eer.	South.	Spe-cious-ly.	Spi-nos-i-ty
So-no-rous.	South-east.	Speck.	Spi-nous.
Son-ship.	South-er-ly.	Speck-le.	Spi-ny.
Soon.	South-ern.	Speck-led.	Spin-ster.
	South-ing.	Spec-ta-cle.	Spir-a-cle.
	South-ron.	Spec-tac-u-lar.	Spi-ral.
	South-ward.	Spec-ta-tor.	Spire.

82

Spir-it.
Spir-it-ed.
Spir-it-less.
Spir-it-u-al.
Spir-it-u-al-i-ty.
Spir-it-u-al-ize.
Spir-it-u-al-ly.
Spir-it-u-ous.
Spirt.
Spir-y.
Spis-si-tude.
Spit.
Spite.
Spite-ful.
Spit-tle.
Spit-toon.
Splash.
Splay-foot-ed.
Spleen.
Spleen-y.
Splen-dent.
Splen-did.
Splen-did-ly.
Splen-dor.
Splen-e-tic.
Splice.
Splint.
Splint-er.
Split.
Splut-ter.
Spoil.
Spoke.
Spo-ken.
Spokes-man.
Spo-li-a-tion.
Spon-da-ic.
Spon-dee.
Sponge.
Spong-er.
Spong-i-ness.
Spong-y.
Spon-sal.
Spon-sion.
Spon-sor.
Spon-ta-ne-i-ty.
Spon-ta-ne ous.
Spon-toon.
Spool.
Spoon.
Spoon-bill.
Spoon-ful.
Spo-rad-ic.
Sport.
Sport-ful.
Sport-ive.
Sports-man.
Spot.
Spot-less.
Spot-ted.
Spouse.

Spous-al.
Spout.
Sprain.
Sprang.
Sprat.
Sprawl.
Spray.
Spread.
Spree.
Sprig.
Spright.
Spright-ful.
Spright-li-ness.
Spright-ly.
Spring.
Spring-bok.
Springe.
Spring-halt.
Spring-i-ness.
Spring-tide.
Spring-y.
Sprink-le.
Sprink-ling.
Sprit.
Sprite.
Sprout.
Spruce.
Spruce-ly.
Spruce-ness.
Sprung.
Spry.
Spume.
Spum-ous.
Spum-y.
Spun.
Spunk.
Spur.
Spurge.
Spu-ri-ous.
Spu-ri-ous-iy.
Spurn.
Spurred.
Spur-ri-er.
Spurt.
Sput-ter.
Spy.
Spy-glass.
Squab.
Squab-ble.
Squad.
Squad-ron.
Squal-id.
Squall.
Squall-y.
Squa-lor.
Squan-der.
Square.
Squash.
Squat.
Squat-ter.

Squaw.
Squeak.
Squeal.
Squeam-ish.
Squeeze.
Squib.
Squill.
Squint.
Squint-eyed.
Squire.
Squirm.
Squir-rel.
Squirt.
Stab.
Sta-bil-i-ty.
Sta-ble.
Sta-bling.
Stack.
Stad-dle.
Staff.
Stag.
Stage.
Stage-coach.
Stage-play.
Stage-play-er.
Stag-ger.
Stag-nan-cy.
Stag-nant.
Stag-nate.
Stag-na-tion.
Staid.
Stain.
Stain-less.
Stair.
Stair-case.
Stake.
Stal-ac-tit-ic.
Sta-lac-tite.
Sta-lag-mite.
Stale.
Stalk.
Stall.
Stall-fed.
Stall-ion.
Stal-wart.
Sta-men.
Stam-mer.
Stamp.
Stam-pede.
Stanch.
Stan-chion.
Stand.
Stand-ard.
Stand-ing.
Stand-ish.
Stan-za.
Sta-ple.
Star.
Star-board.
Starch.

Starch-y.
Stare.
Star-fish.
Stark.
Star-less.
Star-light.
Star-ling.
Star-ry.
Start.
Start-le.
Start-ling.
Starve.
Starve-ling.
State.
Sta-ted.
Sta-ted-ly.
State-li-ness.
State-ly.
State-ment.
State-room.
States-man.
States-man-ship.
Stat-ic.
Stat-ic-al.
Stat-ics.
Sta-tion.
Sta-tion-a-ry.
Sta-tion-er.
Sta-tion-er-y.
Sta-tist-ic.
Sta-tist-ic-al.
Sta-tist-ics.
Stat-u-a-ry.
Stat-ue.
Stat-ure.
Stat-u-ta-ble.
Stat-ute.
Stat-u-to-ry.
Staunch.
Stave.
Stay.
Stead.
Stead-fast.
Stead-fast-ness.
Stead-i-ly.
Stead-i-ness.
Stead-y.
Steak.
Steal.
Stealth.
Stealth-y.
Steam.
Steam-boat.
Steam-er.
Steam-en-gine.
Ste-a-tite.
Steed.
Steel.
Steel-yard.
Steep.

Stee-ple.
Steep-ness.
Steer.
Steer-age.
Steers-man.
Stel-lar.
Stel-late.
Stem.
Stench.
Sten-cil.
Sten-o-graph-ic.
Ste-nog-ra-pher.
Ste-nog-ra-phy.
Sten-to-ri-an.
Step.
Step-child.
Step-fa-ther.
Steppe.
Step-ping-stone.
Step-son.
Ste-re-o-scope.
Ste-re-o-scop-ic.
Ste-re-o-type.
Ste-re-o-typ-er.
Ster-ile.
Ste-ril-i-ty.
Ster-ling.
Stern.
Stern-chase.
Stern-ly.
Stern-ness.
Ster-nu-ta-tion.
Ster-nu-ta-to-ry.
Ster-to-rous.
Steth-o-scope.
Ste-ve-dore.
Stew.
Stew-ard.
Stew-ard-ship.
Stick.
Stick-i-ness.
Stick-le.
Stick-ler.
Stick-y.
Stiff.
Stiff-en.
Stiff-ly.
Stiff-ness.
Stiff-necked.
Sti-fle.
Stig-ma.
Stig-ma-tize.
Sti-let-to.
Still.
Still-born.
Still-ness.
Stil-ly.
Stilt.
Stim-u-lant.
Stim-u-late.

Stim-u-la-tion.
Stim-u-la-tive.
Stim-u-lus.
Sting.
Stin-gi-ly.
Stin-gi-ness.
Stin-gy.
Stink.
Stint.
Sti-pend.
Sti-pend-i-a-ry.
Stip-ple.
Stip-u-late.
Stip-u-la-tion.
Stir.
Stir-rup.
Stitch.
Stive.
Sti-ver.
Stoat.
Stock.
Stock-ade.
Stock-bro-ker.
Stock-fish.
Stock-hold-er.
Stock-ing.
Stock-job-ber.
Stocks.
Stock-still.
Stock-y.
Sto-ic.
Sto-ic-al.
Sto-i-cism.
Stole.
Stolen.
Stol-id.
Sto-lid-i-ty.
Stom-ach.
Stom-a-cher.
Sto-mach-ic.
Stone.
Stone-cut-ter.
Stone-fruit.
Stone-still.
Ston-i-ness.
Ston-y.
Stood.
Stool.
Stoop.
Stop.
Stop-cock.
Stop-page.
Stop-per.
Stop-ple.
Stor-age.
Store.
Store-house.
Sto-ried.
Stork.
Storm.

Storm-y.
Stoup.
Sto-ry.
Stout.
Stout-ly.
Stout-ness.
Stove.
Stow.
Stow-age.
Stra-bis-mus.
Strad-dle.
Strag-gle.
Strag-gler.
Straight.
Straight-en.
Straight-for-ward.
Straight-ly.
Straight-way.
Strain.
Strain-er.
Strait.
Strait-en.
Strait-jack-et.
Strait-laced.
Strake.
Strand.
Strange.
Strange-ly.
Strange-ness.
Stran-ger.
Stran-gle.
Stran-gu-la-tion.
Stran-gu-ry.
Strap.
Strap-ping.
Stra-ta.
Strat-a-gem.
Strat-e-gist.
Strat-e-gy.
Strat-i-fi-ca-tion.
Strat-i-fy.
Stra-tum.
Straw.
Straw-ber-ry.
Stray.
Streak.
Streak-ed.
Streak-y.
Stream.
Stream-er.
Stream-let.
Street.
Strength.
Strength-en.
Stren-u-ous.
Stren-u-ous-ly
Stress.
Stretch.
Stretch-er.

Strew.
Stri-a-ted.
Strick-en.
Strict.
Strict-ly.
Strict-ness.
Strict-ure.
Stride.
Strife.
Strike.
Strik-ing.
String.
Stringed.
Strin-gent.
String-y.
Strip.
Stripe.
Stri-ped.
Strip-ling.
Strive.
Stroke.
Stroll.
Stroll-er.
Strong.
Strong-ly.
Strong-hold.
Strop.
Stro-phe.
Strove.
Strow.
Struck.
Struct-ur-al
Struct-ure.
Strug-gle.
Stru-mous.
Strum-pet.
Strung.
Strut.
Strych-nine.
Stub.
Stub-bed.
Stub-ble.
Stub-born.
Stub-by.
Stuc-co.
Stuck.
Stud.
Stu-dent.
Stud-ied.
Stu-di-o.
Stu-di-ous.
Stu-di-ous-ly.
Stud-y.
Stuff.
Stuff-ing.
Stul-ti-fy.
Stum-ble.
Stum-bling block.
Stump.

Stump-y.
Stun.
Stung.
Stunk.
Stunt.
Stu-pe-fac-tion.
Stu-pe-fy.
Stu-pen-dous.
Stu-pid.
Stu-pid-i-ty.
Stu-pid-ly.
Stu-por
Stur-di-ly.
Stur-dy.
Stur-geon.
Stut-ter.
Stut-ter-er.
Sty.
Styg-i-an.
Sty-lar.
Style.
Styl-ish.
Styp-tic.
Su-ant.
Sua-sion.
Sua-sive.
Sua-so-ry.
Suav-i-ty.
Sub-ac-e-tate.
Sub-ac-id
Sub-al-tern.
Sub-a-que-ous.
Sub-di-vide.
Sub-di-vi-sion.
Sub-duct.
Sub-due.
Sub-ja-cent.
Sub-ject.
Sub-jec-tion.
Sub-ject-ive.
Sub-join.
Sub-ju-gate.
Sub-ju-ga-tion.
Sub-junc-tion.
Sub-junct-ive.
Sub-let.
Sub-li-mate.
Sub-li-ma-tion.
Sub-lime.
Sub-lime-ly.
Sub-lim-i-ty.
Sub-lin-gual.
Sub-lu-na-ry.
Sub-ma-rine.
Sub-merge.
Sub-merse.
Sub-mer-sion.
Sub-mis-sion.
Sub-mis-sive.
Sub-mis-sive-ly.

Sub-mis-sive-ness.
Sub-mit.
Sub-mul-ti-ple.
Sub-or-di-nate.
Sub-or-di-**na**-tion.
Sub-orn.
Sub-or-na-tion.
Sub-pœ-na.
Sub-scribe.
Sub-scrib-er
Sub-scrip-tion.
Sub-se-quence.
Sub-se-quent.
Sub-se-quent-ly.
Sub-serve.
Sub-serv-i-ence.
Sub-serv-i-en-cy.
Sub-serv-i-ent.
Sub-side.
Sub-sid-ence.
Sud-sid-i-a-ry.
Sub-si-dize.
Sub-si-dy.
Sub-sist.
Sub-sist-ence.
Sub-sist-ent.
Sub-soil.
Sub-stance.
Sub-stan-tial.
Sub-stan-tial-ly.
Sub-stan-tials.
Sub-stan-ti-ate.
Sub-stan-tive.
Sub-stan-tive-ly.
Sub-sti-tute.
Sub-sti-tu-tion.
Sub-stra-tum.
Sub-struc-tion.
Sub-tend.
Sub-tense.
Sub-ter-fuge.
Sub-ter-ra-ne-an.
Sub-ter-ra-**ne**-ous.
Sub-tile.
Sub-til-ty.
Sub-til-i-za-tion.
Sub-til-ize.
Sub-tle.
Sub-tle-ty.
Sub-tly.
Sub-tract.
Sub-trac-tion.
Sub-tract-ive.
Sub-tra-hend.
Sub-urb-an.
Sub-urbs.
Sub-ver-sion.

Sub-ver-sive.
Sub-vert.
Suc-ceed.
Suc-cess.
Suc-cess-ful.
Suc-cess-ful-ly.
Suc-ces-sion.
Suc-ces-sive.
Suc-ces-sive-ly.
Suc-ces-sor.
Suc-cinct.
Suc-cinct-ly.
Suc-cor.
Suc-co-tash.
Suc-cu-lence.
Suc-cu-lent.
Suc-cumb.
Such.
Suck.
Suck-er.
Suck-le.
Suck-ling.
Suc-tion.
Suc-to-ri-al.
Sud-den.
Sud-den-ly.
Su-dor-if-ic.
Suds.
Sue.
Su-et.
Suf-fer.
Suf-fer-a-ble.
Suf-fer-ance.
Suf-fer-er.
Suf-fer-ing.
Suf-fice.
Suf-fi-cien-cy.
Suf-fi-cient.
Suf-fi-cient-ly.
Suf-fix.
Suf-fo-cate.
Suf-fo-ca-tion.
Suf-fo-ca-tive.
Suf-fra-gan.
Suf-frage.
Suf-fuse.
Suf-fu-sion.
Sug-ar.
Sug-ar-cane.
Sug-ar-loaf.
Sug-ar-plum.
Sug-ar-y.
Sug-gest.
Sug-ges-tion.
Sug-gest-ive.
Su-i-ci-dal.
Su-i-cide.
Suit.
Suit-a-ble.
Suit-a-ble-ness.

Suit-a-bly.
Suite.
Suit-or.
Sulk-i-ly.
Sulk-i-ness.
Sulk-y.
Sul-len.
Sul-ly.
Sul-phate.
Sul-phur.
Sul-phu-re-ous.
Sul-phur-ous.
Sul-phu-ret.
Sul-phu-ric.
Sul-phur-y.
Sul-tan.
Sul-ta-na.
Sul-ta-ness.
Sul-tri-ness.
Sul-try.
Sum.
Su-mac.
Su-mach.
Sum-ma-ry.
Sum-mer.
Sum-mer-set.
Sum-mit.
Sum-mon.
Sum-mons.
Sump-ter.
Sumpt-u-a-ry.
Sumpt-u-ous.
Sun.
Sun-beam.
Sun-burnt.
Sun-day.
Sun-der.
Sun-di-al.
Sun-dries.
Sun-dry.
Sun-flow-er.
Sung.
Sunk.
Sunk-en.
Sun-less.
Sun-light.
Sun-ny.
Sun-rise.
Sun-set.
Sun-shine.
Sun-shin-y.
Sun-stroke.
Sup.
Su-per-a-bound.
Su-per-a-bund-ance.
Su-per-a-bund-ant.
Su-per-add.
Su-per-an-nu-ate.

Su-per-an-nu-a-ted.
Su-perb.
Su-perb-ly.
Su-per-car-go.
Su-per-cil-i-ous.
Su-per-cil-i-ous-ly.
Su-per-em-i-nence.
Su-per-em-i-nent.
Su-per-er-o-ga-tion.
Su-per-e-rog-a-to-ry.
Su-per-ex-cel-lent.
Su-per-fi-cial.
Su-per-fi-cial-ly.
Su-per-fi-cies.
Su-per-fine.
Su-per-flu-i-ty.
Su-per-flu-ous.
Su-per-hu-man.
Su-per-in-cum-bent.
Su-per-in-duce.
Su-per-in-tend.
Su-per-in-tend-ence.
Su-per-in-**tend**-ent.
Su-pe-ri-or.
Su-pe-ri-or-i-ty.
Su-per-la-tive.
Su-per-nal.
Su-per-nat-u-ral.
Su-per-nu-mer-a-ry.
Su-per-scribe.
Su-per-scrip-tion.
Su-per-sede.
Su-per-sti-tion.
Su-per-sti-tious.
Su-per-sti-tious-ly.
Su-per-struct-ure.
Su-per-vene.
Su-per-vi-sal.
Su-per-vis-ion.
Su-per-vise.
Su-per-vi-sor.
Su-pine.
Su-pine-ly.
Su-pine-ness.
Sup-per.
Sup-per-less.
Sup-plant.

Sup-ple.
Sup-ple-ment.
Sup-ple-ment-al.
Sup-ple-ment-a-ry.
Sup-ple-ness.
Sup-pli-ant.
Sup-pli-cant.
Sup-pli-cate.
Sup-pli-ca-tion.
Sup-pli-ca-to-ry.
Sup-ply.
Sup-port.
Sup-port-a-ble.
Sup-pos-a-ble.
Sup-pose.
Sup-po-si-**tion.**
Sup-**pos-i-ti**-tious.
Sup-press.
Sup-pres-sion.
Sup-pu-rate.
Sup-pu-ra-tion.
Sup-pu-ra-**tive.**
Su-pra-**mun**-dane.
Su-prem-a-cy.
Su-preme.
Su-preme-ly.
Sur-charge.
Sur-cin-gle.
Surd.
Sure.
Sure-ly.
Sure-ty.
Sure-ty-ship.
Surf.
Sur-face.
Sur-feit.
Surge.
Sur-geon.
Sur-ger-y.
Sur-gic-al.
Sur-li-ness.
Sur-loin.
Sur-ly.
Sur-mise.
Sur-mount.
Sur-mount-a-ble.
Sur-name.
Sur-pass.
Sur-pass-ing.
Sur-plice.
Sur-plus.
Sur-plus-age.
Sur-pris-al.
Sur-prise.
Sur-pris-ing.
Sur-ren-der.
Sur-rep-ti-tious.

Sur-rep-ti-tious-ly.
Sur-ro-gate.
Sur-round.
Sur-tout.
Sur-vey.
Sur-vey-ing.
Sur-vey-or.
Sur-vi-val.
Sur-vive.
Sur-viv-or.
Sur-viv-or-ship.
Sus-cep-ti-bil-i-ty.
Sus-cep-ti-ble.
Sus-cep-tive.
Sus-pect.
Sus-pend.
Sus-pend-er.
Sus-pense.
Sus-pen-sion.
Sus-pen-so-ry.
Sus-pi-cion.
Sus-pi-cious.
Sus-pi-cious-ly.
Sus-pi-ra-tion.
Sus-tain.
Sus-te-nance.
Sus-ten-ta-tion.
Sut-ler.
Sut-tee.
Sut-ure.
Swab.
Swad-dle.
Swag.
Swag-ger.
Swain.
Swale.
Swal-low.
Swam.
Swamp.
Swamp-y.
Swan.
Swap.
Sward.
Swarm.
Swarth-i-ly.
Swarth-y.
Swath.
Swathe.
Sway.
Swear.
Swear-ing.
Sweat.
Sweat-y.
Sweep.
Sweep-ings.
Sweep-stakes.
Sweet.
Sweet-bread.

Sweet-bri-ar.
Sweet-en.
Sweet-en-ing.
Sweet-heart.
Sweet-ing.
Sweet-ish.
Sweet-ly.
Sweet-meat.
Sweet-ness.
Swell.
Swell-ing.
Swelt-er.
Swelt-ry.
Swept.
Swerve.
Swift.
Swift-ly.
Swift-ness.
Swig.
Swill.
Swim.
Swim-mer.
Swim-ming.
Swim-ming-ly.
Swin-dle.
Swin-dler.
Swine.
Swine-herd
Swing.
Swinge.
Swin-gle.
Swin-ish.
Swipe.
Swiss.
Switch.
Swiv-el.
Swollen.
Swoon.
Swoop.
Swop.
Sword.
Sword-fish.
Swore.
Sworn.
Swum.
Swung.
Syc-a-more.
Syc-o-phan-cy.
Syc-o-phant.
Syc-o-phant-ic.
Sy-e-nite.
Syl-lab-ic.
Syl-lab-i-ca-tion.
Syl-la-ble.
Syl-la-bub.
Syl-la-bus.
Syl-lo-gism.
Syl-lo-gist-ic.
Sylph.
Syl-van.

Sym-bol.
Sym-bol-ic.
Sym-bol-ic-al.
Sym-bol-ic-al-ly.
Sym-bol-ize.
Sym-bol-ism.
Sym-met-ric-al.
Sym-met-ric-al-ly.
Sym-me-trize.
Sym-me-try.
Sym-pa-thet-ic.
Sym-pa-thet-ic-al
Sym-pa-thize.
Sym-pa-thy.
Sym-pho-ni-ous.
Sym-pho-ny.
Sym-po-si-ac.
Symp-tom
Symp-tom-at-ic.
Syn-ær-e-sis.
Syn-er-e-sis.
Syn-a-gogue.
Syn-chro-nal.
Syn-chron-ic-al.
Syn-chro-nous.
Syn-chro-nism.
Syn-co-pate.
Syn-co-pa-tion.
Syn-co-pe.
Syn-dic
Syn-ec-do-che.
Syn-od.
Syn-od-ic.
Syn-od-ic-al.
Syn-o-nym.
Syn-o-nyme.
Syn-on-y-mize.
Syn-on-y-mous.
Syn-on-y-my.
Syn-op-sis.
Syn-op-tic.
Syn-op-tic-al.
Syn-tac-tic.
Syn-tac-tic-al.
Syn-tax.
Syn-the-sis.
Syn-thet-ic.
Syn-thet-ic-al.
Syn-thet-ic-al-ly.
Syph-i-lis.
Syr-i-ac.
Sy-rin-ga.
Syr-inge.
Sys-tem.
Sys-tem-at-ic.
Sys-tem-at-ic-al-ly.
Sys-tem-a-tize
Sys-to-le.

T

Tab.
Tab-ard.
Tab-by.
Tab-er-na-cle.
Ta-bes.
Tab-la-ture.
Ta-ble.
Tab-leau.
Tab-leaux.
Ta-ble-land.
Tab-let.
Ta-boo.
Ta-bor.
Tab-u-lar.
Tac-it.
Tac-it-ly.
Tac-i-turn.
Tac-i-tur-ni-ty.
Tack.
Tack-le.
Tack-ling.
Tact.
Tac-tic-al.
Tac-ti-cian.
Tac-tics.
Tac-tile.
Tact-u-al.
Tad-pole.
Taff-rail.
Taf-fe-ta.
Taf-fe-ty.
Tag.
Tail.
Tai-lor.
Tai-lor-ess.
Taint.
Take.
Tak-ing.
Talc.
Tale.
Tale-bear-er.
Tal-ent.
Tal-ent-ed.
Tal-is-man.
Tal-is-man-ic.
Talk.
Talk-a-tive.
Tall.
Tall-ness.
Tal-low.
Tal-low-chan-dler.
Tal-ly.
Tal-mud.
Tal-on.
Tam-a-ble.
Tam-a-rind.

Tam-bour.
Tam-bour-ine.
Tame.
Tame-ly.
Tam-my.
Tamp.
Tam-per
Tam-pi-on.
Tan.
Tan-dem.
Tang.
Tan-gent.
Tan-gi-bil-i-ty.
Tan-gi-ble.
Tan-gle.
Tank.
Tank-ard.
Tan-nate.
Tan-ner.
Tan-ner-y.
Tan-nin.
Tan-sy
Tan-ta-lize.
Tan-ta-mount.
Tan-yard.
Tap.
Tape.
Ta-per.
Tap-es-try
Tape-worm.
Tap-i-o-ca.
Tap-house.
Tap-root.
Tap-ster.
Tar.
Ta-ran-tu-la.
Tar-di-ly.
Tar-di-ness.
Tar-dy.
Tare.
Tar-get.
Tar-iff.
Tar-la-tan.
Tar-nish.
Tar-pau-lin.
Tar-ry.
Tart.
Tar-tan.
Tar-tar.
Tar-ta-re-an.
Tar-ta-re-ous.
Tar-tar-ous.
Tar-tar-ic.
Tart-ly.
Tart-ness.
Task.
Task-mas-ter.
Tas-sel.
Taste.
Taste-ful.

Taste-ful-ly.
Taste-less.
Tast-i-ly.
Tast-y.
Tat-ter.
Tat-ter-de-mal-ion.
Tat-tle.
Tat-tler.
Tat-too.
Taught.
Taunt.
Taut.
Tau-to-log-ic-al.
Tau-tol-o-gy.
Tav-ern.
Tav-ern-keep-er.
Taw.
Taw-dri-ly.
Taw-dri-ness.
Taw-dry.
Taw-ny.
Tax.
Tax-a-ble.
Tax-a-tion.
Tax-i-der-my.
Tea.
Teach.
Teach-a-ble.
Teach-er.
Tea-cup.
Teak.
Tea-ket-tle.
Teal.
Team.
Team-ster.
Tea-pot.
Tear.
Tear-ful.
Tear-less.
Tease.
Tea-sel.
Tea-spoon.
Teat.
Tech-nic-al.
Tech-ni-cal-i-ty.
Tech-no-log-ic-al.
Tech-nol-o-gy.
Tech-y.
Tec-ton-ic.
Ted-der.
Te De-um.
Te-di-ous.
Te-di-um.
Teem.
Teens.
Tee-ter.
Teeth.
Tee-to-tal-ism.

87

Teg-u-ment.
Tel-e-gram.
Tel-e-graph.
Tel-e-graph-ic.
Tel-e-phone.
Tel-e-scope.
Tel-e-scop-ic.
Tel-e-scop-ic-al.
Tell.
Tell-er.
Tell-tale.
Te-mer-i-ty.
Tem-per.
Tem-per-a-ment.
Tem-per-ance.
Tem-per-ate.
Tem-per-ate-ly.
Tem-per-a-ture.
Tem-pest.
Tem-pest-u-ous.
Tem-plar.
Tem-ple.
Tem-plet.
Tem-po-ral.
Tem-po-ral-i-ty.
Tem-po-ral-ly.
Tem-po-ra-ri-ly.
Tem-po-ra-ry.
Tem-po-rize.
Tempt.
Temp-ta-tion.
Tempt-er.
Ten.
Ten-a-ble.
Te-na-cious.
Te-nac-i-ty.
Ten-an-cy.
Ten-ant.
Ten-ant-a-ble.
Ten-ant-ry.
Tend.
Tend-en-cy.
Tend-er.
Ten-der.
Ten-der-ly.
Ten-der-loin.
Ten-der-ness.
Ten-di-nous.
Ten-don.
Ten-dril.
Ten-e-ment.
Ten-et.
Ten-fold.
Ten-nis.
Ten-on.
Ten-or.
Tense.
Tense-ness.
Ten-sion.
Tent.

Ten-ta-cle.
Ten-ta-tive.
Tent-ed.
Ten-ter.
Tenth.
Tenth-ly.
Te-nu-i-ty.
Ten-u-ous.
Ten-ure.
Tep-e-fac-tion.
Tep-id.
Te-por.
Ter-a-phim.
Ter-e-binth.
Ter-gi- ver - sa - tion.
Term.
Ter-ma-gan-cy.
Ter-ma-gant.
Ter-mi-na-ble.
Ter-mi-nal.
Ter-mi-nate.
Ter-mi-na-tion.
Ter-mi-nol-o-gy.
Ter-mi-nus.
Ter-mite.
Ter-na-ry.
Ter-race.
Ter-ra Cot-ta.
Ter-ra-pin.
Ter-ra-que-ous.
Ter-rene.
Ter-res-tri-al.
Ter-ri-ble.
Ter-ri-bly.
Ter-ri-er.
Ter-rif-ic.
Ter-ri-fy.
Ter-ri-to-ri-al.
Ter-ri-to-ry.
Ter-ror.
Ter-ror-ism.
Terse.
Terse-ly.
Terse-ness.
Ter-tian.
Ter-ti-a-ry.
Tes-sel-ate.
Tes-sel-a-tion.
Test.
Tes-ta-cean.
Tes-ta-ceous.
Test-a-ment.
Test-a-ment-a-ry.
Test-ate.
Tes-ta-tor.
Tes-ta-trix.
Tes-ter.
Tes-ti-cle.
Tes-ti-fy.

Tes-ti-ly.
Tes-ti-mo-ni-al.
Tes-ti-mo-ny.
Tes-ti-ness.
Tes-ty.
Tet-a-nus.
Tete-a-tete.
Teth-er.
Tet-ra-gon.
Tet-ra-he-dron.
Te-tram-e-ter.
Te-trarch.
Te-trarch-ate.
Tet-rarch-y.
Te-tras-tich.
Tet-ter.
Teu-ton-ic.
Text.
Text-book.
Text-hand.
Tex-tile.
Text-u-al.
Text-u-al-ist.
Text-u-a-ry.
Text-ure.
Than.
Thane.
Thank.
Thank-ful.
Thank-ful-ly.
Thank-ful-ness.
Thank-less.
Thanks.
Thanks-giv-ing.
Thank-wor-thy.
That.
Thatch.
Thaw.
The.
The-a-ter.
The-a-tre.
The-at-ric.
The-at-ric-al.
Thee.
Theft.
Their.
Theirs.
The-ism.
The-ist.
The-ist-ic.
The-ist-ic-al.
Them.
Theme.
Them-selves.
Then.
Thence.
Thence-forth.
Thence-for-ward.
The-oc-ra-cy.
The-o-crat-ic-al.

Tne-od-o-lite.
The-o-lo-gi-an.
The-o-log-ic.
The-o-log-ic-al.
The-ol-o-gy.
The-or-bo.
The-o-rem.
The-o-ret-ic.
The-o-ret-ic-al.
The-o - ret - ic-al-ly.
The-o-rist.
The-o-rize.
The-o-ry.
Ther-a-peu-tic.
There.
There-a-bout.
There-aft-er.
There-at.
There-by.
There-fore.
There-in.
There-of.
There-on.
There-up-on.
There-with.
Ther-mal.
Ther-mom-e-ter.
Ther-mo-met-ric-al.
The-sau-rus.
These.
The-sis.
They.
Thick.
Thick-en.
Thick-et.
Thick-ly.
Thick-ness.
Thick-set.
Thief.
Thieve.
Thiev-er-y.
Thiev-ish.
Thigh.
Thills.
Thim-ble.
Thin.
Thine.
Thing.
Think.
Third.
Third-ly.
Thirst.
Thirst-y.
Thir-teen.
Thir-teenth.
Thir-ti-eth.
Thir-ty.
This.

This-tle.
Thith-er.
Thith-er-ward.
Thole.
Thong.
Tho-rax.
Thorn.
Thorn-y.
Thor-ough.
Thor-ough-fare.
Thor-ough-ly.
Thor-ough-ness.
Those.
Thou.
Though.
Thought.
Thought-ful.
Thought-less.
Thou-sand.
Thou-sandth.
Thrall-dom.
Thral-dom.
Thrash.
Thread.
Thread-bare.
Threat.
Threat-en.
Threat-en-ing.
Three.
Three-fold.
Three-pence.
Three-score.
Thresh.
Thresh-old.
Threw.
Thrice.
Thrid.
Thrift.
Thrift-less.
Thrift-y.
Thrill.
Thrive.
Thriv-ing.
Throat.
Throb.
Throe.
Throne.
Throng.
Throt-tle.
Through.
Through-out.
Throve.
Throw.
Thrum.
Thrush.
Thrust.
Thug.
Thumb.
Thump.
Thun-der.

Thun-der-bolt.
Thun-der-show-er.
Thun-der-struck.
Thurs-day.
Thus.
Thwack.
Thwart.
Thy.
Thyme.
Thy-self.
Ti-a-ra.
Tick.
Tick-en.
Tick-ing.
Tick-et.
Tick-le.
Tick-lish.
Tid-al.
Tid-bit.
Tide.
Tide-wait-er.
Ti-di-ly.
Ti-dings.
Ti-dy.
Tie.
Tier.
Tierce.
Tiff.
Tif-fa-ny.
Ti-ger.
Tight.
Tight-en.
Tight-ly.
Ti-gress.
Til-bu-ry.
Tile.
Till.
Till-age.
Till-er.
Tilt.
Tilt-ham-mer.
Tim-ber.
Tim-brel.
Time.
Time-keep-er.
Time-ly.
Time-piece.
Time-serv-er.
Time-serv-ing.
Tim-id.
Ti-mid-i-ty.
Tim-o-rous.
Tin.
Tinc-al.
Tinct-ure.
Tin-der.
Tine.
Tin-foil.
Ting.

Tinge.
Tin-gle.
Tink-er.
Tink-le.
Tink-ling.
Tin-man.
Tin-ner.
Tin-ny.
Tin-sel.
Tint.
Ti-ny.
Tip.
Tip-pet.
Tip-ple.
Tip-pler.
Tip-staff.
Tip-sy.
Tip-toe.
Ti-rade.
Tire.
Tir-ed.
Tire-some.
Tire-some-ness.
Tis-sue.
Tit.
Tit-bit.
Tithe.
Tith-ing-man.
Tit-il-late.
Tit-il-la-tion.
Ti-tle.
Tit-mouse.
Tit-ter.
Tit-tle.
Tit-tle-tat-tle.
Tit-u-lar.
Tit-u-la-ry.
To.
Toad.
Toad-stool.
Toast.
To-bac-co.
To-bac-co-nist.
Toc-sin.
Tod.
To-day.
Tod-dle.
Tod-dy.
Toe.
To-geth-er.
Tog-gle-joint.
Toil.
Toi-let.
Toil-some.
To-kay.
To-ken.
Told.
Tole.
Tol-er-a-ble.
Tol-er-a-bly.

Tol-er-ance.
Tol-er-ant.
Tol-er-ate.
Tol-er-a-tion.
Toll.
Toll-bridge.
Toll-gate.
Toll-house.
Tom-a-hawk.
To-ma-to.
Comb.
Tom-boy.
Tomb-stone.
Tome.
To-mor-row.
Tom-tit.
Ton.
Tone.
Tongs.
Tongue.
Tongue-tied.
Ton-ic.
To-night.
Ton-nage.
Ton-sil.
Ton-sure.
Ton-tine.
Too.
Took.
Tool.
Toot.
Tooth.
Tooth-ache.
Tooth-less.
Tooth-pick.
Tooth-some.
Top.
To-paz.
To-per.
To-phet.
Top-ic.
Top-ic-al.
Top-knot.
Top-mast.
Top-most.
To-pog-ra-pher.
Top-o-graph-ic.
Top-o-graph-ic-al.
To-pog-ra-phy.
Top-ple.
Torch.
Torch-light.
Tore.
Tor-ment.
Tor-ment-er.
Tor-ment-or.
Torn.
Tor-na-do.
Tor-pe-do.

Tor-pid.
Tor-pid-i-ty.
Tor-pid-ness.
Tor-por.
Tor-re-fy.
Tor-rent.
Tor-rid.
Tor-sion.
Tort.
Tor-toise.
Tort-u-ous.
Tort-ure.
To-ry.
To-ry-ism.
Toss.
To-tal.
To-tal-i-ty.
To-tal-ly.
Tot-ter.
Touch.
Touch-i-ness.
Touch-ing.
Touch-me-not.
Touch-stone.
Touch-wood.
Touch-y.
Tough.
Tough-en.
Tou-pee.
Tour.
Tour-ist.
Tour-na-ment.
Tour-ni-quet.
Touse.
Tow.
Tow-age.
To-ward.
To-wards.
To-ward-ly.
Tow-el.
Tow-er.
Tow-er-ing.
Tow-line.
Town.
Town-ship.
Towns-man.
Town-talk.
Tox-i-col-o-gy.
Toy.
Toy-man.
Toy-shop.
Trace.
Trace-a-ble.
Tra-cer-y.
Tra-che-a.
Track.
Track-less.
Tract.
Tract-a-ble.
Tract-a-bil-i-ty.

Trac-tate.
Tract-ile.
Trac-til-i-ty.
Trac-tion.
Trac-tive.
Trade.
Trad-er.
Trades-man.
Trade-wind.
Tra-di-tion.
Tra-di-tion-al.
Tra-di-tion-a-ry.
Tra-duce.
Traf-fic.
Traf-fick-er.
Tra-ge-di-an.
Trag-e-dy.
Trag-ic.
Trag-ic-al.
Trag-i-com-e-dy.
Trail.
Train.
Train-bands.
Train-oil.
Traipse.
Trait.
Trai-tor.
Trai-tor-ous.
Trai-tress.
Tra-ject.
Tra-jec-tion.
Tra-ject-o-ry.
Tram.
Tram-mel.
Tra-mon-tane.
Tramp.
Tramp-er.
Tram-ple.
Trance.
Tran-quil.
Tran-quil-ize.
Tran-quil-lize.
Tran-quil-li-ty.
Tran-quil-ly.
Trans-act.
Trans-ac-tion.
Trans-act-or.
Trans-al-pine.
Trans-at-lan-tic.
Tran-scend.
Tran-scend-ence.
Tran-scend-ent.
Tran-scend-ent-al.
Tran-scend-ent-ly.
Tran-scribe.
Tran-script.
Tran-scrip-tion.
Tran-sept.

Trans-fer
Trans-fer-a-ble.
Trans-fer-ence.
Trans-fer-rence.
Trans-fer-ri-ble.
Trans - fig - u - ra - tion.
Trans-fig-ure.
Trans-fix.
Trans-form.
Trans - for - ma - tion.
Trans-fuse.
Trans-fu-sion.
Trans-gress.
Trans-gres-sion.
Trans-gress-or.
Tran-sient.
Tran-sient-ly.
Tran-sit.
Tran-si-tion.
Tran-si-tion-al.
Tran-si-tive.
Tran-si-to-ry.
Trans-late.
Trans-la-tion.
Trans-la-tor.
Trans-lu-cent.
Trans-ma-rine.
Trans-mi-grate.
Trans - mi - gra - tion.
Trans-mis-si-ble.
Trans-mis-sion.
Trans-mis-sive.
Trans-mit.
Trans-mit-tal.
Trans-mu-ta-ble.
Trans - mu - ta - tion.
Trans-mute.
Tran-som.
Trans-par-en-cy.
Trans-par-ent.
Trans-pierce.
Tran-spi-ra-tion.
Tran-spire.
Trans-plant.
Trans - plan - ta - tion.
Trans-port.
Trans - por - ta - tion.
Trans-pos-al.
Trans-pose.
Trans-po-si-tion.
Trans-ship.
Tran-sub-stan-ti-a-tion.
Tran-sude.

Trans-verse.
Trap.
Tra-pan.
Trap-door.
Tra-pe-zi-um.
Trap-e-zoid.
Trap-pings.
Trash.
Trash-y.
Trav-ail.
Trav-el.
Trav-el-er.
Trav-el-ler.
Trav-erse.
Trav-es-ty.
Tray.
Treach-er-ous.
Treach-er-y.
Trea-cle.
Tread.
Tread-le.
Tred-dle.
Tread-mill.
Trea-son.
Trea-son-a-ble.
Treas-ure.
Treas-ur-er.
Treas-ur-y.
Treat.
Trea-tise.
Treat-ment.
Trea-ty.
Treb-le.
Treb-ly.
Tree.
Tree-nail.
Tre-foil.
Trel-lis.
Trem-ble.
Tre-men-dous.
Tre-mor.
Trem-u-lous.
Trench.
Tren-chant.
Trench-er.
Trench-er-man
Trend.
Tre-pan.
Tre-phine.
Trep-i-da-tion.
Tres-pass.
Tress.
Tres-tle.
Tret.
Trev-et.
Trey.
Tri-ad.
Tri-al.
Tri-an-gle.
Tri-an-gu-lar.

Tribe.
Trib-u-la-tion.
Tri-bu-nal.
Trib-une.
Trib-u-ta-ry.
Trib-ute.
Trice.
Trick.
Trick-er-y.
Trick-ish.
Trick-le.
Trick-ster.
Tri-col-ored.
Tri-cus-pid.
Tri-dent.
Tri-dent-ate.
Tri-en-ni-al.
Tri-en-ni-al-ly.
Tri-er.
Tri-fid.
Tri-fle.
Tri-fling.
Tri-fo-li-ate.
Tri-form.
Trig.
Trig-ger.
Tri-glyph.
Trig-o-no-met-ric-al.
Trig-o-nom-e-try.
Tri-graph.
Tri-he-dral.
Tri-he-dron.
Tri-lat-er-al.
Tri-lit-er-al.
Trill.
Trill-ion.
Trim.
Trim-mer.
Trim-ming.
Trine.
Trin-i-ta-ri-an.
Trin-i-ty.
Trink-et.
Tri-no-mi-al.
Tri-o.
Trip.
Trip-ar-tite.
Tripe.
Tri-per-son-al.
Trip-ham-mer.
Trip-thong.
Trip-thon-gal.
Trip-le.
Trip-let.
Trip-li-cate.
Tri-plic-i-ty.
Tri-pod.
Tri-sect.

Tri-sec-tion.
Tris-yl-lab-ic.
Tri-syl-la-ble.
Trite.
Tri-the-ism.
Tri-the-ist.
Tri-the-ist-ic.
Trit-u-ra-ble.
Trit-u-rate.
Trit-u-ra-tion.
Tri-umph.
Tri-umph-al.
Tri-umph-ant.
Tri-um-vir.
Tri-um-vi-rate.
Tri-une.
Tri-u-ni-ty.
Triv-et.
Triv-i-al.
Tro-car.
Trod.
Trod-den.
Troll.
Trol-lop.
Trom-bone.
Troop.
Troop-er.
Trope.
Tro-phied.
Tro-phy.
Trop-ic.
Trop-ic-al.
Trot.
Troth.
Trot-ter.
Troub-le.
Troub-le-some.
Troub-lous.
Trough.
Trounce.
Trow-sers.
Trous-seau.
Trout.
Tro-ver.
Trow.
Trow-el.
Troy-weight.
Tru-ant.
Truce.
Truck.
Truck-le.
Truck-le-bed.
Truck-man.
Tru-cu-lence.
Tru-cu-lent.
Trudge.
True.
Truf-fle.
Tru-ism.
Trull.

Tru-ly.
Trump.
Trump-er-y.
Trump-et.
Trump-et-er.
Trun-cate.
Trun-ca-ted.
Trun-ca-tion.
Trun-cheon.
Trun-dle.
Trun-dle-bed.
Trunk.
Trun-nion.
Truss.
Trust.
Trust-ee.
Trust-i-ly.
Trust-i-ness.
Trust-y.
Truth.
Truth-ful.
Try.
Tub.
Tube.
Tu-ber.
Tu-ber-cle.
Tu-ber-cu-lar.
Tu-ber-cu-lous.
Tube-rose.
Tu-ber-ous.
Tu-bu-lar.
Tu-bu-lous.
Tuck.
Tuck-er.
Tues-day.
Tuft.
Tuft-ed.
Tug.
Tu-i-tion.
Tu-lip.
Tum-ble.
Tum-bler.
Tum-brel.
Tu-me-fac-tion.
Tu-me-fy.
Tu-mid.
Tu-mor.
Tu-mu-lar.
Tu-mu-lous.
Tu-mult.
Tu-mult-u-a-ry.
Tu-mult-u-ous.
Tun.
Tune.
Tune-ful.
Tu-nic.
Tu-ni-cle.
Tun-nel.
Tur-ban.
Tur-bid.

Tur-bid-ness.
Tur-bi-na-ted.
Tur-bine.
Tur-bot.
Tur-bu-lence.
Tur-bu-len-cy.
Tur-bu-lent.
Tu-reen.
Turf.
Turf-y.
Tur-ges-cence.
Tur-gid.
Tur-gid-i-ty.
Tur-key.
Tur-kois.
Tur-mer-ic.
Tur-moil.
Turn.
Turn-coat.
Turn-er-y.
Tur nip.
Turn-key.
Turn-pike.
Turn-sole.
Turn-stile.
Tur-pen-tine.
Tur-pi-tude.
Tur-quoise.
Tur-ret.
Tur-ret-ed.
Tur-tle.
Tur-tle-dove
Tus-can.
Tusk.
Tus-sle.
Tu-te-lage.
Tu-te-lar.
Tu-te-la-ry.
Tu-tor.
Tu-tor-age.
Tu-tor-ess.
Twad-dle.
Twain.
Twang.
Twat-tle.
Tweak.
Twee-dle.
Tweeds.
Twee-zers.
Twelfth.
Twelve.
Twelve-month.
Twen-ti-eth.
Twen-ty.
Twice.
Twig.
Twi-light.
Twill.
Twin.
Twine.

91

Twinge.
Twink-le.
Twink-ling.
Twirl.
Twist.
Twit.
Twitch.
Twit-ter.
Two.
Two-edged.
Two-fold.
Tym-bal.
Tym-pan.
Tym-pa-num.
Type.
Ty-phoid.
Ty-phoon.
Ty-phus.
Typ-ic-al.
Typ-ic-al-ly.
Typ-i-fy.
Ty-pog-ra-pher.
Typ-o-graph-ic-al.
Ty-pog-ra-phy.
Ty-ran-nic.
Ty-ran-nic-al.
Ty-ran-nic-al-ly.
Ty-ran-ni-cide.
Tyr-an-nize.
Tyr-an-nous.
Tyr-an-ny.
Ty-rant.
Ty-ro.

U

U-biq-ui-ty.
U-biq-ui-ta-ry.
Ud-der.
Ug-li-ness.
Ug-ly.
Ul-cer.
Ul-cer-ate.
Ul-cer-a-tion.
Ul-cer-ous.
Ul-lage.
Ul-te-ri-or.
Ul-ti-mate.
Ul-ti-mate-ly.
Ul-ti-ma-tum.
Ul-tra.
Ul-tra-ma-rine.
Ul-tra-mon-tane.
Ul-tra-mun-dane.
Um-bel.
Um-bel-**lif-er-ous.**

Um-ber.
Um-bil-ic-al.
Um-bles.
Um-brage.
Um-bra-geous.
Um-brel-la.
Um-pi-rage.
Um-pire.
Un.
Un-a-ble.
Un-ac-cept-a-ble.
Un-ac-count-**a-ble.**
Un-ad-vis-a-ble.
Un-af-fect-ed.
Un-al-loyed.
Un-al-ter-a-ble.
Un-a-mi-a-ble.
Un-a-nim-i-ty.
U-nan-i-mous.
U-nan-i-mous-ly.
Un-an-**swer-a-ble.**
Un-apt.
Un-as-sum-ing.
Un-a-vail-ing.
Un-a-void-a-ble.
Un-a-void-a-bly.
Un-a-ware.
Un-a-wares.
Un-bar.
Un-be-com-ing.
Un-be-lief.
Un-be-liev-er.
Un-be-liev-ing.
Un-bend.
Un-bend-ing.
Un-bi-as.
Un-bind.
Un-blem-ished.
Un-blest.
Un-bolt.
Un-born.
Un-bo-som.
Un-bound-ed.
Un-bri-dle.
Un-bro-ken.
Un-buck-le.
Un-bur-ied.
Un-bur-den.
Un-but-ton.
Un-ceas-ing.
Un-cer-e-mo-ni-**ous.**
Un-cer-tain.
Un-cer-tain-ly.
Un-cer-tain-ty.
Un-chain.
Un-change-a-ble.
Un-change-a-bly.

Un-char-i-ta-ble.
Un-chris-tian.
Un-church.
Un-civ-il.
Un-civ-il-ized.
Un-civ-il-ly.
Un-clasp.
Un-cle.
Un-clean.
Un-clean-ness.
Un-close.
Un-coil.
Un-come-ly.
Un-com-fort-**a-ble.**
Un-com-fort-**a-bly.**
Un-com-mon.
Un-com-mon-ly.
Un-com-pro-mis-ing.
Un-con-cern.
Un-con-cern-ed-ly.
Un-con-di-**tion-al.**
Un-con-quer-**a-ble.**
Un-con-scion-a-ble.
U**n-con-scion-a-bly.**
Un-con-scious.
Un-con-scious-ly.
Un-con-scious-ness.
Un-con-sti-**tu-tion-al.**
Un-con-sti-**tu-tion-al-i-ty.**
Un-con-trol-**la-ble.**
Un-con-vert-ed.
Un-cork.
Un-court-e-ous.
Un-couth.
Un-couth-ness.
Un-cov-er.
Unc-tion.
Unct-u-ous.
Un-curb.
Un-curl.
Un-dat-ed.
Un-daunt-ed.
Un-de-ceive.
Un-de-ni-a-ble.
Un-de-ni-a-bly.
Un-der.
Un-der-a-gent.
Un-der-bid.

Un-der-brush.
Un-der-cur-rent.
Un-der-do.
Un-der-grad-**u-ate.**
Un-der-ground.
Un-der-growth.
Un-der-hand.
Un-der-hand-ed.
Un-der-lay.
Un-der-let.
Un-der-lie.
Un-der-line.
Un-der-ling.
Un-der-mine.
Un-der-neath.
Un-der-pin.
Un-der-pin-ning.
U**n-der-rate.**
Un-der-score.
Un-der-sell.
Un-der-sign.
Un-der-shot.
Un-der-stand.
Un-der-stand-ing.
Un-der-stood.
Un-der-strap-per.
Un-der-take.
Un-der-tak-er.
Un-der-tak-ing.
Un-der-took.
Un-der-tone.
U**n-**der-tow.
Un-der-went.
Un-der-val-ue.
Un-der-wood.
Un-der-work.
Un-der-write.
Un-der-wri-ter.
U**n-**der-sign-ing.
Un-de-vi-a-ting.
Un-di-vid-ed.
Un-do.
Un-do-ing.
Un-done.
Un-doubt-ed.
Un-doubt-ed-ly.
Un-dress.
Un-due.
Un-du-late.
Un-du-la-ted.
Un-du-la-tion.
Un-du-la-to-ry.
Un-du-ly.
Un-dy-ing.
Un-earth.
Un-earth-ly.
Un-ea-si-ness.

Un-ea-sy.
Un-end-ing.
Un-e-qual.
Un-e-qual-ly.
Un-e-quiv-o-cal.
Un-err-ing.
Un-e-ven.
Un-e-ven-ness.
Un-ex-cep-tion-a-ble.
Un-ex-cep-**tion**-a-bly.
Un-ex-pect-ed.
Un-ex-pect-ed-ly
Un-fail-ing.
Un-fair.
Un-fair-ly.
Un-fair-ness.
Un-faith-ful.
Un-faith-ful-ness.
Un-fash-ion-a-ble.
Un-fast-en.
Un-fath-**om**-a-**ble.**
Un-fa-vor-a-ble.
Un-feel-ing.
Un-feigned.
Un-feign-ed-ly.
Un-fil-ial.
Un-fin-ished.
Un-fit.
Un-fix.
Un-fold.
Un-for-giv-ing.
Un-fort-u-nate.
Un-found-ed.
Un-friend-ly.
Un-fruit-ful.
Un-furl.
Un-fur-nish.
Un-gain-ly.
Un-gen-er-ous.
Un-god-li-ness.
Un-god-ly.
Un-gov-ern-a-ble.
Un-grace-ful.
Un-gra-cious.
Un-grate-ful.
Un-guent.
Un-hal-lowed.
Un-hand-some.
Un-hand-some-ly.
Un-hand-y.
Un-hap-pi-ly.
Un-hap-pi-ness.
Un-hap-py.
Un-har-ness.

Un-health-y.
Un-heard.
Un-hinge.
Un-hitch.
Un-ho-li-ness.
Un-ho-ly.
Un-hook.
Un-horse.
Un-hurt.
U-ni-corn.
U-ni-fi-ca-tion.
U-ni-form.
U-ni-form-i-ty.
U-ni-form-ly.
Un-im-peach-a-ble.
Un-in-tel-li-gi-ble.
Un-in-ter-est-ed.
Un-ion.
Un-ion-ist.
U-nip-a-rous.
U-nique.
U-ni-son.
U-nis-o-nant.
U-nis-o-nous.
U-nit.
U-ni-ta-ri-an.
U-ni-ta-ri-an-ism.
U-nite.
U-nit-ed-ly.
U-ni-ty.
U-ni-valve.
U-ni-valv-u-lar.
U-ni-ver-sal.
U-ni-ver-sal-ism.
U-ni-ver-sal-ist.
U-ni-ver-sal-i-ty.
U-ni-ver-sal-ly.
U-ni-verse.
U-ni-ver-si-ty.
Un-just.
Un-just-ly.
Un-kind.
Un-kind-ly.
Un-kind-ness.
Un-knit.
Un-know-ing-ly.
Un-lace.
Un-lade.
Un-law-ful.
Un-law-ful-ly.
Un-law-ful-ness.
Un-learn.
Un-learn-ed.
Un-less.
Un-let-tered.
Un-like.
Un-like-ly.

Un-like-ness.
Un-lim-it-ed.
Un-link.
Un-load.
Un-lock.
Un-love-li-ness.
Un-love-ly.
Un-luck-y.
Un-man.
Un-man-ly.
Un-man-nered.
Un-man-ner-ly.
Un-mask.
Un-mean-ing.
Un-mer-ci-ful.
Un-moor.
Un-nat-ur-al.
Un-nec-es-sa-ri-ly.
Un-nec-es-sa-ry.
Un-neigh-bor-ly.
Un-nerve.
Un-num-bered.
Un-ob-tru-sive.
Un-os-ten-ta-tious.
Un-pack.
Un-pal-a-ta-ble.
Un-par-al-leled.
Un-par-lia-ment-a-ry.
Un-pin.
Un-pleas-ant.
Un-pop-u-lar.
Un-prec-e-dent-ed.
Un-prej-u-diced.
Un-pre-tend-ing.
Un-prin-ci-pled.
Un-pro-duc-tive.
Un-prof-it-a-ble.
Un-prom-is-ing.
Un-pro-pi-tious.
Un-qual-i-fied.
Un-ques-tion-a-ble.
Un-ques-tion-a-bly.
Un-qui-et.
Un-rav-el.
Un-re-al.
Un-rea-son-a-ble.
Un-rea-son-a-ble-ness.
Un-rea-son-a-bly.
Un-re-gen-er-ate.
Un-re-lent-ing.
Un-re-mit-ting.
Un-re-serve.

Un-re-served.
Un-re-serv-ed-ly.
Un-rest.
Un-rig.
Un-right-eous.
Un-right-eous-ness.
Un-ripe.
Un-ri-valed.
Un-ri-valled.
Un-ri-vet.
Un-robe.
Un-roll.
Un-roof.
Un-root.
Un-ruf-fled.
Un-ru-ly.
Un-sad-dle.
Un-safe.
Un-sal-a-ble.
Un-sat-is-fac-to-**ry.**
Un-sav-o-ry.
Un-say.
Un-screw.
Un-scru-pu-lous.
Un-seal.
Un-search-a-ble.
Un-sea-son-a-ble.
Un-sea-son-a-bly.
Un-seat.
Un-seem-ly.
Un-seen.
Un-set-tle.
Un-shack-le.
Un-shak-en.
Un-sheathe.
Un-ship.
Un-sight-ly.
Un-skill-ful.
Un-skil-ful.
Un-skill-ful-ness.
Un-skil-ful-ness.
Un-so-cia-ble.
Un-so-phis-ti-ca-ted.
Un-sound.
Un-sound-ness.
Un-spar-ing.
Un-speak-a-ble.
Un-speak-a-bly.
Un-spot-ted.
Un-sta-ble.
Un-stead-y.
Un-stop.
Un-string.
Un-suc-cess-ful
Un-suit-a-ble.
Un-suit-a-bly
Un-sung.

Un-swathe.	Up-on.	Ut-ter-ly.	Van-dal-ism.
Un-tam-a-ble.	Up-per.	Ut-ter-most.	Van-dyke.
Un-think-ing.	Up-per-hand.	U-ve-ous.	Vane.
Un-thrift-y.	Up-per-most.	Ux-o-ri-ous.	Van-guard.
Un-tie.	Up-raise.		Va-nil-la.
Un-til.	Up-right.		Van-ish.
Un-time-ly.	Up-right-ly.	**V**	Van-i-ty.
Un-tir-ing.	Up-right-ness.		Van-quish.
Un-to.	Up-roar.		Van-tage.
Un-told.	Up-root.	VA-CAN-CY.	Van-tage-ground.
Un-to-ward.	Up-set.	Va-cant.	Vap-id.
Un-tract-a-ble.	Up-shot.	Va-cate.	Va-por.
Un-trav-el-ed.	Up-side.	Va-ca-tion.	Vap-o-ra-tion.
Un-true.	Up-start.	Vac-ci-nate.	Va-por-bath.
Un-tru-ly.	Up-ward.	Vac-ci-na-tion.	Vap-or-ize.
Un-truss.	Up-wards.	Vac-cine.	Va-por-y.
Un-truth.	U-ra-ni-um.	Vac-il-lan-cy.	Va-ri-a-ble.
Un-twine.	U-ran-og-ra-phy.	Vac-il-late.	Va-ri-a-ble-ness.
Un-twist.	U-ran-ol-o-gy.	Vac-il-la-tion.	Va-ri-a-bly.
Un-used.	U-ra-nus.	Va-cu-i-ty.	Va-ri-ance.
Un-u-su-al.	Ur-ban.	Vac-u-um.	Va-ri-a-tion.
Un-ut-ter a-ble.	Ur-bane.	Vag-a-bond.	Var-i-cose.
Un-var-nished.	Ur-ban-i-ty.	Va-ga-ry.	Va-ri-e-gate.
Un-veil	Ur-chin.	Va-gran-cy.	Va-ri-e-ga-tion.
Un-wa-ri-ly.	Urge.	Va-grant.	Va-ri-e-ty.
Un-wa-ri-ness.	Ur-gen-cy.	Vague.	Va-ri-o-loid.
Un-war-rant-a-ble.	Ur-gent.	Vague-ly.	Va-ri-o-lous.
	U-ri-nal.	Vail.	Va-ri-ous.
Un-war-rant-a-bly.	U-ri-na-ry.	Vain.	Va-ri-ous-ly.
	U-rine.	Vain-glo-ri-ous.	Var-let.
Un-wa-ry.	Urn.	Vain-glo-ry.	Var-nish.
Un-wea-ried.	Us.	Vain-ly.	Va-ry.
Un-weave.	Us-age.	Val-ance.	Vas-cu-lar.
Un-well.	Use.	Vale.	Vase.
Un-whole-some.	Use-ful.	Val-e-dic-tion.	Vas-sal.
Un-wield-y.	Use-ful-ly.	Val-e-dic-to-ry.	Vas-sal-age.
Un-will-ing.	Use-ful-ness.	Val-en-tine.	Vast.
Un-wind.	Use-less.	Va-le-ri-an.	Vas-ta-tion.
Un-wise.	Ush-er.	Val-et.	Vast-ly.
Un-wit-ting-ly.	Us-que-baugh.	Val-e-tu-di-na-ri-an.	Vast-ness.
Un-wont-ed.	U-su-al.		Vat.
Un-wor-thi-ly.	U-su-al-ly.	Val-e-tu-di-na-ry.	Va-tic-i-nate.
Un-wor-thi-ness.	U-su-cap-tion.		Va-tic-i-na-tion.
Un-wor-thy.	U-su-fruct.	Val-iant.	Vault.
Un-wreathe.	U-su-rer.	Val-id.	Vault-ed.
Un-writ-ten.	U-su-ri-ous.	Va-lid-i-ty.	Vaunt.
Un-yield-ing.	U-surp.	Va-lise.	Veal
Un-yoke.	U-sur-pa-tion.	Val-la-tion.	Ve-dette.
Up.	U-surp-er.	Val-ley.	Veer.
Up-braid.	U-su-ry.	Val-or.	Veg-e-ta-ble.
Up-cast.	U-ten-sil.	Val-or-ous.	Veg-e-tate.
Up-heave.	U-ter-ine.	Val-u-a-ble.	Veg-e-ta-tion.
Up-heav-al.	U-til-i-ta-ri-an.	Val-u-a-tion.	Veg-e-ta-tive.
Up-hill.	U-til-i-ta-ri-an-ism.	Val-ue.	Ve-he-mence.
Up-hold.		Valve.	Ve-he-ment.
Up-hold-er.	U-til-i-ty.	Valv-u-lar.	Ve-hi-cle.
Up-hol-ster-er.	Ut-most.	Vamp.	Veil.
Up-hol-ster-y.	U-to-pi-an.	Vam-pire.	Vein.
Up-land.	Ut-ter.	Van.	Veined.
Up-lift.	Ut-ter-ance.	Van-dal.	Vein-y.

Vel-ium.	Ver-i-fy.	Vex.	Vin-di-cate.
Ve-loc-i-pede.	Ver-i-ly.	Vex-a-tion.	Vin-di-ca-tion.
Ve-loc-i-ty.	Ver-i-sim-i-lar.	Vex-a-tious.	Vin-di-ca-tive
Vel-vet.	Ver-i-si-mil-i-tude.	Vi-a-ble.	Vin-di-ca-to-ry
Vel-vet-een.		Vi-a-duct.	Vin-di-ca-tor.
Vel-vet-y.	Ver-i-ta-ble.	Vi-al.	Vin-dic-tive.
Ve-nal.	Ver-i-ta-bly.	Vi-ands.	Vine.
Ve-nal-i-ty.	Ver-i-ty.	Vi-brate.	Vin-e-gar.
Vend.	Ver-juice.	Vi-bra-tion.	Vine-yard.
Ven-dee.	Ver-mi-cel-li.	Vi-bra-to-ry.	Vi-nous.
Vend-er.	Ver-mic-u-lar.	Vic-ar.	Vint-age.
Vend-i-ble.	Ver-mic-u-late.	Vic-ar-age.	Vint-a-ger.
Ven-di-tion.	Ver-mic-u-la-tion.	Vi-ca-ri-ous.	Vint-ner.
Ven-due.		Vi-ce.	Vin-y.
Ve-neer.	Ver-mi-fuge.	Vice.	Vi-ol.
Ven-er-a-ble.	Ver-mil-ion.	Vice-ad-mi-ral.	Vi-o-la.
Ven-er-ate.	Ver-min.	Vice-con-sul.	Vi-o-la-ble.
Ven-er-a-tion.	Ver-mip-a-rous.	Vice-ge-rent.	Vi-o-la-ceous.
Ve-ne-re-al.	Ver-miv-o-rous.	Vice-re-gal.	Vi-o-late.
Ven-e-sec-tion.	Ver-nac-u-lar.	Vice-roy.	Vi-o-la-tion.
Venge-ance.	Ver-nal.	Vice-roy-al-ty.	Vi-o-lence.
Venge-ful.	Ver-sa-tile.	Vic-i-nage.	Vi-o-lent.
Ve-ni-al.	Ver-sa-til-i-ty.	Vi-cin-i-ty.	Vi-o-let.
Ven-i-son.	Verse.	Vi-cious.	Vi-o-lin.
Ven-om.	Versed.	Vi-cis-si-tude.	Vi-per.
Ven-om-ous.	Ver-si-fi-ca-tion.	Vic-tim.	Vi-per-ine.
Ve-nous.	Ver-si-fi-er.	Vic-tim-ize.	Vi-ra-go.
Vent.	Ver-si-fy.	Vic-tor.	Vir-gin.
Vent-hole.	Ver-sion.	Vic-to-ri-ous.	Vir-gin-al.
Ven-ti-duct.	Ver-te-bra.	Vic-to-ry.	Vir-gin-i-ty.
Ven-ti-late.	Ver-te-bral.	Vict-ual.	Vi-rid-i-ty
Ven-ti-la-tion.	Ver-te-brate.	Vict-ual-er.	Vi-rile.
Ven-ti-la-tor.	Ver-te-bre.	Vict-uals.	Vi-ril-i-ty.
Ven-tral.	Ver-tex.	Vi-del-i-cet.	Vir-tu.
Ven-tri-cle.	Ver-ti-cal.	Vie.	Virt-u-al.
Ven-tril-o-quism.	Ver-tic-i-ty	View.	Virt-u-al-ly.
Ven-tril-o-quist.	Ver-tig-i-nous.	View-less.	Vir-tue.
Vent-ure.	Ver-ti-go.	Vig-il.	Vir-tu-o-so.
Vent-ure-some.	Ver-vain.	Vig-i-lance.	Virt-u-ous.
Vent-ur-ous.	Ver-y.	Vig-i-lant.	Vir-u-lence.
Ven-ue.	Ves-i-cate.	Vignette.	Vir-u-lent.
Ve-nus.	Ves-i-ca-tion.	Vig-or.	Vi-rus.
Ve-ra-cious.	Ves-i-ca-to-ry.	Vig-or-ous.	Vis-age.
Ve-rac-i-ty.	Ves-i-cle.	Vile.	Vis-cer-a.
Ve-ran-da.	Ve-sic-u-lar.	Vile-ly.	Vis-cer-al.
Verb.	Ves-per.	Vil-i-fi-er.	Vis-cid.
Verb-al.	Ves-sel.	Vil-i-fy.	Vis-cid-i-ty
Verb-al-ly.	Vest.	Vil-la.	Vis-cos-i-ty.
Ver-ba-tim.	Ves-tal.	Vil-lage.	Vis-count.
Ver-bi-age.	Vest-ed.	Vil-la-ger.	Vis-count-ess.
Ver-bose.	Ves-ti-bule.	Vil-lain.	Vis-cous.
Ver-bos-i-ty.	Ves-tige.	Vil-lain-ous.	Vise.
Ver-dan-cy.	Vest-ment.	Vil-lan-ous.	Vis-i-bil-i-ty.
Ver-dant.	Ves-try.	Vil-lain-y.	Vis-i-ble.
Ver-dict.	Vest-ure.	Vil-la-ny.	Vis-i-bly.
Ver-di-gris.	Vetch.	Vil-lan-age	Vis-ion.
Verd-ure.	Vet-er-an.	Vil-lose.	Vis-ion-a-ry.
Verge.	Vet-er-i-na-ri-an.	Vil-lous.	Vis-it.
Verg-er.	Vet-er-i-na-ry.	Vi-min-e-ous.	Vis-it-ant.
Ver-i-fi-ca-tion.	Ve-to.	Vi-na-ceous.	Vis-it-a-tion

Vis-it-or.
Vis-or.
Vis-ta.
Vis-u-al.
Vi-tal.
Vi-tal-i-ty.
Vi-tal-ly.
Vi-tals.
Vi-ti-ate.
Vi-ti-a-tion.
Vit-re-ous.
Vit-ri-fac-tion.
Vit-ri-fy.
Vit-ri-ol.
Vit-ri-ol-ic.
Vi-tu-per-ate.
Vi-tu-per-a-tion.
Vi-tu-per-a-tive.
Vi-va-cious.
Vi-vac-i-ty.
Viv-id.
Viv-i-fi-ca-tion.
Viv-i-fy.
Vi-vip-a-rous.
Vix-en.
Viz-ard.
Viz-ier.
Vo-ca-ble.
Vo-cab-u-la-ry.
Vo-cal.
Vo-cal-ic.
Vo-cal-ist.
Vo-cal-i-ty.
Vo-cal-ize.
Vo-ca-tion.
Voc-a-tive.
Vo-cif-er-ate.
Vo-cif-er-a-tion.
Vo-cif-er-ous.
Vogue.
Voice.
Void.
Void-ance.
Void-er.
Vol-a-tile.
Vol-a-til-i-ty.
Vol-a-til-ize.
Vol-can-ic.
Vol-ca-no.
Vo-li-tion.
Vol-ley.
Vol-u-bil-i-ty.
Vol-u-ble.
Vol-u-bly.
Vol-ume.
Vo-lu-mi-nous.
Vol-un-ta-ri-ly.
Vol-un-ta-ry.
Vol-un-teer.
Vo-lupt-u-a-ry.

Vo-lupt-u-ous.
Vo-lute.
Vom-it.
Vo-ra-cious.
Vo-rac-i-ty.
Vor-tex.
Vor-ti-cal.
Vo-ta-ry.
Vote.
Vot-er.
Vo-tive.
Vouch.
Vouch-er.
Vouch-safe.
Vow.
Vow-el.
Voy-age.
Voy-a-ger.
Vul-can-ize.
Vul-gar.
Vul-gar-ism.
Vul-gar-i-ty.
Vul-gar-ly.
Vul-gate.
Vul-ner-a-ble.
Vul-ner-a-ry.
Vul-pine.
Vult-ure.
Vult-ur-ine.

W

Wab-ble.
Wad.
Wad-ded.
Wad-ding.
Wad-dle.
Wade.
Wa-fer.
Waf-fle.
Waft.
Wag.
Wage.
Wa-ger.
Wa-ges.
Wag-ger-y.
Wag-gish.
Wag-on.
Wag-on-er.
Waif.
Wail.
Wain.
Wain-scot.
Waist.
Waist-band.
Waist-coat.
Wait.
Wait-er.

Wait-ing-maid.
Waive.
Wake.
Wake-ful.
Wak-en.
Wale.
Walk.
Wall.
Wal-let.
Wall-eye.
Wal-lop.
Wal-low.
Wal-nut.
Wal-rus.
Waltz.
Wam-pum.
Wan.
Wand.
Wan-der.
Wan-der-er.
Wane.
Wan-ness.
Want.
Wan-ton.
War.
War-ble.
War-bler.
War-cry.
Ward.
Ward-en.
Ward-er.
Ward-robe.
Ward-room.
Ware.
Wares.
Ware-house.
War-fare.
Wa-ri-ly.
Wa-ri-ness.
War-like.
Warm.
Warmth.
Warn.
Warn-ing.
Warp.
War-rant.
War-rant-a-ble.
War-ran-tee.
War-ran-ty.
War-ren.
War-ri-or.
Wart.
Wart-y.
War-worn.
Wa-ry.
Was.
Wash.
Wash-ball.
Wash-board.
Wash-er.

Wash-er-wom-an.
Wash-ing.
Wash-y.
Wasp.
Wasp-ish.
Was-sail.
Wast.
Waste.
Waste-ful.
Watch.
Watch-er.
Watch-ful.
Watch-house.
Watch-man.
Watch-tow-er.
Watch-word.
Wa-ter.
Wa-ter-col-ors.
Wa-ter-course.
Wa-ter-cress.
Wa-ter-fall.
Wa-ter-fowl.
Wa-ter-i-ness.
Wa-ter-ish.
Wa-ter-man.
Wa-ter-mark.
Wa-ter-mel-on.
Wa-ter-mill.
Wa-ter-pot.
Wa-ter-proof.
Wa-ter-rot.
Wa-ter-spout.
Wa-ter-tight.
Wa-ter-wheel.
Wa-ter-y.
Wat-tle.
Waul.
Wave.
Wave-less.
Wave-of-fer-ing.
Wa-ver.
Wa-vy.
Wax.
Wax-en.
Wax-work.
Wax-y.
Way.
Way-bill.
Way-far-er.
Way-far-ing.
Way-lay.
Way-ward.
We.
Weak.
Weak-en.
Weak-ly.
Weak-ness.
Weal.
Wealth.

Wealth-y	West-er-ly	Whim.	Wick-er.
Wean.	West-ern.	Whim-sey.	Wick-et.
Wean-ling.	West-ward.	Whim-per.	Wide.
Weap-on.	West-ward-ly.	Whim-si-cal.	Wide-ly.
Wear.	Wet.	Whin.	Wid-en.
Wea-ri-some.	Weth-er.	Whine.	Wid-geon.
Wea-ry.	Whale.	Whin-ny.	Wid-ow.
Wea-sand.	Whale-bone.	Whip.	Wid-ow-er.
Wea-sel.	Whale-man.	Whip-ple-tree.	Wid-ow-hood.
Weath-er.	Wharf.	Whip-poor-will.	Width.
Weath-er-cock.	Wharf-in-ger.	Whip-saw.	Wield.
Weath-er-gage.	What.	Whip-stock.	Wife.
Weath-er-glass.	What-ev-er.	Whir.	Wig.
Weath-er-wise.	What-not.	Whirl.	Wight.
Weave.	**What-so-ev-er.**	Whirl-i-gig.	Wig**-wam.**
Weav-er.	**Wheat.**	Whirl-pool.	Wild.
Web.	Wheat-en.	Whirl-wind.	Wild-cat.
Webbed.	Whee-dle.	Whisk.	Wil-der-ness.
Web-bing.	Wheel.	Whisk-er.	Wild-fire.
Web-foot-ed.	Wheel-bar-row.	Whis-ky.	Wild-ly.
Wed.	Wheel-wright.	Whis-key.	Wile.
Wed-ding.	Wheeze.	Whis-per.	Wi-li-ness.
Wedge.	Whelm.	Whist.	Will.
Wed-lock.	Whelp.	Whis-tle.	Will-ful.
Wednes-day.	When.	Whit.	Wil-ful.
Wee.	Whence.	White.	Will-ful-ly.
Weed.	Whence-so-ev-er.	Whit-en.	Wil-ful-ly.
Weed-y.	When-ev-er.	White-ness.	Will-ful-ness.
Week.	When-so-ev-er.	White-swell-ing	Wil-ful-ness.
Week-day.	Where.	White-wash.	Will-ing.
Week-ly.	Where-a-bouts.	Whith-er.	Will-ing-ly.
Ween.	Where-as.	Whith-er-so-**ev-**	Will-ing-ness.
Weep.	Where-at.	er.	Wil-low.
Wee-vil.	Where-by.	Whit-ing.	Wil-low-y.
Weft.	Where-fore.	Whit-ish.	Wilt.
Weigh.	Where-in.	Whit-leath-er.	Wi-ly.
Weight.	Where-in-to.	Whit-low.	Wim-ble.
Weight-y.	Where-of.	Whit-tle.	Win.
Weird.	Where-on.	Whiz.	Wince.
Wel-come.	Where-up-on.	Who.	Winch.
Weld.	Where-so-ev-er.	Who-ev-er.	Wind.
Wel-fare.	Where-to.	Whole.	Wind-age.
Wel-kin.	Where-up-on.	Whole-sale.	Wind-bound.
Well.	Wher-ev-er.	Whole-some.	Wind-fall.
Well-be-ing.	Where-with.	Whol-ly.	Wind-flow-er.
Well-bred.	Wher-ry.	Whom.	Wind-gall.
Well-nigh.	Whet.	Whom-so-ev-er.	Wind-gun.
Well-spent.	Wheth-er.	Whoop.	Wind-ing-sheet.
Well-sweep.	Whet-stone.	Whoop - **ing** -	Wind-lass.
Well-wish-er.	Whey.	cough.	Wind-mill.
Welsh.	Which.	Whore.	Win-dow.
Welt.	Whiff.	Whor-tle-ber-ry.	Wind-pipe.
Wel-ter.	Whif-fle.	Whose.	Wind-row.
Wen.	Whif-fle-tree.	Who-so-ev-er.	Wind-ward.
Wench.	Whig.	Whur.	Wind-y.
Went.	Whig-gish.	Why.	Wine.
Wept.	Whig-gism.	Wick.	Wine-bib-ber.
Were.	Whig-ger-y.	Wick-ed.	Wine-glass.
Wert.	While.	Wick-ed-**ly.**	Wing
West.	Whilst.	Wick-ed-ness.	**W**ink.

Win-ner.
Win-ning.
Win-now.
Win-ter.
Win-ter-green.
Win-ter-kill.
Win-ter-y.
Win-try.
Wipe.
Wip-er.
Wire.
Wire-draw-er.
Wire-pull-er.
Wir-y.
Wis-dom.
Wise.
Wise-a-cre.
Wish.
Wish-ful.
Wisp.
Wist-ful.
Wit.
Witch.
Witch-craft.
Witch-er-y.
With.
With-al.
With-draw.
With-draw-al.
Withe.
With-er.
With-ers.
With-hold.
With-in.
With-out.
With-stand.
With-y.
Wit-less.
Wit-ling.
Wit-ness.
Wit-ti-cism.
Wit-ti-ly.
Wit-ting-ly.
Wit-ty.
Wives.
Wiz-ard.
Wiz-en.
Woad.
Woe.
Woe-be-gone.
Wo-ful.
Woe-ful.
Wolf.
Wolf-ish.
Wolf's-bane.
Wom-an.
Wom-an-hood.
Wom-an-ly.
Womb.
Wom-en.

Won.
Won-der.
Won-der-ful.
Won-drous.
Wont.
Wont-ed.
Woo.
Wood.
Wood-bine.
Wood-chuck.
Wood-cock.
Wood-cut.
Wood-ed.
Wood-en.
Wood-house.
Wood-land.
Wood-nymph.
Wood-peck-er.
Wood-y.
Woo-er.
Woof.
Wool.
Wool-en.
Wool-len.
Wool-li-ness.
Wool-ly.
Wool-sack.
Word.
Word-i-ness.
Word-ing.
Word-y.
Wore.
Work.
Work-house.
Work-ing.
Work-man.
Work-man-ship.
Work-shop.
World.
World-li-ness.
World-ling.
World-ly.
Worm.
Worm-wood.
Worm-y.
Worn.
Wor-ry.
Worse.
Wor-ship.
Wor-ship-er.
Wor-ship-per.
Wor-ship-ful.
Worst.
Worst-ed.
Wort.
Worth.
Wor-thi-ly.
Worth-less.
Wor-thy.
Would.

Wound.
Wove.
Wov-en.
Wran-gle.
Wran-gler.
Wrap.
Wrap-per.
Wrap-ping.
Wrath.
Wrath-ful.
Wrath-y.
Wreak.
Wreath.
Wreathe.
Wreck.
Wreck-er.
Wren.
Wrench.
Wrest.
Wres-tle.
Wres-tler.
Wrest-ling.
Wretch.
Wretch-ed.
Wrig-gle.
Wrig-gler.
Wright.
Wring.
Wring-er.
Wrink-le.
Wrist.
Wrist-band.
Writ.
Write.
Writ-er.
Writhe.
Writ-ing.
Writ-ten.
Wrong.
Wrong-ful.
Wrong-head-ed.
Wrong-ly.
Wrote.
Wroth.
Wrought.
Wrung.
Wry.
Wry-ness.

X

Xan-thic.
Xe-bec.
Xy-log-ra-pher.
Xy-lo-graph-ic.
Xy-lo-graph-ic-al
Xy-log-ra-phy.
Xy-loph-a-geos.

Y

Yacht.
Yacht-ing.
Yam.
Yan-kee.
Yard.
Yard-arm.
Yard-stick.
Yard-wand.
Yarn.
Yar-row.
Yaw.
Yawl.
Yawn.
Ye.
Yea.
Yean.
Yean-ling.
Year.
Year-ling.
Year-ly.
Yearn.
Yearn-ing.
Yeast.
Yeast-y.
Yelk.
Yell.
Yel-low.
Yel-low Fe-ver.
Yel-low-ish.
Yel-lows.
Yelp.
Yeo-man.
Yeo-man-ry.
Yerk.
Yes.
Yest.
Yes-ter.
Yes-ter-day.
Yet.
Yew.
Yield.
Yield-ing.
Yoke.
Yoke-fel-low.
Yoke-mate.
Yolk.
Yon.
Yon-der.
Yore.
You.
Young.
Youn-ger.
Youn-gest.
Young-ish.
Young-ling.
Young-ster.
Your.

Your-self.	Zain.	Zest.	Zo-o-log-ic-al.
Youth.	Zam-bo.	Ze-tet-ic.	Zo-ol-o-gist.
Youth-ful.	Za-ny.	Zig-zag.	Zo-ol-o-gy.
Yule.	Zeal.	Zinc.	Zo-on-o-my.
	Zeal-ot.	Zinck-y.	Zo-o-phyte.
	Zeal-ous.	Zi-on.	Zo-o-phyt-ic.
Z	Ze-bra.	Zo-di-ac.	Zo-ot-o-mist.
	Ze-bu.	Zo-di-ac-al.	Zo-ot-o-my.
	Zend-a-ves-ta.	Zone.	Zouave.
Zap-fer.	Ze-nith.	Zo-og-ra-pher.	Zyg-o-mat-ic.
Zaim.	Zeph-yr.	Zo-o-graph-ic-al.	Zy-mol-o-gy.
Zaim-et.	Ze-ro.	Zo-og-ra-phy.	Zy-mot-ic.

OLD TYPE WANTED.

In the casting of new type we can use a part old worn type in the metal, adding our Nickel Alloy. We will accept any quantity of old type AT 10 CENTS PER POUND, in payment for new goods from our Catalogue. Ship the type by freight, prepaid, packed in strong boxes well nailed, or in heavy canvas bags.

KELSEY PRESS CO.,
Meriden, Connecticut.

NEW STAR JOBBER.
$60.00 ONLY.

Chase 7x11 inches. Cheapest and best press in the world. Costs little to run and little to buy. Speed 3500. Ink Fountain, if desired, $10.00.

$3. BINDING Machine.

For binding books of from 2 to 100 leaves with bright wire staples. Self feeding. Binds 500 an hour. Price with full directions, $3.00 [If mailed 35c extra.] Wire Staples 35c per 1000 or 10,000 for $3.00.

OUR $5.00 CUTTER.
For Brass Rules and Leads.
...Also...
Has Arrangement To Mitre Rules.

THE KELSEY PRESS CO.
Meriden, Conn., U. S. A.

SELF-INKING HAND PRESSES.

3 by 5 inch,	. .	$ 5.00
5 by 8 "	. .	18.00
6 by 10 "	. .	25.00
9 by 13 "	. .	45.00
11 by 16 "	. .	80.00

UNION
JOB PRESS.

Best Low Price Rotary Job Press in the world.

CHASE 10 x 14 INCHES.

Price $100.00

Write for our full Catalogue of Presses, Type, Rules, Paper, Cards, etc.

$12

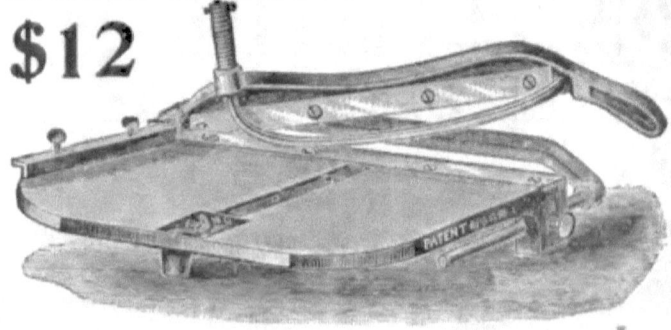

Card and Paper Cutter

2½ inch Blades.

www.ingramcontent.com/pod-product-compliance
Lightning Source LLC
Chambersburg PA
CBHW020136170426
43199CB00010B/766